The Best Test Preparation for the

ELM

Entry Level Mathematics

ELM EDITORIAL BOARD

Archibald Sia, Ph.D.
Associate Professor of Elementary Education
California State University, Northridge
Northridge, California

Hugo Sun, Ph.D.
Professor of Mathematics
California State University, Fresno
Fresno, California

Robert S. Wilson, Ph.D.
Instructor of Mathematics
Sonoma State University
Rohnert Park, California

Research & Education Association
61 Ethel Road West • Piscataway, New Jersey 08854

The Best Test Preparation for the
ELM (Entry Level Mathematics)

Printed in the United States of America

Library of Congress Catalog Card Number 97-65003

International Standard Book Number 0-87891-909-0

Research & Education Association
61 Ethel Road West
Piscataway, New Jersey 08854

REA supports the effort to conserve and protect environmental resources by printing on recycled papers.

Contents

ELM

Entry Level Mathematics

Study Schedule

STUDY SCHEDULE

It is important for you to discover the time and place for studying that works best for you. Some students may set aside a certain number of hours every morning to study, while others may choose to study at night before going to sleep. Other students may study during the day, while waiting in line, or they may find another convenient time to do their studying. Only you will be able to know when and where your studying is most effective. Keep in mind that the most important factor is consistency. Use your time wisely. Work out a study routine and stick to it!

You may want to follow a schedule similar to the one below. The following schedule consists of a nine-week program. You can always condense the schedule, if necessary, by combining two weeks into one.

Week 1	Take the diagnostic quiz for each review (Arithmetic, Elementary Algebra, Geometry, Intermediate Algebra, and Word Problems). Rank your score on each quiz. On whichever quiz you scored the lowest, plan to study that review first. Make a list of the reviews in the order in which you plan to study them. Then read the introduction of this book for study hints and to learn more about the ELM.
Week 2	Study the subject which corresponds to the quiz on which you scored the lowest. Make sure you complete all the drills in the review and work out the example problems on your own to learn the processes involved in each type of problem.
Week 3	Study your next-to-lowest scoring area this week. Again, be sure to complete all the drills in the review and work out example problems so that you learn the processes involved in each type of problem.
Week 4	Study your third weakest area during Week 4. Completing all the drills and example problems will increase your ability to perform well on these types of problems.

Week 5	Study your second-to-strongest area this week. Since you probably did fairly well in this area, you may feel much more confident in this area than you have in other areas you studied in previous weeks. This may tempt you not to be as thorough in your studying habits this week, but taking the drills and studying the examples will only increase your chances of answering questions in this area correctly during the actual ELM test.
Week 6	Study your strongest subject this week. Temptation to merely skim or even skip this chapter might be strong, but if you study thoroughly, you are bound to learn something new about this subject. Perhaps you will discover an easier way to approach a problem or a tip which will save you precious minutes during the actual test.
Week 7	Take ELM Practice Test 1 and grade yourself. Read the detailed explanations of answers. Try to find a pattern in those questions you answered incorrectly. Did you consistently answer questions incorrectly on the Pythagorean Theorem, for example? Perhaps you should review this subject to refresh your memory.
Week 8	Take ELM Practice Test 2 and grade yourself. Read the detailed explanations of answers. Did you improve in any of the areas from the last test? If there are areas which continue to trouble you, re-take some of the drill questions or ask a teacher to explain some of those concepts to you.
Week 9	Take ELM Practice Test 3 and grade yourself. This should be your best score yet. Any subjects in which you still feel weak should be re-studied. Feel free to take one or more of the tests again if you want to improve your test-taking skills or your ability to complete the test within the given 75-minute time frame.

About Research & Education Association

Research and Education Association (REA) is an organization of educators, scientists, and engineers specializing in various academic fields. Founded in 1959 with the purpose of disseminating the most recently developed scientific information to groups in industry, government, and universities, REA has since become a successful and highly respected publisher of study aids, test preps, handbooks, and reference works.

REA's Test Preparation series includes study guides for all academic levels in almost all disciplines. Research and Education Association publishes test preps for students who have not yet completed high school, as well as high school students preparing to enter college. Students from countries around the world seeking to attend college in the United States will find the assistance they need in REA's publications. For college students seeking advanced degrees, REA publishes test preps for many major graduate school admission examinations in a wide variety of disciplines, including engineering, law, and medicine. Students at every level, in every field, with every ambition can find what they are looking for among REA's publications.

Unlike most Test Preparation books that present only a few practice tests which bear little resemblance to the actual exams, REA's series presents tests which accurately depict the official exams in both degree of difficulty and types of questions. REA's practice tests are always based upon the most recently administered exams, and include every type of question that can be expected on the actual exams.

REA's publications and educational materials are highly regarded and continually receive an unprecedented amount of praise from professionals, instructors, librarians, parents, and students. Our authors are as diverse as the subjects and fields represented in the books we publish. They are well-known in their respective fields and serve on the faculties of prestigious universities throughout the United States.

Acknowledgments

In addition to our authors, we would like to thank Dr. Max Fogiel, President, for his overall guidance which has brought this publication to its completion; Stacey A. Daly, Managing Editor, for directing the editorial staff throughout each phase of the project; and Jeffrey C. Turbitt, Revisions Editor, for his editorial contributions.

ABOUT THE ELM
(Entry Level Mathematics Test)

The ELM (Entry Level Mathematics Test) is required by the California State University campus system for incoming freshmen who have not obtained an exemption by earning one of the following: a score of 3 or above on the College Board Advanced Placement (AP) Mathematics examination, a score of 530 or above on the Mathematics section of the Scholastic Aptitude Test (SAT), a score of 23 or above on the ACT-E (enhanced) Mathematics Test, a score of 520 or above on the College Board Math Achievement Test, Level 1, or a score of 540 or above on the College Board Math Achievement Test, Level 2. If you have not met the requirements, you are not exempt and must take the ELM before your freshman year.

Once you take the ELM, your score is used to place you into an appropriate freshman mathematics class. The higher your score, the more choices you are given regarding your freshman mathematics class. Lower scores result in placement into remedial mathematics. While being placed into remedial mathematics does not effect your admission to a CSU campus, and while students are not surcharged for being placed in this course, it is not considered college-level, and you will not receive credit for the course. Therefore, it is in your best interests to pass the test with as high a score as possible, so that you will be placed into a higher-level course.

The ELM contains 65 multiple-choice questions which you must answer in 75 minutes. The questions range in difficulty level from arithmetic, to geometry, to elementary and intermediate algebra, to word problems. Of the 65 multiple-choice questions, five questions are Field Test Questions and are not considered in your score. You will not know which questions are Field Test Questions, so it is to your advantage to treat every question as though it counts.

HOW TO PREPARE FOR AND DO YOUR BEST
ON THE ELM

By reviewing and studying this book, you can achieve a top score on the ELM. The ELM assesses the mathematical skills which you have developed over your high school career. Most of the knowledge tested by the ELM is covered in your high school mathematics classes. You may find that some of the questions are on a higher level than your high school classes; that is because not everyone takes the same level of math during high school. At the same time, you may find that some of the math presented is at a level much lower than your high school math classes; that is because the ability to perform higher level math problems is tied directly to your understanding of lower-level arithmetical concepts.

The purpose of our book is to properly prepare you for the ELM by providing three full-length exams which accurately reflect the ELM in both types of questions and degree of difficulty. The exams are provided based on the most recently administered ELMs and include every type of question that can be expected on the ELM. Following each exam is an answer key complete with detailed explanations and solutions. Designed specifically to clarify the material for the student, the explanations not only provide the correct answers, but also explain why the answer to a particular question is more acceptable than any other answer choice. By completing all three exams and studying the explanations which follow, your strengths and weaknesses can be discovered. This knowledge will allow you to concentrate on the sections of the exam you find to be most difficult.

ABOUT THE TEST EXPERTS

Our Editorial Board, all professors of mathematics or education from California State University, carefully examined and edited our tests and subject reviews, which were designed by a mathematics expert. They have examined and researched the mechanics of the actual ELM to see what types of practice questions accurately depict the exam and challenge the student. Our experts are highly regarded in the educational community, having studied at the doctoral level and taught in their respective fields at California State University. They have an in-depth knowledge of the subjects presented in the book, and provide accurate questions which appeal to the student's interest. Each question is clearly explained in order to help the student achieve a top score on the ELM.

ABOUT THE REVIEW SECTIONS

Our ELM Test Preparation book offers five reviews which correspond to the subject areas you will find on the exam. These include Arithmetic, Elementary Algebra, Geometry, Intermediate Algebra, and Word Problems. Using our review will provide focus and structure and will allow you to choose a particular subject or subtopic to study. Each review provides a diagnostic quiz which will help you determine your strengths and weaknesses in the subject before you begin studying. The reviews consist of the following:

Arithmetic Review
- Integers and Real Numbers
- Fractions
- Decimals
- Percentages
- Radicals
- Exponents and Scientific Notation

Elementary Algebra
- Operations with Polynomials
- Simplifying Algebraic Expressions
- Rational Expressions
- Equations and Linear Equations
- Two Linear Equations
- Quadratic Equations
- Inequalities
- Graphs

Geometry Review
- Points, Lines, and Angles
- Triangles
- Quadrilaterals
- Circles
- Solids
- Geometry Formulas

Intermediate Algebra
- Quadratic Equations
- Complex Numbers
- Linear Equations and Rational Expressions
- Absolute Value Equations
- Equations of Higher Degree
- Elementary Functions
- Fractional Expressions
- Sequences and Series
- Graphs

Word Problems
- Algebraic Word Problems
- Rate
- Work
- Mixture
- Interest
- Discount
- Profit
- Ratios and Proportions
- Geometry-based Word Problems
- Averages
- Data Interpretation

PARTICIPATE IN STUDY GROUPS

As a final word on how to study for this exam, you may want to study with others. This will allow you to share knowledge and obtain feedback from other members of your study group. Study groups may make preparing for the exam more enjoyable.

SCORING THE EXAM

To pass the ELM, you must earn a score of 65% on the exam. In raw numbers, this means you must achieve 39 correct responses out of the 60 scored questions on the test. When you receive your actual ELM test score, it will be a scaled score ranging from 100 to 700, however, it will be based on the following raw score information. If you score above 65% (39 problems correct out of 60), you will be eligible for placement in baccalaureate-level mathematics classes. If you answer less than 39 questions correctly, you will be placed in remedial mathematics.

You also will receive two subscores. One subscore is for all the algebra problems on the test, and the other subscore is for all the geometry problems on the test. While these scores are not used in determining a "passing" grade on the test, they are useful for placement so that school officials will know where your strengths and weaknesses in mathematics may lie.

Determining your score on our sample tests is very easy. Simply go to the answer key and mark your correct and incorrect answers. Circle those numbers which correspond with Field Test Questions. DO NOT COUNT FIELD TEST QUESTIONS toward your score. Simply count the number of questions (other than Field Test Questions) which you answered correctly. If you answered over 39 questions correctly, you have passed the sample test.

ELM TEST-TAKING STRATEGIES
How to Beat the Clock

Every second counts and you will want to use the available test time in the most efficient manner. Here's how:

1. Memorize the test directions. You do not want to waste valuable time reading directions on the day of the exam. Your time should be spent answering the questions.

2. Bring a watch to the exam and pace yourself. (Make sure you don't wear a calculator watch, as it most likely will be confiscated.) Work carefully and quickly. Do not spend too much time on any one question. If, after a few minutes, you cannot answer a particular question, make a note of it and continue. You can go back to it after you have completed easier questions first.

3. As you work on the test, be sure that your answers correspond with the proper numbers and letters on the answer sheet.

ELM

Entry Level Mathematics

Chapter 1
Arithmetic Review

ARITHMETIC DIAGNOSTIC TEST

16 Questions

(Answer sheets appear at the back of the book.)

DIRECTIONS: Each question has five multiple-choice answers. Select the single best answer.

1. $10^3 + 10^5 =$

    (A) 10^8 (B) 10^{15}

    (C) 20^8 (D) 2^{15}

    (E) $101{,}000$

2. Evaluate the following: $48 - 24 \div 3 + 5 \times 2$.

    (A) 6   (B) 12

    (C) 18   (D) 26

    (E) 50

3. Divide $3^1/_5$ by $1^1/_3$.

    (A) $2^2/_5$ (B) $3^1/_{15}$

    (C) $3^3/_5$ (D) $4^4/_{15}$

    (E) 8

4. Simplify $6\sqrt{7} + 4\sqrt{7} - \sqrt{5} + 5\sqrt{7}$.

    (A) $10\sqrt{7}$ (B) $15\sqrt{7} - \sqrt{5}$

(C) $15\sqrt{21} - \sqrt{5}$ (D) $15\sqrt{16}$

(E) 60

5. Find the sum of $5^3/_4$, $2^{11}/_{16}$, $7^1/_8$.

(A) $14^8/_{17}$ (B) $14^{15}/_{16}$

(C) $15^1/_2$ (D) $15^{15}/_{28}$

(E) $15^9/_{16}$

6. Simplify $7.5 \times 1^7/_9 \div 1.333...$

(A) $^1/_{18}$ (B) $5^5/_8$

(C) $6^2/_3$ (D) 10

(E) $17^7/_9$

7. Simplify $9.223 \div 4.01$.

(A) .023   (B) 2.3

(C) 23   (D) 230

(E) .23

8. Change the fraction $^7/_8$ to a decimal.

(A) .666   (B) .75

(C) .777   (D) .875

(E) 1.142

9. Which is the smallest number?

(A) $5 \times 10^{-3} / (3 \times 10^{-3})$ (B) $.3 / .2$

(C) $.3 / (3 \times 10^{-3})$ (D) $(5 \times 10^{-2}) / .1$

(E) $.3 / (3 \times 10^{-1})$

10. Simplify $\sqrt{36}$.

    (A) 3   (B) 6

    (C) 12   (D) 18

    (E) 72

11. Evaluate $\dfrac{-4+(-2)[-1+(-2)]}{-2}$.

    (A) -7 (B) -2

    (C) -1 (D) 4

    (E) 9

12. 46.863 rounded to the nearest hundredth is

    (A) 100.   (B) 46.8.

    (C) 46.9.   (D) 46.86.

    (E) 46.87.

13. $7.04 \times 2.5 =$

    (A) 17.6   (B) 176

    (C) 9.25   (D) 1.76

    (E) 17.51

14. $451 + 21 + 689 =$

    (A) 1,051   (B) 1,081

    (C) 1,161   (D) 1,261

    (E) 1,281

15. $\sqrt{.04} =$

    (A) .0016   (B) .08

    (C) .02   (D) .2

    (E) .16

16. Find 10% of 250.

    (A) 25   (B) 125

    (C) 175   (D) 225

    (E) 275

ARITHMETIC DIAGNOSTIC TEST

ANSWER KEY

1. (E)	5. (E)	9. (D)	13. (A)
2. (E)	6. (D)	10. (B)	14. (C)
3. (A)	7. (B)	11. (C)	15. (D)
4. (B)	8. (D)	12. (D)	16. (A)

DETERMINE YOUR STRENGTHS AND WEAKNESSES

ARITHMETIC

Question Type	Question #	See Pages . . .
Integers	2, 11, 14	14–25
Fractions	3, 5, 6	25–36
Decimals and Fraction-Decimal Conversions	6, 7, 8, 9, 12, 13, 15	37–45
Percentages	16	46–53
Square Root	4, 10, 15	53–58
Exponents and Scientific Notation	1, 9	59–65

DETAILED EXPLANATIONS OF ANSWERS

ARITHMETIC DIAGNOSTIC TEST

1. **(E)**

$$10^3 = 1,000 \text{ and } 10^5 = 100,000$$

$$10^3 + 10^5 = 101,000$$

2. **(E)** When evaluating an expression without grouping symbols to indicate what operation should be done first, always do all multiplication and division first as they appear from left to right, then do any addition and subtraction, again as they appear from left to right. Therefore,

$$48 - 24 \div 3 + 5 \times 2 =$$

$$48 - 8 + 10 =$$

$$40 + 10 = 50$$

3. **(A)** In order to divide $3^1/_5$ by $1^1/_3$, we must first change both mixed numbers into improper fractions.

$$\frac{16}{5} \div \frac{4}{5} = \frac{16}{5} \times \frac{3}{4}$$

$$= \frac{4}{5} \times \frac{3}{1} = \frac{12}{5}$$

Since the result is an improper fraction, we must convert it back into a mixed number.

$$\frac{12}{5} = \frac{10}{5} + \frac{2}{5} = 2 + \frac{2}{5}$$

Therefore, the correct answer is $2^2/_5$.

4. (B) To combine radicals, the radicands (the value under the radical sign) must be equal. The distributive property allows you to add and subtract radicals.

$$(6\sqrt{7} + 4\sqrt{7}) - \sqrt{5} + 5\sqrt{7}$$
$$(6 + 4)\sqrt{7} - \sqrt{5} + 5\sqrt{7}$$
$$10\sqrt{7} - \sqrt{5} + 5\sqrt{7}$$
$$(10 + 5)\sqrt{7} - \sqrt{5}$$
$$15\sqrt{7} - \sqrt{5}$$

5. (E) Since the lowest common denominator for $^3/_4$, $^{11}/_{16}$, and $^1/_8$ is 16, we change each fraction into equivalent fractions having a common denominator of 16.

$$5\frac{3}{4} = 5\frac{12}{16}$$
$$2\frac{11}{16} = 2\frac{11}{16}$$
$$7\frac{1}{8} = 7\frac{2}{16}$$

Adding the whole numbers 5, 2, and 7 yields

$$5 + 2 + 7 = 14.$$

Adding the numerators 12, 11, and 2 yields

$$12 + 11 + 2 = 25.$$

Writing this sum over the common denominator gives $^{25}/_{16}$, which changes to the proper fraction $1^9/_{16}$.
Adding this with the sum of the whole numbers

$$14 + 1\frac{9}{16} = 15\frac{9}{16}.$$

The correct answer is therefore $15^9/_{16}$.

6. **(D)** First, change all the numbers to the same form. All are easily converted to fractions and simplified:

$$7.5 \times 1\frac{7}{9} \div 1.333... = 7\frac{1}{2} \times \frac{16}{9} \div 1\frac{1}{3}$$

$$= \frac{15}{2} \times \frac{16}{9} \div \frac{4}{3}$$

$$= \frac{15}{2} \times \frac{16}{9} \times \frac{3}{4}$$

$$= 10$$

7. **(B)** To divide make the divisor a whole number by moving the decimal point. Make sure that the decimal point of the dividend is moved the same number of places.

$$
\begin{array}{r}
2.3 \\
4.01.\overline{)9.22.3} \\
\underline{802} \\
1203 \\
\underline{1203}
\end{array}
$$

8. **(D)** To change a fraction to a decimal, divide the numerator (7) by the denominator (8)

$$7 \div 8$$

Add a decimal point after the 7 and necessary zeros.

$$
\begin{array}{r}
.875 \\
8\overline{)7.000} \\
\underline{-64} \\
60 \\
\underline{-56} \\
40 \\
\underline{-40} \\
0
\end{array}
$$

9. **(D)** To find the smallest number we will calculate each one.

(A) $\dfrac{5 \times 10^{-3}}{3 \times 10^{-3}} = \dfrac{5}{3} = 1.6$

(B) $\dfrac{.3}{.2} = 1.5$

(C) $\dfrac{.3}{3 \times 10^{-3}} = \dfrac{.3 \times 10^3}{3} = \dfrac{3 \times 10^2}{3} = 100$

(D) $\dfrac{5 \times 10^{-2}}{.1} = \dfrac{5 \times 10^{-2}}{10^{-1}} = 5 \times 10^{-1} = .5$

(E) $\dfrac{.3}{3 \times 10^{-1}} = \dfrac{.3 \times 10}{3} = \dfrac{3}{3} = 1$

10. **(B)** Remember

$$36 = 6 \times 6$$

Therefore, the square root of 36 equals 6.

11. **(C)** When evaluating a problem, do what is inside the parentheses first. Continue doing the multiplication and division with addition and subtraction last.

$$\dfrac{-4 + (-2)[-1 + (-2)]}{-2} = \dfrac{-4 - 2[-1 - 2]}{-2}$$

$$= \dfrac{-4 - 2[-3]}{-2}$$

$$= \dfrac{-4 + 6}{-2}$$

$$= \dfrac{2}{-2} = -1$$

12. **(D)** Rounding off means to drop everything to the right of the place requested. If the number following it is equal to or greater than 5 add 1 to the number and the following numbers are dropped. The hundredth place is the second number to the *right* of the decimal. Since 3 in the thousandth's place is less than 5, drop it. Therefore, the answer is 46.86.

13. **(A)**

$$
\begin{array}{r}
7.04 \quad \text{(2 decimal places)} \\
\times\ 2.5 \quad \text{(1 decimal place)} \\
\hline
3520 \\
1408 \\
\hline
17.600
\end{array}
$$

Remember to put the decimal point in the correct place (3 decimal places).

14. **(C)**

$$
\begin{array}{r}
451 \\
21 \\
689 \\
\hline
1161
\end{array}
$$

Remember to add digits in correct places (tens and hundreds).

15. **(D)** Remember $2 \times 2 = 4$. Then figure out where to put the decimal point

.2	×	.2	=	.04
1	+	1	=	2
decimal		decimal		decimal
place		place		places

16. **(A)** Change 10% to a decimal.

$$10\% = \frac{10}{100} = 0.10$$

10% of $250 = 0.10 \times 250 = 25$

ARITHMETIC REVIEW

1. INTEGERS AND REAL NUMBERS

Most of the numbers used in algebra belong to a set called the **real numbers** or **reals**. This set can be represented graphically by the real number line.

Given the number line below, we arbitrarily fix a point and label it with the number 0. In a similar manner, we can label any point on the line with one of the real numbers, depending on its position relative to 0. Numbers to the right of 0 are positive, while those to the left are negative. Value increases from left to right, so that if a is to the right of b, it is said to be greater than b.

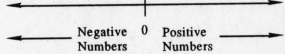

If we now divide the number line into equal segments, we can label the points on this line with real numbers. For example, the point 2 lengths to the left of 0 is -2, while the point 3 lengths to the right of 0 is $+3$ (the $+$ sign is usually assumed, so $+3$ is written simply as 3). The number line now looks like this:

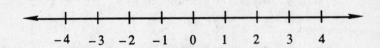

These boundary points represent the subset of the reals known as the **integers**. The set of integers is made up of both the positive and negative whole numbers: $\{..., -4, -3, -2, -1, 0, 1, 2, 3, 4, ...\}$. Some subsets of integers are:

Natural Numbers or Positive Numbers — the set of integers starting with 1 and increasing:

$\mathcal{N} = \{1, 2, 3, 4, ...\}$.

Whole Numbers — the set of integers starting with 0 and increasing:

$\mathcal{W} = \{0, 1, 2, 3, ...\}$.

Negative Numbers — the set of integers starting with –1 and decreasing:

$$Z = \{-1, -2, -3, \ldots\}.$$

Prime Numbers — the set of positive integers greater than 1 that are divisible only by 1 and themselves:

$$\{2, 3, 5, 7, 11, \ldots\}.$$

Even Integers — the set of integers divisible by 2:

$$\{\ldots, -4, -2, 0, 2, 4, 6, \ldots\}.$$

Odd Integers — the set of integers not divisible by 2:

$$\{\ldots, -3, -1, 1, 3, 5, 7, \ldots\}.$$

PROBLEM

Classify each of the following numbers into as many different sets as possible. Example: real, integer ...

(1) 0

(2) 9

(3) $\sqrt{6}$

(4) $1/2$

(5) $2/3$

(6) 1.5

Solution

(1) 0 is a real number and an integer.

(2) 9 is a real, natural number, and an integer.

(3) $\sqrt{6}$ is a real number.

(4) $1/2$ is a real number.

(5) $2/3$ is a real number.

(6) 1.5 is a real number and a decimal.

Absolute Value

The **absolute value** of a number is represented by two vertical lines around the number, and is equal to the given number, regardless of sign.

The absolute value of a real number A is defined as follows:

$$|A| = \begin{cases} A \text{ if } A \geq 0 \\ -A \text{ if } A < 0 \end{cases}$$

EXAMPLE

$$|5| = 5, \quad |-8| = -(-8) = 8$$

Absolute values follow the given rules:

(A) $|-A| = |A|$

(B) $|A| \geq 0$, equality holding only if $A = 0$

(C) $\left|\dfrac{A}{B}\right| = \dfrac{|A|}{|B|}, \; B \neq 0$

(D) $|AB| = |A| \times |B|$

(E) $|A|^2 = A^2$

Absolute value can also be expressed on the real number line as the distance of the point represented by the real number from the point labeled 0.

3 unit lengths

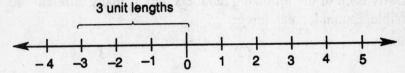

So $|-3| = 3$ because -3 is 3 units to the left of 0.

PROBLEM

Classify each of the following statements as true or false. If it is false, explain why.

(1) $|-120| > 1$

(2) $|4 - 12| = |4| - |12|$

(3) $|4 - 9| = 9 - 4$

(4) $|12 - 3| = 12 - 3$

(5) $|-12a| = 12|a|$

Solution

(1) True

(2) False, $\quad |4 - 12| = |4| - |12|$

$$|-8| = 4 - 12$$

$$8 \neq -8$$

In general, $|a + b| \neq |a| + |b|$

(3) True

(4) True

(5) True

PROBLEM

Find the absolute value for each of the following:

(1) $|0|$ (2) $|-\pi|$

(3) $|4|$ (4) $|a|$, where a is a real number

Solution

(1) $|0| = 0$

(2) $|-\pi| = \pi$

(3) $|4| = 4$

(4) for $a > 0, |a| = a$

for $a = 0, |a| = 0$

for $a < 0, |a| = -a$

$$\text{i.e., } |a| = \begin{cases} a \text{ if } a > 0 \\ 0 \text{ if } a = 0 \\ -a \text{ if } a < 0 \end{cases}$$

Positive and Negative Numbers

(A) **To add two numbers with like signs,** add their absolute values and write the sum with the common sign. So,

$$6 + 2 = 8, (-6) + (-2) = -8$$

(B) **To add two numbers with unlike signs,** find the difference between their absolute values, and write the result with the sign of the number with the greater absolute value. So,

$$(-4) + 6 = 2, 15 + (-19) = -4$$

(C) **To subtract a number b from another number a,** change the sign of b and add to a. Examples:

$$10 - (3) = 10 + (-3) = 7 \tag{1}$$

$$2 - (-6) = 2 + 6 = 8 \tag{2}$$

$$(-5) - (-2) = -5 + 2 = -3 \tag{3}$$

(D) **To multiply (or divide) two numbers having like signs,** multiply (or divide) their absolute values and write the result with a positive sign. Examples:

$$(5)(3) = 15 \tag{1}$$

$$-6 / -3 = 2 \tag{2}$$

(E) **To multiply (or divide) two numbers having unlike signs,** multiply (or divide) their absolute values and write the result with a negative sign. Examples:

$$(-2)(8) = -16 \tag{1}$$

$$9 / -3 = -3 \tag{2}$$

According to the law of signs for real numbers, the square of a positive or negative number is always positive. This means that it is impossible to take the square root of a negative number in the real number system.

Properties of Real Numbers

Commutative Law

$a + b = b + a$ for addition

$ab = ba$ for multiplication

Associative Law

$(a + b) + c = a + (b + c)$ for addition

$(ab)c = a(bc)$ for multiplication

Distributive Law

$a(b + c) = ab + ac$

Identity Law

$a + 0 = a$ for addition

$b \times 1 = b$ for multiplication

Inverse Law

$$a + (-a) = 0 \qquad \text{for addition}$$

$$b \times {}^1/_b = 1 \text{ (if } b \neq 0) \qquad \text{for multiplication}$$

The number ${}^1/_b$ is the **multiplicative inverse** or the **reciprocal of** b. It follows that b is the reciprocal of ${}^1/_b$.

Order of Operations

To simplify an expression containing parentheses, multiplication, powers, addition, etc, use the rules for the **order of operations**, as follows:

1. parentheses or absolute value

2. powers

3. multiplication or division

4. addition or subtraction

PROBLEM

Calculate the value of each of the following expressions:

(1) $||2 - 5| + 6 - 14|$

(2) $|-5| \times |4| + \dfrac{|-12|}{4}$

Solution

(1) $||-3| + 6 - 14| = |3 + 6 - 14|$

$$= |9 - 14|$$

$$= |-5|$$

$$= 5$$

(2) $(5 \times 4) + 12/4 = 20 + 3$

$$= 23$$

Drill 1: Integers and Real Numbers

Addition

1. Simplify $4 + (-7) + 2 + (-5)$.

    (A) -6 (B) -4

    (C) 0 (D) 6

    (E) 18

2. Simplify $144 + (-317) + 213$.

    (A) -357 (B) -40

    (C) 40 (D) 357

    (E) 674

3. Simplify $|4 + (-3)| + |-2|$.

    (A) -2 (B) -1

    (C) 1 (D) 3

    (E) 9

4. What integer makes the equation $-13 + 12 + 7 + ? = 10$ a true statement?

    (A) -22 (B) -10

    (C) 4 (D) 6

    (E) 10

5. Simplify $4 + 17 + (-29) + 13 + (-22) + (-3)$.

    (A) -44 (B) -20

    (C) 23 (D) 34

    (E) 78

Subtraction

6. Simplify $319 - 428$.

    (A) -111 (B) -109

(C) – 99　　　　　　　　　　　　　(D) 109

(E) 747

7. Simplify 91,203 – 37,904 + 1,073.

(A) 54,372　　　　　　　　　　　(B) 64,701

(C) 128,034　　　　　　　　　　(D) 129,107

(E) 130,180

8. Simplify $| 43 – 62 | – | – 17 – 3 |$.

(A) – 39　　　　　　　　　　　　(B) – 19

(C) – 1　　　　　　　　　　　　　(D) 1

(E) 39

9. Simplify $– (– 4 – 7) + (– 2)$.

(A) – 22　　　　　　　　　　　　(B) – 13

(C) – 9　　　　　　　　　　　　　(D) 7

(E) 9

10. In the Great Smoky Mountains National Park, Mt. Le Conte rises from 1,292 feet above sea level to 6,593 feet above sea level. How tall is Mt. Le Conte?

(A) 4,009 ft　　　　　　　　　　(B) 5,301 ft

(C) 5,699 ft　　　　　　　　　　(D) 6,464 ft

(E) 7,885 ft

Multiplication

11. Simplify $(– 3) \times (– 18) \times (– 1)$.

(A) – 108　　　　　　　　　　　(B) – 54

(C) – 48　　　　　　　　　　　　(D) 48

(E) 54

12. Simplify $| – 42 | \times | 7 |$.

(A) – 294　　　　　　　　　　　(B) – 49

(C) – 35   (D) 284

(E) 294

13. Simplify (– 6) × 5 × (– 10) × (– 4) × 0 × 2.

(A) – 2,400   (B) – 240

(C) 0   (D) 280

(E) 2,700

14. Simplify – |(– 6) × 8|.

(A) – 48   (B) – 42

(C) 2   (D) 42

(E) 48

15. A city in Georgia had a record low temperature of – 3°F one winter. During the same year, a city in Michigan experienced a record low that was nine times the record low set in Georgia. What was the record low in Michigan that year?

(A) – 31°F   (B) – 27°F

(C) – 21°F   (D) – 12°F

(E) – 6°F

Division

16. Simplify – 24 / 8.

(A) – 4   (B) – 3

(C) – 2   (D) 3

(E) 4

17. Simplify (– 180) / (– 12).

(A) – 30   (B) – 15

(C) 1.5   (D) 15

(E) 216

18. Simplify $|-76|/|-4|$.

    (A) -21 (B) -19

    (C) 13   (D) 19

    (E) 21.5

19. Simplify $|216/(-6)|$.

    (A) -36 (B) -12

    (C) 36   (D) 38

    (E) 43

20. At the end of the year, a small firm has $2,996 in its account for bonuses. If the entire amount is equally divided among the 14 employees, how much does each one receive?

    (A) $107   (B) $114

    (C) $170   (D) $210

    (E) $214

Order of Operations

21. Simplify $\dfrac{4+8\times2}{5-1}$.

    (A) 4   (B) 5

    (C) 6   (D) 8

    (E) 12

22. $96 \div 3 + 4 \div 2 =$

    (A) 65   (B) 64

    (C) 16   (D) 8

    (E) 4

23. $3 + 4 \times 2 - 6 \div 3 =$

    (A) -1 (B) $^5/_3$

    (C) $^8/_3$ (D) 9

    (E) 12

24. $[(4 + 8) \times 3] \div 9 =$

   (A) 4   (B) 8

   (C) 12   (D) 24

   (E) 36

25. $18 + 3 \times 4 \div 3 =$

   (A) 3   (B) 5

   (C) 10   (D) 22

   (E) 28

26. $(29 - 17 + 4) \div 4 + |-2| =$

   (A) $2^2/_3$ (B) 4

   (C) $4^2/_3$ (D) 6

   (E) 15

27. $(-3) \times 5 - 20 \div 4 =$

   (A) -75 (B) -20

   (C) -10 (D) $-8^3/_4$

   (E) 20

28. $\dfrac{11 \times 2 + 2}{16 - 2 \times 2} =$

   (A) $^{11}/_{16}$ (B) 1

   (C) 2   (D) $3^2/_3$

   (E) 4

29. $|-8 - 4| \div 3 \times 6 + (-4) =$

   (A) 20   (B) 26

   (C) 32   (D) 62

   (E) 212

30. $32 \div 2 + 4 - 15 \div 3 =$

(A) 0   (B) 7

(C) 15   (D) 23

(E) 63

2. FRACTIONS

The fraction, a/b, where the **numerator** is a and the **denominator** is b, implies that a is being divided by b. The denominator of a fraction can never be zero since a number divided by zero is not defined. If the numerator is less than the denominator, the fraction is called a **proper fraction**. If the numerator is greater than the denominator, the fraction is called an **improper fraction**. A **mixed number** is the sum of a whole number and a fraction, i.e., $4^3/_8 = 4 + {}^3/_8$.

Operations with Fractions

(A) **To change a mixed number to an improper fraction,** multiply the whole number by the denominator of the fraction and add the numerator. This product becomes the numerator of the result and the denominator remains the same, e.g.,

$$5\frac{2}{3} = \frac{(5 \times 3) + 2}{3} = \frac{15 + 2}{3} = \frac{17}{3}$$

To change an improper fraction to a mixed number, divide the numerator by the denominator. The remainder becomes the numerator of the fractional part of the mixed number, and the denominator remains the same, e.g.,

$$\frac{35}{4} = 35 \div 4 = 8\frac{3}{4}$$

To check your work, change your result back to an improper fraction to see if it matches the original fraction.

(B) **To find the sum of two fractions having a common denominator,** add together the numerators of the given fractions and put this sum over the common denominator.

$$\frac{11}{3} + \frac{5}{3} = \frac{11 + 5}{3} = \frac{16}{3}$$

Similarly for subtraction,

$$\frac{11}{3} - \frac{5}{3} = \frac{11-5}{3} = \frac{6}{3} = 2$$

(C) **To find the sum of the two fractions having different denominators,** it is necessary to find the **lowest common denominator (LCD)** of the different denominators using a process called **factoring**.

To **factor** a number means to find two or more numbers that when multiplied together have a product equal to the original number. These two numbers are then said to be **factors** of the original number. For example, the factors of 6 are

  (1) 1 and 6 since $1 \times 6 = 6$.

  (2) 2 and 3 since $2 \times 3 = 6$.

Every number is the product of itself and 1. A **prime factor** is a number that does not have any factors besides itself and 1. This is important when finding the LCD of two fractions having different denominators.

To find the LCD of $^{11}/_6$ and $^5/_{16}$, we must first find the prime factors of each of the two denominators.

  $6 = 2 \times 3$

  $16 = 2 \times 2 \times 2 \times 2$

  $\text{LCD} = 2 \times 2 \times 2 \times 2 \times 3 = 48$

Note that we do not need to repeat the 2 that appears in both the factors of 6 and 16.

Once we have determined the LCD of the denominators, each of the fractions must be converted into equivalent fractions having the LCD as a denominator.

Rewrite $^{11}/_6$ and $^5/_{16}$ to have 48 as their denominators.

  $6 \times ? = 48$ $16 \times ? = 48$

  $6 \times 8 = 48$ $16 \times 3 = 48$

If the numerator and denominator of each fraction is multiplied (or divided) by the same number, the value of the fraction will not change. This is because a fraction b/b, b being any number, is equal to the multiplicative identity, 1.

Therefore,

$$\frac{11}{6} \times \frac{8}{8} = \frac{88}{48} \qquad \frac{5}{16} \times \frac{3}{3} = \frac{15}{48}$$

We may now find

$$\frac{11}{6} + \frac{5}{16} = \frac{88}{48} + \frac{15}{48} = \frac{103}{48}$$

Similarly for subtraction,

$$\frac{11}{6} - \frac{5}{16} = \frac{88}{48} - \frac{15}{48} = \frac{73}{48}$$

(D) **To find the product of two or more fractions,** multiply the numerators of the given fractions to find the numerator of the product and multiply the denominators of the given fractions to find the denominator of the product, e.g.,

$$\frac{2}{3} \times \frac{1}{5} \times \frac{4}{7} = \frac{2 \times 1 \times 4}{3 \times 5 \times 7} = \frac{8}{105}$$

(E) **To find the quotient of two fractions,** invert the divisor and multiply, e.g.,

$$\frac{8}{9} \div \frac{1}{3} = \frac{8}{9} \times \frac{3}{1} = \frac{24}{9} = \frac{8}{3}$$

(F) **To simplify a fraction** is to convert it into a form in which the numerator and denominator have no common factor other than 1, e.g.,

$$\frac{12}{18} = \frac{12 \div 6}{18 \div 6} = \frac{2}{3}$$

(G) **A compound fraction** is a fraction whose numerator and/or denominator is made up of fractions. To simplify the fraction, find the LCD of all the fractions. Multiply both the numerator and denominator by this number and simplify.

PROBLEM

If $a = 4$ and $b = 7$, find the value of $\dfrac{a + \frac{a}{b}}{a - \frac{a}{b}}$.

Solution

By substitution,

$$\frac{a + \frac{a}{b}}{a - \frac{a}{b}} = \frac{4 + \frac{4}{7}}{4 - \frac{4}{7}}$$

In order to combine the terms, we must find the LCD of 1 and 7. Since both are prime factors, the LCD = $1 \times 7 = 7$.

Multiplying both the numerator and denominator by 7, we get

$$\frac{7(4 + \frac{4}{7})}{7(4 - \frac{4}{7})} = \frac{28 + 4}{28 - 4} = \frac{32}{24}$$

By dividing both the numerator and denominator by 8, $^{32}/_{24}$ can be reduced to $^4/_3$.

Drill 2: Fractions

Fractions

DIRECTIONS: Add and write the answer in its *simplest* form.

1. $^5/_{12} + {}^3/_{12} =$

   (A) $^5/_{24}$ (B) $^1/_3$

   (C) $^9/_{12}$ (D) $^2/_3$

   (E) $1^1/_3$

2. $^5/_8 + {}^7/_8 + {}^3/_8 =$

   (A) $^{15}/_{24}$ (B) $^3/_4$

   (C) $^5/_6$ (D) $^7/_8$

   (E) $1^7/_8$

3. $131^2/_{15} + 28^3/_{15} =$

   (A) $159^1/_6$ (B) $159^1/_5$

   (C) $159^1/_3$ (D) $159^1/_2$

   (E) $159^3/_5$

4. $3^5/_{18} + 2^1/_{18} + 8^7/_{18} =$

   (A) $13^{13}/_{18}$ (B) $13^3/_4$

   (C) $13^7/_9$ (D) $14^1/_6$

   (E) $14^2/_9$

5. $17^9/_{20} + 4^3/_{20} + 8^{11}/_{20} =$

   (A) $29^{23}/_{60}$ (B) $30^{23}/_{20}$

   (C) $30^3/_{20}$ (D) $30^1/_5$

   (E) $30^3/_5$

Subtracting Fractions with the Same Denominator

DIRECTIONS: Subtract and write the answer in its *simplest* form.

6. $4^7/_8 - 3^1/_8 =$

   (A) $1^1/_4$ (B) $1^1/_2$

   (C) $1^3/_4$ (D) $1^7/_8$

   (E) 2

7. $132^5/_{12} - 37^3/_{12} =$

   (A) $94^1/_6$ (B) $95^1/_{12}$

   (C) $95^1/_6$ (D) $105^1/_6$

   (E) $169^2/_3$

8. $19^1/_3 - 2^2/_3 =$

   (A) $16^2/_3$ (B) $16^5/_6$

   (C) $17^1/_3$ (D) $17^2/_3$

   (E) $17^5/_6$

9. $^8/_{21} - ^5/_{21} =$

   (A) $^1/_{21}$ (B) $^1/_7$

   (C) $^3/_{21}$ (D) $^2/_7$

   (E) $^3/_7$

10. $82^7/_{10} - 38^9/_{10} =$

(A) $43^4/_5$ (B) $44^1/_5$

(C) $44^2/_5$ (D) $45^1/_5$

(E) $45^2/_{10}$

Finding the LCD

DIRECTIONS: Find the lowest common denominator of each group of fractions.

11. $^2/_3$, $^5/_9$, and $^1/_6$.

(A) 9   (B) 18

(C) 27   (D) 54

(E) 162

12. $^1/_2$, $^5/_6$, and $^3/_4$.

(A) 2   (B) 4

(C) 6   (D) 12

(E) 48

13. $^7/_{16}$, $^5/_6$, and $^2/_3$.

(A) 3   (B) 6

(C) 12   (D) 24

(E) 48

14. $^8/_{15}$, $^2/_5$, and $^{12}/_{25}$.

(A) 5   (B) 15

(C) 25   (D) 75

(E) 375

15. $^2/_3$, $^1/_5$, and $^5/_6$.

(A) 15   (B) 30

(C) 48   (D) 90

(E) 120

16. $^1/_3$, $^9/_{42}$, and $^4/_{21}$.

    (A) 21   (B) 42

    (C) 126   (D) 378

    (E) 4,000

17. $^4/_9$, $^2/_5$, and $^1/_3$.

    (A) 15   (B) 17

    (C) 27   (D) 45

    (E) 135

18. $^7/_{12}$, $^{11}/_{36}$, and $^1/_9$.

    (A) 12   (B) 36

    (C) 108   (D) 324

    (E) 432

19. $^3/_7$, $^5/_{21}$, and $^2/_3$.

    (A) 21   (B) 42

    (C) 31   (D) 63

    (E) 441

20. $^{13}/_{16}$, $^5/_8$, and $^1/_4$.

    (A) 4   (B) 8

    (C) 16   (D) 32

    (E) 64

Adding Fractions with Different Denominators

DIRECTIONS: Add and write the answer in its *simplest* form.

21. $^1/_3 + ^5/_{12} =$

    (A) $^2/_5$ (B) $^1/_2$

    (C) $^6/_{12}$ (D) $^3/_4$

    (E) $1^1/_3$

22. $3^5/_9 + 2^1/_3 =$

    (A) $5^1/_2$ (B) $5^2/_3$

    (C) $5^8/_9$ (D) $6^1/_9$

    (E) $6^2/_3$

23. $12^9/_{16} + 17^3/_4 + 8^1/_8 =$

    (A) $37^7/_{16}$ (B) $38^7/_{16}$

    (C) $38^1/_2$ (D) $38^2/_3$

    (E) $39^3/_{16}$

24. $28^4/_5 + 11^{16}/_{25} =$

    (A) $39^2/_3$ (B) $39^4/_5$

    (C) $40^9/_{25}$ (D) $40^2/_5$

    (E) $40^{11}/_{25}$

25. $2^1/_8 + 1^3/_{16} + {}^5/_{12} =$

    (A) $3^{35}/_{48}$ (B) $3^3/_4$

    (C) $3^{19}/_{24}$ (D) $3^{13}/_{16}$

    (E) $4^1/_{12}$

Subtracting Fractions with Different Denominators

DIRECTIONS: Subtract and write the answer in its *simplest* form.

26. $8^9/_{12} - 2^2/_3 =$

    (A) $6^1/_{12}$ (B) $6^1/_6$

    (C) $6^1/_3$ (D) $6^7/_{12}$

    (E) $6^2/_3$

27. $185^{11}/_{15} - 107^2/_5 =$

    (A) $77^2/_{15}$ (B) $78^1/_5$

    (C) $78^3/_{10}$ (D) $78^1/_3$

    (E) $78^9/_{15}$

28. $34^2/_3 - 16^5/_6 =$

    (A) 16   (B) $16^1/_3$

    (C) $17^1/_2$ (D) 17

    (E) $17^5/_6$

29. $3^{11}/_{48} - 2^3/_{16} =$

    (A) $^{47}/_{48}$ (B) $1^1/_{48}$

    (C) $1^1/_{24}$ (D) $1^8/_{48}$

    (E) $1^7/_{24}$

30. $81^4/_{21} - 32^1/_3 =$

    (A) $47^3/_7$ (B) $48^6/_7$

    (C) $49^1/_6$ (D) $49^5/_7$

    (E) $49^{13}/_{21}$

Multiplication

DIRECTIONS: Multiply and reduce the answer.

31. $^2/_3 \times ^4/_5 =$

    (A) $^6/_8$ (B) $^3/_4$

    (C) $^8/_{15}$ (D) $^{10}/_{12}$

    (E) $^6/_5$

32. $^7/_{10} \times ^4/_{21} =$

    (A) $^2/_{15}$ (B) $^{11}/_{31}$

    (C) $^{28}/_{210}$ (D) $^1/_6$

    (E) $^4/_{15}$

33. $5^1/_3 \times ^3/_8 =$

    (A) $^4/_{11}$ (B) 2

    (C) $^8/_5$ (D) $5^1/_8$

    (E) $5^{17}/_{24}$

34. $6^1/_2 \times 3 =$

    (A) $9^1/_2$ (B) $18^1/_2$

    (C) $19^1/_2$ (D) 20

    (E) $12^1/_2$

35. $3^1/_4 \times 2^1/_3 =$

    (A) $5^7/_{12}$ (B) $6^2/_7$

    (C) $6^5/_7$ (D) $7^7/_{12}$

    (E) $7^{11}/_{12}$

Division

DIRECTIONS: Divide and reduce the answer.

36. $^3/_{16} \div ^3/_4 =$

    (A) $^9/_{64}$ (B) $^1/_4$

    (C) $^6/_{16}$ (D) $^9/_{16}$

    (E) $^3/_4$

37. $^4/_9 \div ^2/_3 =$

    (A) $^1/_3$ (B) $^1/_2$

    (C) $^2/_3$ (D) $^7/_{11}$

    (E) $^8/_9$

38. $5^1/_4 \div ^7/_{10} =$

    (A) $2^4/_7$ (B) $3^{27}/_{40}$

    (C) $5^{19}/_{20}$ (D) $7^1/_2$

    (E) $8^1/_4$

39. $4^2/_3 \div ^7/_9 =$

    (A) $2^{24}/_{27}$ (B) $3^2/_9$

    (C) $4^{14}/_{27}$ (D) $5^{12}/_{27}$

    (E) 6

40. $3^2/_5 + 1^7/_{10} =$

    (A) 2   (B) $3^4/_7$

    (C) $4^7/_{25}$ (D) $5^1/_{10}$

    (E) $5^2/_7$

Changing an Improper Fraction to a Mixed Number

DIRECTIONS: Write each improper fraction as a mixed number in *simplest* form.

41. $^{50}/_4$

    (A) $10^1/_4$ (B) $11^1/_2$

    (C) $12^1/_4$ (D) $12^1/_2$

    (E) 25

42. $^{17}/_5$

    (A) $3^2/_5$ (B) $3^3/_5$

    (C) $3^4/_5$ (D) $4^1/_5$

    (E) $4^2/_5$

43. $^{42}/_3$

    (A) $10^2/_3$ (B) 12

    (C) $13^1/_3$ (D) 14

    (E) $21^1/_3$

44. $^{85}/_6$

    (A) $9^1/_6$ (B) $10^5/_6$

    (C) $11^1/_2$ (D) 12

    (E) $14^1/_{16}$

45. $^{151}/_7$

    (A) $19^6/_7$ (B) $20^1/_7$

    (C) $21^4/_7$ (D) $31^2/_7$

    (E) $31^4/_7$

Changing a Mixed Number to an Improper Fraction

DIRECTIONS: Change each mixed number to an improper fraction in *simplest* form.

46. $2^3/_5$

    (A) $^4/_5$ (B) $^6/_5$

    (C) $^{11}/_5$ (D) $^{13}/_5$

    (E) $^{17}/_5$

47. $4^3/_4$

    (A) $^7/_4$ (B) $^{13}/_4$

    (C) $^{16}/_3$ (D) $^{19}/_4$

    (E) $^{21}/_4$

48. $6^7/_6$

    (A) $^{13}/_6$ (B) $^{43}/_6$

    (C) $^{19}/_{36}$ (D) $^{42}/_{36}$

    (E) $^{48}/_6$

49. $12^3/_7$

    (A) $^{87}/_7$ (B) $^{39}/_7$

    (C) $^{34}/_3$ (D) $^{187}/_{21}$

    (E) $^{252}/_7$

50. $21^1/_2$

    (A) $^{11}/_2$ (B) $^{22}/_2$

    (C) $^{24}/_2$ (D) $^{42}/_2$

    (E) $^{43}/_2$

3. DECIMALS

When we divide the denominator of a fraction into its numerator, the result is a **decimal**. The decimal is based upon a fraction with a denominator of 10, 100, 1,000, ... and is written with a **decimal point**. Whole numbers are placed to the left of the decimal point where the first place to the left is the units place; the second to the left is the tens; the third to the left is the hundreds, etc. The fractions are placed on the right where the first place to the right is the tenths; the second to the right is the hundredths, etc.

EXAMPLES

$$12\frac{3}{10} = 12.3 \quad 4\frac{17}{100} = 4.17 \quad \frac{3}{100} = .03$$

Since a **rational number** is of the form a/b, $b \neq 0$, then all rational numbers can be expressed as decimals by dividing b into a. The result is either a **terminating decimal**, meaning that b divides a with a remainder of 0 after a certain point; or **repeating decimal**, meaning that b continues to divide a so that the decimal has a repeating pattern of integers.

EXAMPLES

(A) $1/2 = .5$

(B) $1/3 = .333...$

(C) $11/16 = .6875$

(D) $2/7 = .285714285714...$

(A) and (C) are terminating decimals; (B) and (D) are repeating decimals. This explanation allows us to define **irrational numbers** as numbers whose decimal form is non-terminating and non-repeating, e.g.,

$$\sqrt{2} = 1.414...$$
$$\sqrt{3} = 1.732...$$

PROBLEM

Express $- 10/20$ as a decimal.

Solution

$$- 10/20 = - 50/100 = - .5$$

PROBLEM

Write $2/7$ as a repeating decimal.

Solution

To write a fraction as a repeating decimal divide the numerator by the denominator until a pattern of repeated digits appears.

$$2 \div 7 = .285714285714\ldots$$

Identify the entire portion of the decimal which is repeated. The repeating decimal can then be written in the shortened form:

$$2/7 = .\overline{285714}$$

Operations with Decimals

(A) **To add numbers containing decimals,** write the numbers in a column making sure the decimal points are lined up, one beneath the other. Add the numbers as usual, placing the decimal point in the sum so that it is still in line with the others. It is important not to mix the digits in the tenths place with the digits in the hundredths place, and so on.

EXAMPLES

$$2.558 + 6.391 \qquad 57.51 + 6.2$$

$$
\begin{array}{r}
2.558 \\
+ 6.391 \\
\hline
8.949
\end{array}
\qquad
\begin{array}{r}
57.51 \\
+ 6.20 \\
\hline
63.71
\end{array}
$$

Similarly with subtraction,

$$78.54 - 21.33 \qquad 7.11 - 4.2$$

$$
\begin{array}{r}
78.54 \\
- 21.33 \\
\hline
57.21
\end{array}
\qquad
\begin{array}{r}
7.11 \\
- 4.20 \\
\hline
2.91
\end{array}
$$

Note that if two numbers differ according to the amount of digits to the right of the decimal point, zeros must be added.

$$.63 - .214 \qquad 15.224 - 3.6891$$

$$
\begin{array}{r}
.630 \\
- .214 \\
\hline
.416
\end{array}
\qquad
\begin{array}{r}
15.2240 \\
- 3.6891 \\
\hline
11.5349
\end{array}
$$

(B) **To multiply numbers with decimals,** multiply as usual. Then, to figure out the number of decimal places that belong in the product, find the total number of decimal places in the numbers being multiplied.

EXAMPLES

6.555	(3 decimal places)	5.32	(2 decimal places)
× 4.5	(1 decimal place)	× .04	(2 decimal places)
32775		2128	
26220		000	
294975		2128	
29.4975	(4 decimal places)	.2128	(4 decimal places)

(C) **To divide numbers with decimals,** you must first make the divisor a whole number by moving the decimal point the appropriate number of places to the right. The decimal point of the dividend should also be moved the same number of places. Place a decimal point in the quotient, directly in line with the decimal point in the dividend.

EXAMPLES

12.92 / 3.4

```
        3.8
3.4. | 12.9.2
     -102
       272
      -272
         0
```

40.376 / 7.21

```
          5.6
7.21. | 40.37.6
      -3605
        4326
       -4326
          0
```

If the question asks you to find the correct answer to two decimal places, simply divide until you have three decimal places and then round off. If the third decimal place is a 5 or larger, the number in the second decimal place is increased by 1. If the third decimal place is less than 5, that number is simply dropped.

PROBLEM

Find the answer to the following to 2 decimal places:

(1) 44.3 / 3   (2) 56.99 / 6

Solution

(1)

```
            14.766
    3 | 44.300
       -3
        14
       -12
         23
        -21
         20
        -18
          20
         -18
           2
```

(2)

```
           9.498
    6 | 56.990
       -54
        29
       -24
         59
        -54
         50
        -48
          2
```

14.766 can be rounded off to 14.77.

9.498 can be rounded off to 9.50.

(D) **When comparing two numbers with decimals to see which is the larger, first look at the tenths place.** The larger digit in this place represents the larger number. If the two digits are the same, however, take a look at the digits in the hundredths place, and so on.

EXAMPLES

.518 and .216

5 is larger than 2, therefore

.518 is larger than .216

.723 and .726

6 is larger than 3, therefore

.726 is larger than .723

Drill 3: Decimals

Addition

1. 1.032 + 0.987 + 3.07 =

    (A) 4.089

    (B) 5.089

    (C) 5.189

    (D) 6.189

    (E) 13.972

2. 132.03 + 97.1483 =

    (A) 98.4686

    (B) 110.3513

(C) 209.1783   (D) 229.1486

(E) 229.1783

3. 7.1 + 0.62 + 4.03827 + 5.813 =

(A) 0.2315127   (B) 16.45433

(C) 17.57127   (D) 18.561

(E) 40.4543

4. 8 + 17.43 + 9.2 =

(A) 34.63   (B) 34.86

(C) 35.63   (D) 176.63

(E) 189.43

5. 1036.173 + 289.04 =

(A) 382.6573   (B) 392.6573

(C) 1065.077   (D) 1325.213

(E) 3926.573

Subtraction

6. 3.972 – 2.04 =

(A) 1.932   (B) 1.942

(C) 1.976   (D) 2.013

(E) 2.113

7. 16.047 – 13.06 =

(A) 2.887   (B) 2.987

(C) 3.041   (D) 3.141

(E) 4.741

8. 87.4 – 56.27 =

(A) 30.27   (B) 30.67

(C) 31.1   (D) 31.13

(E) 31.27

9. $1046.8 - 639.14 =$

  (A) 303.84   (B) 313.74

  (C) 407.66   (D) 489.74

  (E) 535.54

10. $10,000 - 842.91 =$

  (A) 157.09   (B) 942.91

  (C) 5236.09   (D) 9057.91

  (E) 9157.09

Multiplication

11. $1.03 \times 2.6 =$

  (A) 2.18   (B) 2.678

  (C) 2.78   (D) 3.38

  (E) 3.63

12. $93 \times 4.2 =$

  (A) 39.06   (B) 97.2

  (C) 223.2   (D) 390.6

  (E) 3,906

13. $0.04 \times 0.23 =$

  (A) 0.0092   (B) 0.092

  (C) 0.27   (D) 0.87

  (E) 0.920

14. $0.0186 \times 0.03 =$

  (A) 0.000348   (B) 0.000558

  (C) 0.0548   (D) 0.0848

  (E) 0.558

15. $51.2 \times 0.17 =$

   (A) 5.29   (B) 8.534

   (C) 8.704   (D) 36.352

   (E) 36.991

Division

16. $123.39 / 3 =$

   (A) 31.12   (B) 41.13

   (C) 401.13   (D) 411.3

   (E) 4,113

17. $1428.6 / 6 =$

   (A) 0.2381   (B) 2.381

   (C) 23.81   (D) 238.1

   (E) 2,381

18. $25.2 / 0.3 =$

   (A) 0.84   (B) 8.04

   (C) 8.4   (D) 84

   (E) 840

19. $14.95 / 6.5 =$

   (A) 2.3   (B) 20.3

   (C) 23   (D) 230

   (E) 2,300

20. $46.33 / 1.13 =$

   (A) 0.41   (B) 4.1

   (C) 41   (D) 410

   (E) 4,100

Comparing

21. Which is the **largest** number in this set — {0.8, 0.823, 0.089, 0.807, 0.852}?

    (A) 0.8   (B) 0.823

    (C) 0.089   (D) 0.807

    (E) 0.852

22. Which is the **smallest** number in this set — {32.98, 32.099, 32.047, 32.5, 32.304}?

    (A) 32.98   (B) 32.099

    (C) 32.047   (D) 32.5

    (E) 32.304

23. In which set below are the numbers arranged correctly from smallest to largest?

    (A) {0.98, 0.9, 0.993}   (B) {0.113, 0.3, 0.31}

    (C) {7.04, 7.26, 7.2}   (D) {0.006, 0.061, 0.06}

    (E) {12.84, 12.801, 12.6}

24. In which set below are the numbers arranged correctly from largest to smallest?

    (A) {1.018, 1.63, 1.368}   (B) {4.219, 4.29, 4.9}

    (C) {0.62, 0.6043, 0.643}   (D) {16.34, 16.304, 16.3}

    (E) {12.98, 12.601, 12.86}

25. Which is the **largest** number in this set — {0.87, 0.89, 0.889, 0.8, 0.987}?

    (A) 0.87   (B) 0.89

    (C) 0.889   (D) 0.8

    (E) 0.987

Changing a Fraction to a Decimal

26. What is $1/4$ written as a decimal?

    (A) 1.4   (B) 0.14

    (C) 0.2   (D) 0.25

    (E) 0.3

27. What is $3/5$ written as a decimal?

    (A) 0.3   (B) 0.35

    (C) 0.6   (D) 0.65

    (E) 0.8

28. What is $7/20$ written as a decimal?

    (A) 0.35   (B) 0.4

    (C) 0.72   (D) 0.75

    (E) 0.9

29. What is $2/3$ written as a decimal?

    (A) 0.23   (B) 0.33

    (C) 0.5   (D) 0.6

    (E) $0.\overline{6}$

30. What is $11/25$ written as a decimal?

    (A) 0.1125   (B) 0.25

    (C) 0.4   (D) 0.44

    (E) 0.5

4. PERCENTAGES

A **percent** is a way of expressing the relationship between part and whole, where whole is defined as 100%. A percent can be defined by a fraction with a denominator of 100. Decimals can also represent a percent. For instance,

$$56\% = 0.56 = {}^{56}/_{100}$$

PROBLEM

Compute the value.

(1) 90% of 400

(2) 180% of 400

(3) 50% of 500

(4) 200% of 4

Solution

The symbol % means per hundred, therefore $5\% = {}^{5}/_{100}$.

(1) 90% of $400 = 90/100 \times 400 = 90 \times 4 = 360$

(2) 180% of $400 = 180/100 \times 400 = 180 \times 4 = 720$

(3) 50% of $500 = 50/100 \times 500 = 50 \times 5 = 250$

(4) 200% of $4 = 200/100 \times 4 = 2 \times 4 = 8$

PROBLEM

What percent of

(1) 100 is 99.5?

(2) 200 is 4?

Solution

(1) $99.5 = x \times 100$

$99.5 = 100x$

$.995 = x;$

but this is the value of x per hundred. Therefore,

$$x = 99.5\%$$

(2) $4 = x \times 200$

$4 = 200x$

$.02 = x.$

Again this must be changed to percent, so

$$2\% = x$$

Equivalent Forms of a Number

Some problems may call for converting numbers into an equivalent or simplified form in order to make the solution more convenient.

1. Converting a fraction to a decimal:

   $$^1/_2 = 0.50$$

   Divide the numerator by the denominator:

   $$\begin{array}{r} .50 \\ 2\overline{\smash{\big)}\ 1.00} \\ \underline{-10} \\ 00 \end{array}$$

2. Converting a number to a percent:

   $$0.50 = 50\%$$

   Multiply by 100:

   $$0.50 = (0.50 \times 100)\% = 50\%$$

3. Converting a percent to a decimal:

   $$30\% = 0.30$$

   Divide by 100:

   $$30\% = 30/100 = 0.30$$

4. Converting a decimal to a fraction:

   $$0.500 = {}^1/_2$$

   Convert .500 to 500/1,000 and then simplify the fraction by dividing the numerator and denominator by common factors:

   $$\frac{2 \times 2 \times 5 \times 5 \times 5}{2 \times 2 \times 2 \times 5 \times 5 \times 5}$$

   and then cancel out the common numbers to get $^1/_2$.

PROBLEM

Express

(1) 1.65 as a percent.

(2) 0.7 as a fraction.

(3) $-\frac{10}{20}$ as a decimal.

(4) $\frac{4}{2}$ as an integer.

Solution

(1) $1.65 \times 100 = 165\%$

(2) $0.7 = \frac{7}{10}$

(3) $-\frac{10}{20} = -0.5$

(4) $\frac{4}{2} = 2$

Drill 4: Percentages

Finding Percents

1.   Find 3% of 80.

(A) 0.24

(B) 2.4

(C) 24

(D) 240

(E) 2,400

2.   Find 50% of 182.

(A) 9

(B) 90

(C) 91

(D) 910

(E) 9,100

3.   Find 83% of 166.

(A) 0.137

(B) 1.377

(C) 13.778

(D) 137

(E) 137.78

4.   Find 125% of 400.

(A) 425

(B) 500

(C) 525   (D) 600

(E) 825

5. Find 300% of 4.

(A) 12   (B) 120

(C) 1,200   (D) 12,000

(E) 120,000

6. Forty-eight percent of the 1,200 students at Central High are males. How many male students are there at Central High?

(A) 57   (B) 576

(C) 580   (D) 600

(E) 648

7. For 35% of the last 40 days, there has been measurable rainfall. How many days out of the last 40 days have had measurable rainfall?

(A) 14   (B) 20

(C) 25   (D) 35

(E) 40

8. Of every 1,000 people who take a certain medicine, 0.2% develop severe side effects. How many people out of every 1,000 who take the medicine develop the side effects?

(A) 0.2   (B) 2

(C) 20   (D) 22

(E) 200

9. Of 220 applicants for a job, 75% were offered an initial interview. How many people were offered an initial interview?

(A) 75   (B) 110

(C) 120   (D) 155

(E) 165

10. Find 0.05% of 4,000.

    (A) 0.05   (B) 0.5

    (C) 2   (D) 20

    (E) 400

Changing Percents to Fractions

11. What is 25% written as a fraction?

    (A) $^1/_{25}$ (B) $^1/_5$

    (C) $^1/_4$ (D) $^1/_3$

    (E) $^1/_2$

12. What is $33^1/_3$% written as a fraction?

    (A) $^1/_4$ (B) $^1/_3$

    (C) $^1/_2$ (D) $^2/_3$

    (E) $^5/_9$

13. What is 200% written as a fraction?

    (A) $^1/_2$ (B) $^2/_1$

    (C) $^{20}/_1$ (D) $^{200}/_1$

    (E) $^{2,000}/_1$

14. What is 84% written as a fraction?

    (A) $^1/_{84}$ (B) $^4/_8$

    (C) $^{17}/_{25}$ (D) $^{21}/_{25}$

    (E) $^{44}/_{50}$

15. What is 2% written as a fraction?

    (A) $^1/_{50}$ (B) $^1/_{25}$

    (C) $^1/_{10}$ (D) $^1/_4$

    (E) $^1/_2$

Changing Fractions to Percents

16. What is $^2/_3$ written as a percent?

    (A) 23%   (B) 32%

    (C) $33^1/_3$%   (D) $57^1/_3$%

    (E) $66^2/_3$%

17. What is $^3/_5$ written as a percent?

    (A) 30%   (B) 35%

    (C) 53%   (D) 60%

    (E) 65%

18. What is $^{17}/_{20}$ written as a percent?

    (A) 17%   (B) 70%

    (C) 75%   (D) 80%

    (E) 85%

19. What is $^{45}/_{50}$ written as a percent?

    (A) 45%   (B) 50%

    (C) 90%   (D) 95%

    (E) 97%

20. What is $1^1/_4$ written as a percent?

    (A) 114%   (B) 120%

    (C) 125%   (D) 127%

    (E) 133%

Changing Percents to Decimals

21. What is 42% written as a decimal?

    (A) 0.42   (B) 4.2

    (C) 42   (D) 420

    (E) 422

22. What is 0.3% written as a decimal?

    (A) 0.0003   (B) 0.003

    (C) 0.03   (D) 0.3

    (E) 3

23. What is 8% written as a decimal?

    (A) 0.0008   (B) 0.008

    (C) 0.08   (D) 0.80

    (E) 8

24. What is 175% written as a decimal?

    (A) 0.175   (B) 1.75

    (C) 17.5   (D) 175

    (E) 17,500

25. What is 34% written as a decimal?

    (A) 0.00034   (B) 0.0034

    (C) 0.034   (D) 0.34

    (E) 3.4

Changing Decimals to Percents

26. What is 0.43 written as a percent?

    (A) 0.0043%   (B) 0.043%

    (C) 4.3%   (D) 43%

    (E) 430%

27. What is 1 written as a percent?

    (A) 1%   (B) 10%

    (C) 100%   (D) 111%

    (E) 150%

28. What is 0.08 written as a percent?

    (A) 0.08%   (B) 8%

    (C) 8.8%   (D) 80%

    (E) 800%

29. What is 3.4 written as a percent?

    (A) 0.0034%   (B) 3.4%

    (C) 34%   (D) 304%

    (E) 340%

30. What is 0.645 written as a percent?

    (A) 64.5%   (B) 65%

    (C) 69%   (D) 70%

    (E) 645%

5. RADICALS

The **square root** of a number is a number that when multiplied by itself results in the original number. So, the square root of 81 is 9 since 9 × 9 = 81. However, − 9 is also a root of 81 since (− 9) (− 9) = 81. Every positive number will have two roots. Yet, the principal root is the positive one. Zero has only one square root, while negative numbers do not have real numbers as their roots.

A **radical sign** indicates that the root of a number or expression will be taken. The **radicand** is the number of which the root will be taken. The **index** tells how many times the root needs to be multiplied by itself to equal the radicand, e.g.,

index

radical sign → radicand

(1) $\sqrt[3]{64}$;

       3 is the index and 64 is the radicand. Since

       $4 \times 4 \times 4 = 64$, $\sqrt[3]{64} = 4$

(2) $\sqrt[5]{32}$;

5 is the index and 32 is the radicand. Since

$$2 \times 2 \times 2 \times 2 \times 2 = 32, \sqrt[5]{32} = 2$$

Operations with Radicals

(A) **To multiply two or more radicals,** we utilize the law that states

$$\sqrt{a} \times \sqrt{b} = \sqrt{ab}.$$

Simply multiply the whole numbers as usual. Then, multiply the radicands and put the product under the radical sign and simplify, e.g.,

(1) $\sqrt{12} \times \sqrt{5} = \sqrt{60} = \sqrt{4 \times 15} = \sqrt{4}\sqrt{15} = 2\sqrt{15}$

(2) $3\sqrt{2} \times 4\sqrt{8} = 12\sqrt{16} = 48$

(3) $2\sqrt{10} \times 6\sqrt{5} = 12\sqrt{50} = 60\sqrt{2}$

(B) **To divide radicals,** simplify both the numerator and the denominator. By multiplying the radical in the denominator by itself, you can make the denominator a rational number. The numerator, however, must also be multiplied by this radical so that the value of the expression does not change. You must choose as many factors as necessary to rationalize the denominator, e.g.,

(1) $\dfrac{\sqrt{128}}{\sqrt{2}} = \dfrac{\sqrt{64} \times \sqrt{2}}{\sqrt{2}} = \dfrac{8\sqrt{2}}{\sqrt{2}} = 8$

(2) $\dfrac{\sqrt{10}}{\sqrt{3}} = \dfrac{\sqrt{10} \times \sqrt{3}}{\sqrt{3} \times \sqrt{3}} = \dfrac{\sqrt{30}}{3}$

(3) $\dfrac{\sqrt{8}}{2\sqrt{3}} = \dfrac{\sqrt{8} \times \sqrt{3}}{2\sqrt{3} \times \sqrt{3}} = \dfrac{\sqrt{24}}{2 \times 3} = \dfrac{2\sqrt{6}}{6} = \dfrac{\sqrt{6}}{3}$

(C) **To add two or more radicals,** the radicals must have the same index and the same radicand. Only where the radicals are simplified can these similarities be determined, e.g.,

(1) $6\sqrt{2} + 2\sqrt{2} = (6 + 2)\sqrt{2} = 8\sqrt{2}$

(2) $\sqrt{27} + 5\sqrt{3} = \sqrt{9}\sqrt{3} + 5\sqrt{3} = 3\sqrt{3} + 5\sqrt{3} = 8\sqrt{3}$

(3) $7\sqrt{3} + 8\sqrt{2} + 5\sqrt{3} = 12\sqrt{3} + 8\sqrt{2}$

Similarly to subtract,

(1) $12\sqrt{3} - 7\sqrt{3} = (12 - 7)\sqrt{3} = 5\sqrt{3}$

(2) $\sqrt{90} - \sqrt{20} = \sqrt{16}\sqrt{5} - \sqrt{4}\sqrt{5} = 4\sqrt{5} - 2\sqrt{5} = 2\sqrt{5}$

(3) $\sqrt{50} - \sqrt{3} = 5\sqrt{2} - \sqrt{3}$

Drill 5: Radicals

Multiplication

DIRECTIONS: Multiply and simplify each answer.

1. $\sqrt{6} \times \sqrt{5} =$

   (A) $\sqrt{11}$ (B) $\sqrt{30}$

   (C) $2\sqrt{5}$ (D) $3\sqrt{10}$

   (E) $2\sqrt{3}$

2. $\sqrt{3} \times \sqrt{12} =$

   (A) 3   (B) $\sqrt{15}$

   (C) $\sqrt{36}$ (D) 6

   (E) 8

3. $\sqrt{7} \times \sqrt{7} =$

   (A) 7   (B) 49

   (C) $\sqrt{14}$ (D) $2\sqrt{7}$

   (E) $2\sqrt{14}$

4. $3\sqrt{5} \times 2\sqrt{5} =$

   (A) $5\sqrt{5}$ (B) 25

   (C) 30   (D) $5\sqrt{25}$

   (E) $6\sqrt{5}$

5. $4\sqrt{6} \times \sqrt{2} =$

   (A) $4\sqrt{8}$ (B) $8\sqrt{2}$

   (C) $5\sqrt{8}$ (D) $4\sqrt{12}$

   (E) $8\sqrt{3}$

Division

DIRECTIONS: Divide and simplify each answer.

6. $\sqrt{10} \div \sqrt{2} =$

   (A) $\sqrt{8}$ (B) $2\sqrt{2}$

   (C) $\sqrt{5}$ (D) $2\sqrt{5}$

   (E) $2\sqrt{3}$

7. $\sqrt{30} \div \sqrt{15} =$

   (A) $\sqrt{2}$ (B) $\sqrt{45}$

   (C) $3\sqrt{5}$ (D) $\sqrt{15}$

   (E) $5\sqrt{3}$

8. $\sqrt{100} \div \sqrt{25} =$

   (A) $\sqrt{4}$ (B) $5\sqrt{5}$

   (C) $5\sqrt{3}$ (D) 2

   (E) 4

9. $\sqrt{48} \div \sqrt{8} =$

   (A) $4\sqrt{3}$ (B) $3\sqrt{2}$

   (C) $\sqrt{6}$ (D) 6

   (E) 12

10. $3\sqrt{12} \div \sqrt{3} =$

    (A) $3\sqrt{15}$ (B) 6

    (C) 9 (D) 12

    (E) $3\sqrt{36}$

Addition

DIRECTIONS: Simplify each radical and add.

11. $\sqrt{7} + 3\sqrt{7} =$

    (A) $3\sqrt{7}$ (B) $4\sqrt{7}$

    (C) $3\sqrt{14}$ (D) $4\sqrt{14}$

    (E) $3\sqrt{21}$

12. $\sqrt{5} + 6\sqrt{5} + 3\sqrt{5} =$

    (A) $9\sqrt{5}$ (B) $9\sqrt{15}$

    (C) $5\sqrt{10}$ (D) $10\sqrt{5}$

    (E) $18\sqrt{15}$

13. $3\sqrt{32} + 2\sqrt{2} =$

    (A) $5\sqrt{2}$ (B) $\sqrt{34}$

    (C) $14\sqrt{2}$ (D) $5\sqrt{34}$

    (E) $6\sqrt{64}$

14. $6\sqrt{15} + 8\sqrt{15} + 16\sqrt{15} =$

    (A) $15\sqrt{30}$ (B) $30\sqrt{45}$

    (C) $30\sqrt{30}$ (D) $15\sqrt{45}$

    (E) $30\sqrt{15}$

15. $6\sqrt{5} + 2\sqrt{45} =$

    (A) $12\sqrt{5}$ (B) $8\sqrt{50}$

    (C) $40\sqrt{2}$ (D) $12\sqrt{50}$

    (E) $8\sqrt{5}$

Subtraction

DIRECTIONS: Simplify each radical and subtract.

16. $8\sqrt{5} - 6\sqrt{5} =$

   (A) $2\sqrt{5}$ (B) $3\sqrt{5}$
   (C) $4\sqrt{5}$ (D) $14\sqrt{5}$
   (E) $48\sqrt{5}$

17. $16\sqrt{33} - 5\sqrt{33} =$

   (A) $3\sqrt{33}$ (B) $33\sqrt{11}$
   (C) $11\sqrt{33}$ (D) $11\sqrt{0}$
   (E) $\sqrt{33}$

18. $14\sqrt{2} - 19\sqrt{2} =$

   (A) $5\sqrt{2}$ (B) $-5\sqrt{2}$
   (C) $-33\sqrt{2}$ (D) $33\sqrt{2}$
   (E) $-4\sqrt{2}$

19. $10\sqrt{2} - 3\sqrt{8} =$

   (A) $6\sqrt{6}$ (B) $-2\sqrt{2}$
   (C) $7\sqrt{6}$ (D) $4\sqrt{2}$
   (E) $-6\sqrt{6}$

20. $4\sqrt{3} - 2\sqrt{12} =$

   (A) $-2\sqrt{9}$ (B) $-6\sqrt{15}$
   (C) 0 (D) $6\sqrt{15}$
   (E) $2\sqrt{12}$

6. EXPONENTS AND SCIENTIFIC NOTATION

When a number is multiplied by itself a specific number of times, it is said to be **raised to a power**. The way this is written is

$$a^n = b$$

where a is the number or **base**, n is the **exponent** or **power** that indicates the number of times a is to be multiplied by itself, and b is the product of this multiplication.

In the expression 3^2, 3 is the base and 2 is the exponent. This means that 3 is multiplied by itself 2 times and the product is 9.

$$3^2 = 3 \times 3 = 9$$

An exponent can be either positive or negative. A negative exponent implies a fraction. Such that, if n is a positive integer

$$a^{-n} = \frac{1}{a^n}, \ a \neq 0. \text{ So, } 2^{-4} = \frac{1}{2^4} = \frac{1}{16}.$$

An exponent that is 0 gives a result of 1, assuming that the base is not equal to 0.

$$a^0 = 1, a \neq 0.$$

An exponent can also be a fraction. If m and n are positive integers,

$$a^{\frac{m}{n}} = \sqrt[n]{a^m}$$

The numerator remains the exponent of a, but the denominator tells what root to take. For example,

(1) $\quad 4^{\frac{3}{2}} = \sqrt[2]{4^3} = \sqrt{64} = 8$ (2) $\quad 3^{\frac{4}{2}} = \sqrt[2]{3^4} = \sqrt{81} = 9$

If a fractional exponent were negative, the same operation would take place, but the result would be a fraction. For example,

(1) $\quad 27^{-\frac{2}{3}} = \frac{1}{27^{2/3}} = \frac{1}{\sqrt[3]{27^2}} = \frac{1}{\sqrt[3]{729}} = \frac{1}{9}$

PROBLEM

Simplify the following expressions.

(1) -3^{-2}

(2) $(-3)^{-2}$

(3) $\dfrac{-3}{4^{-1}}$

Solution

(1)   Here the exponent applies only to 3. Since

$$x^{-y} = \frac{1}{x^y}, \; -3^{-2} = -(3)^{-2} = -\frac{1}{3^2} = -\frac{1}{9}$$

(2)   In this case the exponent applies to the negative base. Thus,

$$(-3)^{-2} = \frac{1}{(-3)^2} = \frac{1}{(-3)(-3)} = \frac{1}{9}$$

(3) $\dfrac{-3}{4^{-1}} = \dfrac{-3}{\left(\dfrac{1}{4}\right)^1} = \dfrac{-3}{\dfrac{1}{4^1}} = \dfrac{-3}{\dfrac{1}{4}}$

Division by a fraction is equivalent to multiplication by that fraction's reciprocal, thus

$$\frac{-3}{\dfrac{1}{4}} = -3 \times \frac{4}{1} = -12 \text{ and } \frac{-3}{4^{-1}} = -12$$

General Laws of Exponents

(A) $a^p a^q = a^{p+q}$

$$4^2 4^3 = 4^{2+3} = 1,024$$

(B) $(a^p)^q = a^{pq}$

$$(2^3)^2 = 2^6 = 64$$

(C) $\dfrac{a^p}{a^q} = a^{p-q}$

$$\frac{3^6}{3^2} = 3^4 = 81$$

(D) $(ab)^p = a^p b^p$

$$(3 \times 2)^2 = 3^2 \times 2^2 = (9)(4) = 36$$

(E) $\left(\dfrac{a}{b}\right)^p = \dfrac{a^p}{b^p}$, $b \neq 0$

$$\left(\frac{4}{5}\right)^2 = \frac{4^2}{5^2} = \frac{16}{25}$$

Scientific Notation

In **scientific notation** there is only one digit before the decimal point, and the remaining digits follow it. The base, a, is 10 and the exponent, n, is how many places the decimal point has been shifted. A negative exponent means the decimal point was shifted to the right and a positive exponent means the decimal point was shifted to the left.

EXAMPLES

$$5.23 \times 10^2 = 523$$

$$8.9 \times 10^{-4} = 0.00089$$

PROBLEM

Convert to scientific notation.

(1) 0.0042   (2) 25×10^3

Solution

(1)   0.004.2

Move the decimal point 3 places to the right.

$$4.2 \times 10^{-3}$$

(2) $25 \times 10^3 = 25 \times 1{,}000 = 2.5000.$

Move the decimal point 4 places to the left.

$$2.5 \times 10^4$$

Drill 6: Exponents and Scientific Notation

Multiplication

DIRECTIONS: Simplify.

1. $4^6 \times 4^2 =$

    (A) 4^4 (B) 4^8

    (C) 4^{12} (D) 16^8

    (E) 16^{12}

2. $2^2 \times 2^5 \times 2^3 =$

    (A) 2^{10} (B) 4^{10}

    (C) 8^{10} (D) 2^{30}

    (E) 8^{30}

3. $6^6 \times 6^2 \times 6^4 =$

    (A) 18^8 (B) 18^{12}

    (C) 6^{12} (D) 6^{48}

    (E) 18^{48}

4. $a^4b^2 \times a^3b =$

    (A) ab (B) $2a^7b^2$

    (C) $2a^{12}b$ (D) a^7b^3

    (E) a^7b^2

5. $m^8n^3 \times m^2n \times m^4n^2 =$

    (A) $3m^{16}n^6$ (B) $m^{14}n^6$

    (C) $3m^{14}n^5$ (D) $3m^{14}n^5$

    (E) m^2

Division

DIRECTIONS: Simplify.

6. $6^5 \div 6^3 =$

(A) 0   (B) 1

(C) 6   (D) 12

(E) 36

7. $11^8 \div 11^5 =$

(A) 1^3 (B) 11^3

(C) 11^{13} (D) 11^{40}

(E) 88^5

8. $x^{10}y^8 \div x^7y^3 =$

(A) x^2y^5 (B) x^3y^4

(C) x^3y^5 (D) x^2y^4

(E) x^5y^3

9. $a^{14} \div a^9 =$

(A) 1^5 (B) a^5

(C) $2a^5$ (D) a^{23}

(E) $2a^{23}$

10. $c^{17}d^{12}e^4 \div c^{12}d^8e =$

(A) $c^4d^5e^3$ (B) $c^4d^4e^3$

(C) $c^5d^8e^4$ (D) $c^5d^4e^3$

(E) $c^5d^4e^4$

Power to a Power

DIRECTIONS: Simplify.

11. $(3^6)^2 =$

    (A) 3^4 (B) 3^8

    (C) 3^{12} (D) 9^6

    (E) 9^8

12. $(4^3)^5 =$

    (A) 4^2 (B) 2^{15}

    (C) 4^8 (D) 20^3

    (E) 4^{15}

13. $(a^4b^3)^2 =$

    (A) $(ab)^9$ (B) a^8b^6

    (C) $(ab)^{24}$ (D) a^6b^5

    (E) $2a^4b^3$

14. $(r^3p^6)^3 =$

    (A) r^9p^{18} (B) $(rp)^{12}$

    (C) r^6p^9 (D) $3r^3p^6$

    (E) $3r^9p^{18}$

15. $(m^6n^5q^3)^2 =$

    (A) $2m^6n^5q^3$ (B) m^4n^3q

    (C) $m^8n^7q^5$ (D) $m^{12}n^{10}q^6$

    (E) $2m^{12}n^{10}q^6$

Scientific Notation

DIRECTIONS: Convert to scientific notation.

16. 0.0000415

    (A) 4.15×10^5 (B) 4.15×10^{-4}

    (C) 4.15×10^{-7} (D) 4.15×10^{-5}

    (E) 4.15×10^{-6}

17. $12.1 \times \dfrac{1}{10^5}$

    (A) 1.21×10^{-5} (B) 1.21×10^6

    (C) 1.21×10^{-6} (D) 1.21×10^5

    (E) 1.21×10^{-4}

18. 50100.0

    (A) 5.01×10^{-1} (B) 5.01×10^3

    (C) 5.01×10^4 (D) 5.01×10^5

    (E) 5.01×10^6

19. 10.5

    (A) 1.05×10^1 (B) 1.05×10^2

    (C) 1.05×10^{-2} (D) 1.05×10^3

    (E) 1.05×10^{-1}

20. $\dfrac{1}{2,000}$

    (A) 2^3 (B) 2^{-3}

    (C) 5.0×10^{-3} (D) 5.0×10^{-4}

    (E) 2.0×10^{-3}

ARITHMETIC DRILLS

ANSWER KEY

Drill 1 – Integers and Real Numbers

1.	(A)	9.	(E)	17.	(D)	25.	(D)
2.	(C)	10.	(B)	18.	(D)	26.	(D)
3.	(D)	11.	(B)	19.	(C)	27.	(B)
4.	(C)	12.	(E)	20.	(E)	28.	(C)
5.	(B)	13.	(C)	21.	(B)	29.	(A)
6.	(B)	14.	(A)	22.	(E)	30.	(C)
7.	(A)	15.	(B)	23.	(D)		
8.	(C)	16.	(B)	24.	(A)		

Drill 2 – Fractions

1.	(D)	14.	(D)	27.	(D)	40.	(A)
2.	(E)	15.	(B)	28.	(E)	41.	(D)
3.	(C)	16.	(B)	29.	(C)	42.	(A)
4.	(A)	17.	(D)	30.	(B)	43.	(D)
5.	(C)	18.	(B)	31.	(C)	44.	(E)
6.	(C)	19.	(A)	32.	(A)	45.	(C)
7.	(C)	20.	(C)	33.	(B)	46.	(D)
8.	(A)	21.	(D)	34.	(C)	47.	(D)
9.	(B)	22.	(C)	35.	(D)	48.	(B)
10.	(A)	23.	(B)	36.	(B)	49.	(A)
11.	(B)	24.	(E)	37.	(C)	50.	(E)
12.	(D)	25.	(A)	38.	(D)		
13.	(E)	26.	(A)	39.	(E)		

Drill 3 – Decimals

1. (B)	9. (C)	17. (D)	25. (E)
2. (E)	10. (E)	18. (D)	26. (D)
3. (C)	11. (B)	19. (A)	27. (C)
4. (A)	12. (D)	20. (C)	28. (A)
5. (D)	13. (A)	21. (E)	29. (E)
6. (A)	14. (B)	22. (C)	30. (D)
7. (B)	15. (C)	23. (B)	
8. (D)	16. (B)	24. (D)	

Drill 4 – Percentages

1. (B)	9. (E)	17. (D)	25. (D)
2. (C)	10. (C)	18. (E)	26. (D)
3. (E)	11. (C)	19. (C)	27. (C)
4. (B)	12. (B)	20. (C)	28. (B)
5. (A)	13. (B)	21. (A)	29. (E)
6. (B)	14. (D)	22. (B)	30. (A)
7. (A)	15. (A)	23. (C)	
8. (B)	16. (E)	24. (B)	

Drill 5 – Radicals

1. (B)	6. (C)	11. (B)	16. (A)
2. (D)	7. (A)	12. (D)	17. (C)
3. (A)	8. (D)	13. (C)	18. (B)
4. (C)	9. (C)	14. (E)	19. (D)
5. (E)	10. (B)	15. (A)	20. (C)

Drill 6 – Exponents and Scientific Notation

1. (B)	6. (E)	11. (C)	16. (D)
2. (A)	7. (B)	12. (E)	17. (E)
3. (C)	8. (C)	13. (B)	18. (C)
4. (D)	9. (B)	14. (A)	19. (A)
5. (B)	10. (D)	15. (D)	20. (D)

ELM

Entry Level Mathematics

Chapter 2
Elementary Algebra
Review

ELEMENTARY ALGEBRA DIAGNOSTIC TEST

12 Questions

(Answer sheets appear at the back of the book.)

> **DIRECTIONS:** Each question has five multiple-choice answers. Select the single best answer.

1. Solve for the value of y:

   $3x + 2y = 12$

   $2x - 2y = 8$

   (A) 0   (B) 2

   (C) 3   (D) 4

   (E) 5

2. Simplify $(-4a^3x^4)^2$.

   (A) $-4a^5x^6$ (B) $8a^5x^6$

   (C) $8a^6x^8$ (D) $16a^6x^8$

   (E) $-16a^6x^8$

3. What is the factorization of $x^2 + ax - 2x - 2a$?

   (A) $(x + 2)(x - a)$ (B) $(x - 2)(x + a)$

   (C) $(x + 2)(x + a)$ (D) $(x - 2)(x - a)$

   (E) None of these

4. If $abc \neq 0$, then $\dfrac{3a^2bc^3 + 9a^3b^2c}{27ab^2c + 15a^2b^2c^3} =$

(A) $\dfrac{ab(c^2 + 3)}{c(9 + 5a)}$

(B) $\dfrac{a(c^2 + 3ab)}{b(9 + 5ac^2)}$

(C) $\dfrac{a(c^2 + 3ab)}{c(9 + ac^2)}$

(D) $\dfrac{c^2 + 3ab}{9 + 5ac^2}$

(E) $\dfrac{a}{b(9 + 5ac^2)}$

5. Find the sum of:

$$8x^2 - 4xy - y^2 - 4x^2 - 5xy - x^2 - 4xy + y^2 - 7y^2 + 2x^2$$

(A) $3x^2 - 9xy - 4y^2 - 2$

(B) $6x^2 - 13xy - 7y^2$

(C) $-18x^2y^2xy$

(D) $5x^2 - 13xy - 7y^2$

(E) $-13xy - 1$

6. $\dfrac{\dfrac{1}{x} - \dfrac{1}{y}}{\dfrac{1}{x^2} - \dfrac{1}{y^2}} =$

(A) $\dfrac{x^2y^2}{x^2 + y^2}$

(B) $\dfrac{xy}{x + y}$

(C) $\dfrac{xy}{(x + y)^2}$

(D) $\dfrac{xy}{y^2 - x^2}$

(E) $\left(\dfrac{xy}{x + y}\right)^2$

7. Find the roots of the following equation:

    $x^2 - 5x + 6 = 0$

    (A) 1 and 5   (B) 1 and 6

    (C) 2 and 3   (D) 2 and 5

    (E) 3 and 5

8. Find the solution set of the following pair of equations:

    $$\begin{cases} 3x + 4y = -6 \\ 5x + 6y = -8 \end{cases}$$

    (A) $\{(1, 2)\}$ (B) $\{(1, 3)\}$

    (C) $\{(2, 3)\}$ (D) $\{(2, -3)\}$

    (E) $\{(3, -3)\}$

9. Solve $3(x + 2) < 5x$.

    (A) $x = 3$ (B) $x > 3$

    (C) $x < 3$ (D) $x \geq 2$

    (E) $x < -6$

10. Simplify $\dfrac{x^2 - y^2}{x^3 - x^2 y}$.

    (A) $\dfrac{y}{x}$ (B) $\dfrac{x + y}{y}$

    (C) $\dfrac{x - y}{x^2}$ (D) $\dfrac{x + y}{x^2}$

    (E) $\dfrac{-y}{x - x^2}$

11. Find the roots of $x^2 - 10x + 21 = 0$.

    (A) 10, 21   (B) $-3, -7$

    (C) 3, 7   (D) 1, 21

    (E) 0, 2.1

12. Which of the following is an equation of line 1?

    (A) $y = -3$

    (B) $x = 3$

    (C) $x = -3$

    (D) $y = 3$

    (E) $y = 3x$

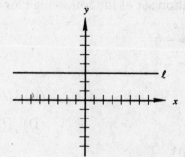

ELEMENTARY ALGEBRA DIAGNOSTIC TEST

ANSWER KEY

1.	(A)	4.	(B)	7.	(C)	10.	(D)
2.	(D)	5.	(D)	8.	(D)	11.	(C)
3.	(B)	6.	(B)	9.	(B)	12.	(D)

DETERMINE YOUR STRENGTHS AND WEAKNESSES

ELEMENTARY ALGEBRA

Question Type	Question #	See Pages . . .
Operations with Polynomials	2, 5	81–88
Simplifying Algebraic Expressions	3, 6, 7, 10, 11	88–93
Rational Expressions	4, 6, 10	93–100
Linear Equations	1, 8	100–106
Two Linear Equations	1, 8	106–113
Quadratic Equations	7, 11	114–119
Inequalities	9	119–123
Graphs	12	123–127

DETAILED EXPLANATIONS OF ANSWERS

ELEMENTARY ALGEBRA DIAGNOSTIC TEST

1. **(A)**
    Add like terms, and notice that the y column is eliminated.

$$3x + 2y = 12$$
$$\underline{2x - 2y = 8}$$
$$5x = 20$$
$$x = 4$$

Substitute the 4 for the x in the equation $3x + 2y = 12$.

$$3(4) + 2y = 12$$
$$12 + 2y = 12$$
$$2y = 0$$
$$y = 0$$

2. **(D)**
    Rewrite each constant and variable separately.

$$(-4a^3x^4)^2 = (-4)^2\,(a^3)^2\,(x^4)^2$$

From the General Laws of Exponents

$$(a^p)^q = a^{pq}.$$

Therefore, the variables equal a^6x^8. Squaring a negative gives a positive number. Therefore, the correct answer is $16a^6x^8$.

3. **(B)**
    First, group the expression and then find the monomial factor for each group as follows:

$$(x^2 + ax) + (-2x - 2a) = x(x + a) + (-2)(x + a).$$

Then, the final factorization is formed by using $(x + a)$ and $(x - 2)$. So,

$$x^2 + ax - 2x - 2a = (x - 2)(x + a).$$

4.   **(B)**

$$\frac{3a^2bc^3 + 9a^3b^2c}{27ab^2c + 15a^2b^2c^3} = \frac{3a^2bc(c^2 + 3ab)}{3ab^2c(9 + 5ac^2)}$$

$$= \frac{a(c^2 + 3ab)}{b(9 + 5ac^2)}$$

5.   **(D)**
Write each term under other like terms (like terms = expressions that contain exactly the same variables and the same exponents, but possibly different coefficients). In the terms y^2 and $-y^2$, the coefficient 1 is usually not written: $(y^2 = 1y^2, -y^2 = -1y^2)$.

$$8x^2 - 4xy - y^2$$
$$-4x^2 - 5xy$$
$$-x^2 - 4xy + y^2$$
$$+2x^2 \qquad -7y^2$$
_____

To add the like terms, find the sum of the numerical coefficients and affix the common variable.

$$(8 - 4 - 1 + 2)x^2 + (-4 - 5 - 4)xy + (-1 + 1 - 7)y^2$$
$$= 5x^2 - 13xy - 7y^2$$

6.   **(B)**

$$\frac{\dfrac{1}{x} - \dfrac{1}{y}}{\dfrac{1}{x^2} - \dfrac{1}{y^2}} = \frac{\dfrac{y - x}{xy}}{\dfrac{y^2 - x^2}{x^2 y^2}}$$

$$= \left(\frac{y-x}{xy}\right)\left(\frac{x^2y^2}{y^2-x^2}\right)$$

$$= (y-x)\left(\frac{xy}{(y+x)(y-x)}\right)$$

$$= \frac{xy}{x+y}$$

7. **(C)**

$$x^2 - 5x + 6 = 0$$

$$(x-2)(x-3) = 0$$

$$x = 2 \quad \text{or} \quad x = 3$$

8. **(D)**

$$\begin{cases} 3x + 4y = -6 & (1) \\ 5x + 6y = -8 & (2) \end{cases}$$

Multiply equation (1) by 3 and equation (2) by 2. Subtract equation (2) from equation (1):

$$9x + 12y = -18$$

$$-(10x + 12y = -16)$$

$$-x = -2$$

$$x = 2$$

Substitute $x = 2$ into (1):

$$3(2) + 4y = -6$$

$$4y = -12$$

$$y = -3$$

Therefore, the solution set is $\{(2, -3)\}$.

9. **(B)**

$$3(x + 2) < 5x$$

$$3x + 6 < 5x$$

$$6 < 2x$$

Subtracting $3x$ from both sides.

$$3 < x$$

Dividing both sides by 2.

10. **(D)**

$$\frac{x^2 - y^2}{x^3 - x^2y} = \frac{(x - y)(x + y)}{x^2(x - y)}$$

Factoring the numerator and denominator.

$$= \frac{x + y}{x^2}$$

11. **(C)**

$$x^2 - 10x + 21 = 0$$

$$(x - 3)(x - 7) = 0$$

$$x = 3 \quad \text{or} \quad x = 7$$

12. **(D)**
    Look at some values of x and y.

x	y
0	3
-4	3
3	3

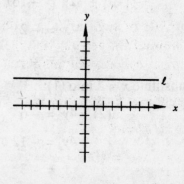

The value of x has no effect on y which is 3. This gives the equation $y = 3$.

ELEMENTARY ALGEBRA REVIEW

In algebra, letters or variables are used to represent numbers. A **variable** is defined as a placeholder, which can take on any of several values at a given time. A **constant**, on the other hand, is a symbol which takes on only one value at a given time. A **term** is a constant, a variable, or a combination of constants and variables. For example: 7.76, $3x$, xyz, $5z/x$, $(0.99)x^2$ are terms. If a term is a combination of constants and variables, the constant part of the term is referred to as the **coefficient** of the variable. If a variable is written without a coefficient, the coefficient is assumed to be 1.

EXAMPLES

$3x^2$ y^3

coefficient: 3   coefficient: 1

variable: x variable: y

An **expression** is a collection of one or more terms. If the number of terms is greater than 1, the expression is said to be the sum of the terms.

EXAMPLES

$9, 9xy, 6x + x/3, 8yz - 2x$

An algebraic expression consisting of only one term is called a **monomial**; of two terms is called a **binomial**; of three terms is called a **trinomial**. In general, an algebraic expression consisting of two or more terms is called a **polynomial**.

Review of Exponents with Variables

1. $a^p a^q = a^{p+q}$

    $x^2 x^3 = x^{2+3} = x^5$

2. $(a^p)^q = a^{pq}$

    $(y^4)^3 = y^{12}$

3. $\dfrac{a^p}{a^q} = a^{p-q}$

$\dfrac{z^5}{z^3} = z^{5-3} = z^2$

4. $(ab)^p = a^p b^p$

$(xy)^4 = x^4 y^4$

5. $\left(\dfrac{a}{b}\right)^p = \dfrac{a^p}{b^p}$, $b \neq 0$

$\left(\dfrac{y}{z}\right)^3 = \dfrac{y^3}{z^3}$

1. OPERATIONS WITH POLYNOMIALS

(A) **Addition of polynomials** is achieved by combining like terms, terms which differ only in their numerical coefficients. For example,

$$P(x) = (x^2 - 3x + 5) + (4x^2 + 6x - 3)$$

Note that the parentheses are used to distinguish the polynomials.

By using the commutative and associative laws, we can rewrite $P(x)$ as:

$$P(x) = (x^2 + 4x^2) + (6x - 3x) + (5 - 3)$$

Using the distributive law, $ab + ac = a(b + c)$, yields:

$$(1 + 4)x^2 + (6 - 3)x + (5 - 3) = 5x^2 + 3x + 2$$

(B) **Subtraction of two polynomials** is achieved by first changing the sign of all terms in the expression which is being subtracted and then adding this result to the other expression. For example,

$$(5x^2 + 4y^2 + 3z^2) - (4xy + 7y^2 - 3z^2 + 1)$$

$$= 5x^2 + 4y^2 + 3z^2 - 4xy - 7y^2 + 3z^2 - 1$$

$$= (5x^2) + (4y^2 - 7y^2) + (3z^2 + 3z^2) - 4xy - 1$$

$$= 5x^2 - 3y^2 + 6z^2 - 4xy - 1$$

(C) **Multiplication of two or more monomials** is achieved by using the laws of exponents, the rules of signs, and the commutative and associative laws of multiplication. Begin by multiplying the coefficients and then multiply the variables according to the laws of exponents. For example,

$(y^2) (5) (6y^2) (yz) (2z^2)$

$= (1) (5) (6) (1) (2) (y^2) (y^2) (yz) (z^2)$

$= 60[(y^2) (y^2) (y)] [(z) (z^2)]$

$= 60(y^5) (z^3)$

$= 60y^5z^3$

(D) **Multiplication of a polynomial by a monomial** is achieved by multiplying each term of the polynomial by the monomial and combining the results. For example,

$(4x^2 + 3y) (6xz^2)$

$= (4x^2) (6xz^2) + (3y) (6xz^2)$

$= 24x^3z^2 + 18xyz^2$

(E) **Multiplication of a polynomial by a polynomial** is achieved by multiplying each of the terms of one polynomial by each of the terms of the other polynomial and combining the results. For example,

$(5y + z + 1) (y^2 + 2y)$

$[(5y) (y^2) + (5y) (2y)] + [(z) (y^2) + (z) (2y)] + [(1) (y^2) + (1) (2y)]$

$= (5y^3 + 10y^2) + (y^2z + 2yz) + (y^2 + 2y)$

$= (5y^3) + (10y^2 + y^2) + (y^2z) + (2yz) + (2y)$

$= 5y^3 + 11y^2 + y^2z + 2yz + 2y$

(F) **Division of a monomial by a monomial** is achieved by first dividing the constant coefficients and the variable factors separately, and then multiplying these quotients. For example,

$6xyz^2 \div 2y^2z$

$= (6/2) (x/1) (y/y^2) (z^2/z)$

$= 3xy^{-1}z$

$= 3xz/y$

(G) **Division of a polynomial by a polynomial** is achieved by following the given procedure called long division.

Step 1: The terms of both the polynomials are arranged in order of ascending or descending powers of one variable.

Step 2: The first term of the dividend is divided by the first term of the divisor which gives the first term of the quotient.

Step 3: This first term of the quotient is multiplied by the entire divisor and the result is subtracted from the dividend.

Step 4: Using the remainder obtained from Step 3 as the new dividend, Steps 2 and 3 are repeated until the remainder is zero or the degree of the remainder is less than the degree of the divisor.

Step 5: The result is written as follows:

$$\frac{\text{dividend}}{\text{divisor}} = \text{quotient} + \frac{\text{remainder}}{\text{divisor}}$$

divisor $\neq 0$

e.g., $(2x^2 + x + 6) \div (x + 1)$

$$
\begin{array}{r}
2x - 1 \\
x + 1 \overline{\smash{\big)}\ 2x^2 + x + 6} \\
\underline{-(2x^2 + 2x)} \\
-x + 6 \\
\underline{-(-x - 1)} \\
7
\end{array}
$$

The result is

$$(2x^2 + x + 6) \div (x + 1) = 2x - 1 + \frac{7}{x+1}$$

Drill 1: Operations with Polynomials

Addition

1. $9a^2b + 3c + 2a^2b + 5c =$

    (A) $19a^2bc$ (B) $11a^2b + 8c$

    (C) $11a^4b^2 + 8c^2$ (D) $19a^4b^2c^2$

    (E) $12a^2b + 8c^2$

2. $14m^2n^3 + 6m^2n^3 + 3m^2n^3 =$

   (A) $20m^2n^3$ (B) $23m^6n^9$

   (C) $23m^2n^3$ (D) $32m^6n^9$

   (E) $23m^8n^{27}$

3. $3x + 2y + 16x + 3z + 6y =$

   (A) $19x + 8y$ (B) $19x + 11yz$

   (C) $19x + 8y + 3z$ (D) $11xy + 19xz$

   (E) $30xyz$

4. $(4d^2 + 7e^3 + 12f) + (3d^2 + 6e^3 + 2f) =$

   (A) $23d^2e^3f$ (B) $33d^2e^2f$

   (C) $33d^4e^6f^2$ (D) $7d^2 + 13e^3 + 14f$

   (E) $23d^2 + 11e^3f$

5. $3ac^2 + 2b^2c + 7ac^2 + 2ac^2 + b^2c =$

   (A) $12ac^2 + 3b^2c$ (B) $14ab^2c^2$

   (C) $11ac^2 + 4ab^2c$ (D) $15ab^2c^2$

   (E) $15a^2b^4c^4$

Subtraction

6. $14m^2n - 6m^2n =$

   (A) $20m^2n$ (B) $8m^2n$

   (C) $8m$ (D) 8

   (E) $8m^4n^2$

7. $3x^3y^2 - 4xz - 6x^3y^2 =$

   (A) $-7x^2y^2z$ (B) $3x^3y^2 - 10x^4y^2z$

   (C) $-3x^3y^2 - 4xz$ (D) $-x^2y^2z - 6x^3y^2$

   (E) $-7xyz$

8. $9g^2 + 6h - 2g^2 - 5h =$

   (A) $15g^2h - 7g^2h$ (B) $7g^4h^2$

   (C) $11g^2 + 7h$ (D) $11g^2 - 7h^2$

   (E) $7g^2 + h$

9. $7b^3 - 4c^2 - 6b^3 + 3c^2 =$

   (A) $b^3 - c^2$ (B) $-11b^2 - 3c^2$

   (C) $13b^3 - c$ (D) $7b - c$

   (E) 0

10. $11q^2r - 4q^2r - 8q^2r =$

   (A) $22q^2r$ (B) q^2r

   (C) $-2q^2r$ (D) $-q^2r$

   (E) $2q^2r$

Multiplication

11. $5p^2t \times 3p^2t =$

   (A) $15p^2t$ (B) $15p^4t$

   (C) $15p^4t^2$ (D) $8p^2t$

   (E) $8p^4t^2$

12. $(2r + s)\,14r =$

   (A) $28rs$ (B) $28r^2 + 14sr$

   (C) $16r^2 + 14rs$ (D) $28r + 14sr$

   (E) $17r^2s$

13. $(4m + p)(3m - 2p) =$

   (A) $12m^2 + 5mp + 2p^2$ (B) $12m^2 - 2mp + 2p^2$

   (C) $7m - p$ (D) $12m - 2p$

   (E) $12m^2 - 5mp - 2p^2$

14. $(2a + b)(3a^2 + ab + b^2) =$

    (A) $6a^3 + 5a^2b + 3ab^2 + b^3$

    (B) $5a^3 + 3ab + b^3$

    (C) $6a^3 + 2a^2b + 2ab^2$

    (D) $3a^2 + 2a + ab + b + b^2$

    (E) $6a^3 + 3a^2b + 5ab^2 + b^3$

15. $(6t^2 + 2t + 1)\,3t =$

    (A) $9t^2 + 5t + 3$ (B) $18t^2 + 6t + 3$

    (C) $9t^3 + 6t^2 + 3t$ (D) $18t^3 + 6t^2 + 3t$

    (E) $12t^3 + 6t^2 + 3t$

Division

16. $(x^2 + x - 6) \div (x - 2) =$

    (A) $x - 3$ (B) $x + 2$

    (C) $x + 3$ (D) $x - 2$

    (E) $2x + 2$

17. $24b^4c^3 \div 6b^2c =$

    (A) $3b^2c^2$ (B) $4b^4c^3$

    (C) $4b^3c^2$ (D) $4b^2c^2$

    (E) $3b^4c^3$

18. $(3p^2 + pq - 2q^2) \div (p + q) =$

    (A) $3p + 2q$ (B) $2q - 3p$

    (C) $3p - q$ (D) $2q + 3p$

    (E) $3p - 2q$

19. $(y^3 - 2y^2 - y + 2) \div (y - 2) =$

    (A) $(y - 1)^2$ (B) $y^2 - 1$

    (C) $(y + 2)(y - 1)$ (D) $(y + 1)^2$

    (E) $(y + 1)(y - 2)$

20. $(m^2 + m - 14) \div (m + 4) =$

   (A) $m - 2$ (B) $m - 3 + \dfrac{-2}{m + 4}$

   (C) $m - 3 + \dfrac{4}{m + 4}$ (D) $m - 3$

   (E) $m - 2 + \dfrac{-3}{m + 4}$

2. SIMPLIFYING ALGEBRAIC EXPRESSIONS

To factor a polynomial completely is to find the prime factors of the polynomial with respect to a specified set of numbers.

The following concepts are important while factoring or simplifying expressions.

1. The factors of an algebraic expression consist of two or more algebraic expressions which when multiplied together produce the given algebraic expression.

2. A **prime factor** is a polynomial with no factors other than itself and 1. The **least common multiple (LCM)** for a set of numbers is the smallest quantity divisible by every number of the set. For algebraic expressions the least common numerical coefficients for each of the given expressions will be a factor.

3. The **greatest common factor (GCF)** for a set of numbers is the largest factor that is common to all members of the set. For algebraic expressions, the greatest common factor is the polynomial of highest degree and the largest numerical coefficient which is a factor of all the given expressions.

Some important formulae useful for the factoring of polynomials are listed below.

(A) $ac + ad = a(c + d)$

   Remember to factor out all common monomial factors first.

      $3x^2 - 6x = 3x(x - 2)$

(B) $a^2 - b^2 = (a + b)(a - b)$

    $a^3 + b^3 = (a + b)(a^2 - ab + b^2)$

$$a^3 - b^3 = (a - b)(a^2 + ab + b^2)$$

Look for easily recognizable patterns: the **difference of the squares,** the **sum of two cubes,** and the **difference of two cubes.**

$$w^2 - 16 = (w + 4)(w - 4)$$

$$a^3 - 125 = (a - 5)(a^2 + 5b + 25)$$

Here are the perfect square integers less than 300:

1, 4, 9, 16, 25, 36, 49, 64, 81, 100, 121, 144, 169, 196, 225, 256, and 289.

Here are the perfect cubes less than 600:

1, 8, 27, 64, 125, 216, 343, and 512.

If a perfect square is with a squared variable, look to factor by using the formula for the difference of the squares. If a perfect cube is with a cubed variable, look to factor by the difference of two cubes or the sum of two cubes.

(C) $a^2 + 2ab + b^2 = (a + b)^2 = (a + b)(a + b)$

$a^2 - 2ab + b^2 = (a - b)^2 = (a - b)(a - b)$

A **perfect square trinomial** is another special product formula.

$$z^2 + 6z + 9 = z^2 + 2(3)z + 3^2$$

$$= (z + 3)(z + 3) = (z + 3)^2$$

(D) $x^2 + (a + b)x + ab = (x + a)(x + b)$

To factor binomials with the lead coefficient of one just list the factors of the third term of the trinomial. Then pick the factorization in which the sum of factors is the coefficient of the middle term.

$$x^2 - 6x + 8$$

The factors of the third term are

$8(1), 4(2), -8(-1),$ and $-4(-2)$.

The sums of the factors are

$9, 6, -9,$ and -6.

Therefore, the factorization of $x^2 - 6x + 8 =$

$(x - 4)(x - 2)$.

(E) $acx^2 + (ad + bc)x + bd = (ax + b)(cx + d)$

$5x^2 + 7x + 2 = (5x + 2)(x + 1)$

If the trinomial is of the form $ax^2 + bx + c$, the trinomial will factor into two binomials with integer coefficients if the value of $b^2 - 4ac$ is a perfect square. Using the example above $a = 5$, $b = 7$, and $c = 2$.

$7^2 - 4(5)(2) = 49 - 40 = 9$

which is a perfect square.

(F) $ac + bc + ad + bd = (a + b)(c + d)$

Sometimes **factoring by grouping** can be used although there is no factor common to all four terms.

$3x^3y - 4x^2y^2 - 6x^2y + 8xy^2$

$xy(3x^2 - 4xy - 6x + 8y)$

Factor out all common monomial factors.

$xy(x(3x - 4y) - 2(3x - 4y))$

Factor by grouping.

$xy(x - 2)(3x - 4y)$

(G) $(a + b)^3 = a^3 + 3a^2b + 3ab^2 + b^3 = (a + b)(a + b)(a + b)$

$(a - b)^3 = a^3 - 3a^2b + 3ab^2 - b^3 = (a - b)(a - b)(a - b)$

$a^2 + b^2 + c^2 + 2ab + 2ac + 2bc = (a + b + c)^2$

$a^4 - b^4 = (a - b)(a^3 + a^2b + ab^2 + b^3)$

$a^5 - b^5 = (a - b)(a^4 + a^3b + a^2b^2 + ab^3 + b^4)$

$a^6 - b^6 = (a - b)(a^5 + a^4b + a^3b^2 + a^2b^3 + ab^4 + b^5)$

$a^n - b^n = (a - b)(a^{n-1} + a^{n-2}b + a^{n-3}b^2 + \ldots + ab^{n-2} + b^{n-1})$

where n is any positive integer (1, 2, 3, 4, …).

$a^n + b^n = (a + b)(a^{n-1} - a^{n-2}b + a^{n-3}b^2 - \ldots - ab^{n-2} + b^{n-1})$

where n is any positive odd integer (1, 3, 5, 7, …).

The above lists some formulae that are common with higher degree polynomials. Become familiar with what they look like. Concentrate on the methods (A) through (F) since most expressions will be simplified using those formulae.

The procedure for factoring an algebraic expression completely is as follows:

Step 1: First find the greatest common factor if there is any. Then examine each factor remaining for greatest common factors.

Step 2: Continue factoring the factors obtained in Step 1 until all factors other than monomial factors are prime.

EXAMPLE

Factoring $4 - 16x^2$,

$$4 - 16x^2 = 4(1 - 4x^2) = 4(1 + 2x)(1 - 2x)$$

PROBLEM

Express each of the following as a single term.

(1) $3x^2 + 2x^2 - 4x^2$

(2) $5axy^2 - 7axy^2 - 3xy^2$

Solution

(1) Factor x^2 in the expression.

$$3x^2 + 2x^2 - 4x^2 = (3 + 2 - 4)x^2 = 1x^2 = x^2$$

(2) Factor xy^2 in the expression and then factor a.

$$5axy^2 - 7axy^2 - 3xy^2 = (5a - 7a - 3)xy^2$$
$$= [(5 - 7)a - 3]xy^2$$
$$= (-2a - 3)xy^2$$

Drill 2: Simplifying Algebraic Expressions

1. $16b^2 - 25z^2 =$

    (A) $(4b - 5z)^2$ (B) $(4b + 5z)^2$

    (C) $(4b - 5z)(4b + 5z)$ (D) $(16b - 25z)^2$

    (E) $(5z - 4b)(5z + 4b)$

2. $x^2 - 2x - 8 =$

    (A) $(x-4)^2$ (B) $(x-6)(x-2)$

    (C) $(x+4)(x-2)$ (D) $(x-4)(x+2)$

    (E) $(x-4)(x-2)$

3. $2c^2 + 5cd - 3d^2 =$

    (A) $(c-3d)(c+2d)$ (B) $(2c-d)(c+3d)$

    (C) $(c-d)(2c+3d)$ (D) $(2c+d)(c+3d)$

    (E) Not possible

4. $4t^3 - 20t =$

    (A) $4t(t^2-5)$ (B) $4t^2(t-20)$

    (C) $4t(t+4)(t-5)$ (D) $2t(2t^2-10)$

    (E) Not possible

5. $x^2 + xy - 2y^2 =$

    (A) $(x-2y)(x+y)$ (B) $(x-2y)(x-y)$

    (C) $(x+2y)(x+y)$ (D) $(x+2y)(x-y)$

    (E) Not possible

6. $5b^2 + 17bd + 6d^2 =$

    (A) $(5b+d)(b+6d)$ (B) $(5b+2d)(b+3d)$

    (C) $(5b-2d)(b-3d)$ (D) $(5b-2d)(b+3d)$

    (E) Not possible

7. $x^2 + x + 1 =$

    (A) $(x+1)^2$ (B) $(x+2)(x-1)$

    (C) $(x-2)(x+1)$ (D) $(x+1)(x-1)$

    (E) Not possible

8. $3z^3 + 6z^2 =$

    (A) $3(z^3+2z^2)$ (B) $3z^2(z+2)$

    (C) $3z(z^2 + 2z)$ (D) $z^2(3z + 6)$

    (E) $3z^2(1 + 2z)$

9. $m^2p^2 + mpq - 6q^2 =$

    (A) $(mp - 2q)(mp + 3q)$ (B) $mp(mp - 2q)(mp + 3q)$

    (C) $mpq(1 - 6q)$ (D) $(mp + 2q)(mp + 3q)$

    (E) Not possible

10. $2h^3 + 2h^2t - 4ht^2 =$

    (A) $2(h^3 - t)(h + t)$ (B) $2h(h - 2t)^2$

    (C) $4h(ht - t^2)$ (D) $2h(h + t) - 4ht^2$

    (E) $2h(h + 2t)(h - t)$

3. RATIONAL EXPRESSIONS

A **rational expression** is an algebraic fraction such as

$$\frac{x^2 + 3}{x - 4}.$$

Operations with rational expressions use the same principles as arithmetic fractions.

(A) **To simplify a rational expression** means to reduce it to its lowest terms. To do this factor both the numerator and the denominator and divide out all common factors. For example,

$$\frac{x^2 - 1}{x^2 + 2x + 1} = \frac{(x+1)(x - 1)}{(x + 1)(x+1)} = \frac{x - 1}{x + 1}$$

(B) **To multiply and divide rational expressions** use factoring. Remember division is carried out by inverting the divisor and multiplying. For example,

$$\left(\frac{x^2 + 2x + 1}{x}\right)\left(\frac{x^2 - x}{x^2 - 1}\right)$$

$$\left(\frac{(x + 1)(x+1)}{x}\right)\left(\frac{x(x-1)}{(x-1)(x+1)}\right) = x + 1$$

$$\frac{3x^2 - x - 2}{6x^2 - 5x - 6} \div \frac{2x^2 + 5x + 3}{4x^2 - 9}$$

$$\left(\frac{3x^2 - x - 2}{6x^2 - 5x - 6}\right)\left(\frac{4x^2 - 9}{2x^2 + 5x + 3}\right)$$

$$\left(\frac{(3x+2)(x - 1)}{(2x-3)(3x+2)}\right)\left(\frac{(2x-3)(2x+3)}{(2x+3)(x + 1)}\right) = \frac{x - 1}{x + 1}$$

(C) **To add or subtract rational expressions,** a common denominator must be found. As in arithmetic fractions the Lowest Common Denominator (LCD) is used. For example,

$$\frac{x}{x + 1} + \frac{2}{x^2 - 1}$$

Factor $x^2 - 1 = (x + 1)(x - 1)$. Therefore, the LCD is $(x + 1)(x - 1)$.

$$\frac{x(x - 1)}{(x + 1)(x - 1)} + \frac{2}{(x + 1)(x - 1)} = \frac{x^2 - x + 2}{(x + 1)(x - 1)}$$

$$= \frac{(x - 2)(x+1)}{(x+1)(x - 1)}$$

$$= \frac{x - 2}{x - 1}$$

Note: By keeping the denominator in factored form it is easier to see if any further simplification can be done after the addition or subtraction.

PROBLEM

Simplify $\dfrac{\dfrac{1}{x-1} - \dfrac{1}{x-2}}{\dfrac{1}{x-2} + \dfrac{1}{x-3}}$.

Solution

Simplify the expression in the numerator by using the addition rule:

$$\frac{a}{b} + \frac{c}{d} = \frac{ad + bc}{bd}$$

Notice *bd* is the Lowest Common Denominator, LCD. We obtain

$$\frac{x-2-(x-1)}{(x-1)(x-2)} = \frac{-1}{(x-1)(x-2)}$$

in the numerator.

Repeat this procedure for the expression in the denominator:

$$\frac{x-3-(x-2)}{(x-2)(x-3)} = \frac{-1}{(x-2)(x-3)}$$

We now have

$$\frac{\dfrac{-1}{(x-1)(x-2)}}{\dfrac{-1}{(x-2)(x-3)}}$$

which is simplified by inverting the fraction in the denominator and multiplying it by the numerator and cancelling like terms.

$$\frac{-1}{(x-1)(x-2)} \times \frac{(x-2)(x-3)}{-1} = \frac{x-3}{x-1}$$

A form of simplification of rational expressions that is easy to simplify is

$$\frac{a-b}{b-a}.$$

To simplify factor (-1) from the numerator.

$$\frac{(-1)(-a+b)}{(b-a)} = -1$$

Recognizing this form when working with rational expressions will be helpful in finding the simplest solution.

Drill 3: Rational Expressions

Simplification

1. $\dfrac{x+y}{x^2-y^2} =$

   (A) $x^3 - y^3$ (B) $\dfrac{1}{x-y}$

   (C) $x - y$ (D) $\dfrac{1}{y-x}$

   (E) $\dfrac{1}{x^2-y^2}$

2. $\dfrac{-24x^3y^4}{18x^4y^3} =$

   (A) $\dfrac{-4x}{3y}$ (B) $\dfrac{4y^7}{3x^7}$

   (C) $\dfrac{-4y}{3x}$ (D) $\dfrac{6y}{x}$

   (E) $\dfrac{-4}{3x^7y^7}$

3. $\dfrac{4x^2+8x+3}{6+x-2x^2} =$

   (A) $\dfrac{2x+1}{2-x}$ (B) $2x^2 + 9x + 9$

   (C) $\dfrac{2x+3}{2-x}$ (D) $\dfrac{2x+1}{3+2x}$

   (E) $\dfrac{(2x+3)^2}{2-x}$

4. $\dfrac{x^2 - 9}{x^2 - x - 6} =$

   (A) $\dfrac{x - 3}{x + 2}$ (B) $\dfrac{2x^2}{-x}$

   (C) $\dfrac{x + 3}{x - 3}$ (D) $\dfrac{-3}{x}$

   (E) $\dfrac{x + 3}{x + 2}$

5. $\dfrac{(5x + 5y)(2x - y)}{y - 2x} =$

   (A) $-5(x + y)$ (B) $5(2x - y)$

   (C) $-5(x - y)$ (D) $5(x + y)$

   (E) $10xy$

Multiplication and Division

6. $(x + 1)\left(\dfrac{1}{x^2 + 2x + 1}\right) =$

   (A) $\dfrac{1}{(x + 1)^3}$ (B) $(x + 1)^3$

   (C) $\dfrac{1}{x^2 + x}$ (D) $\dfrac{1}{x + 1}$

   (E) $(x + 1)$

7. $\dfrac{x^2 - 16}{x^2 - 25} \div \dfrac{x + 4}{x - 5} =$

   (A) $\dfrac{(x + 4)^2}{(x - 5)^2}$ (B) $\dfrac{(x - 4)}{(x + 5)}$

(C) $\dfrac{(x+4)}{(x-5)}$

(D) $\dfrac{(x+5)}{(x-4)}$

(E) $\dfrac{(x-4)}{(x-5)}$

8. $\dfrac{\dfrac{x-1}{x+2}}{\dfrac{x^2-x}{x^2+2x}} =$

(A) -1

(B) $2x$

(C) $\dfrac{(x-1)^2}{(x+2)^2}$

(D) $\dfrac{x^2+x-1}{x^2+2}$

(E) 1

9. $\left(\dfrac{2x^2}{y}\right)\left(\dfrac{y^2}{x^3}\right) =$

(A) $\dfrac{2x^5}{y^3}$

(B) $\dfrac{y}{2x}$

(C) $\dfrac{2y}{x}$

(D) $\dfrac{2x^2+y^2}{y+x^3}$

(E) $2x-y$

10. $\left(\dfrac{a+3}{a-5}\right)\left(\dfrac{2a-10}{3a+9}\right) =$

(A) $\dfrac{2}{3}$

(B) $\dfrac{(a+3)^2}{(a-5)^2}$

(C) $\dfrac{2a+3}{3a-5}$

(D) $\dfrac{2(a+3)}{3(a-5)}$

(E) $\dfrac{3}{2}$

Addition and Subtraction

11. $\dfrac{2}{x-3} + \dfrac{5}{x+2} =$

    (A) $\dfrac{7}{(x-3)(x+2)}$ (B) $\dfrac{7}{2x-1}$

    (C) $\dfrac{7x-11}{(x-3)(x+2)}$ (D) $\dfrac{7x+3}{(x-3)(x+2)}$

    (E) $\dfrac{2(x+2)}{5(x-3)}$

12. $\dfrac{x+8}{x-3} - \dfrac{x-14}{3-x} =$

    (A) -2 (B) $\dfrac{6}{(x-3)^2}$

    (C) $\dfrac{x+8}{x-14}$ (D) 6

    (E) 2

13. $\dfrac{3x}{x-1} - 2x - x^2 =$

    (A) $\dfrac{-x^3 - x^2 + 5x}{x-1}$ (B) $\dfrac{-x^2 + x}{x-1}$

    (C) $\dfrac{x^3 - x^2 + 5x}{x-1}$ (D) $\dfrac{3x}{x-1}$

    (E) $\dfrac{x^2 + x}{x-1}$

14. $\dfrac{3}{x+2} + \dfrac{5}{x-4} =$

(A) $\dfrac{8x-2}{(x+2)(x-4)}$ 　　　　　(B) -4

(C) $\dfrac{8x-14}{(x+2)(x-4)}$ 　　　　　(D) $\dfrac{15(x-4)}{(x+2)}$

(E) $\dfrac{6x}{(x+2)(x-4)}$

15. $\dfrac{x+2}{x+5} - \dfrac{x-3}{x+7} =$

(A) $\dfrac{-1}{2}$ 　　　　　(B) $\dfrac{3x+31}{(x+5)(x+7)}$

(C) $\dfrac{2x^2+11x-1}{(x+5)\,(x+7)}$ 　　　　　(D) $\dfrac{7x+29}{(x+5)(x+7)}$

(E) $\dfrac{7x+29}{(x+2)(x-3)}$

4. EQUATIONS

An **equation** is defined as a statement that two separate expressions are equal.

A **solution** to the equation is a number that makes the equation true when it is substituted for the variable. For example, in the equation $3x = 18$, 6 is the solution since $3(6) = 18$. Depending on the equation, there can be more than one solution. The set of numbers that are permissible values for a variable is the **domain**. The numbers in the domain that satisfy the equation are in the **solution set** of the equation. Equations with the same solutions are said to be **equivalent equations**. An equation without a solution is said to have a solution set that is the **empty** or **null** set and is represented by ϕ.

Replacing an expression within an equation by an equivalent expression will result in a new equation with solutions equivalent to the original equation. Given the equation below

$$3x + y + x + 2y = 15$$

by combining like terms, we get,

$$3x + y + x + 2y = 4x + 3y$$

Since these two expressions are equivalent, we can substitute the simpler form into the equation to get

$$4x + 3y = 15.$$

Performing the same operation to both sides of an equation by the same expression will result in a new equation that is equivalent to the original equation.

1. **Addition or subtraction**

$$y + 6 = 10$$

We can add (-6) to both sides.

$$y + 6 + (-6) = 10 + (-6)$$

$$y + 0 = 10 - 6$$

$$y = 4$$

2. **Multiplication or division**

$$3x = 6$$

$$3x/3 = 6/3$$

$$x = 2$$

$3x = 6$ is equivalent to $x = 2$.

3. **Raising to a power**

$$a = x^2y$$

$$a^2 = (x^2y)^2$$

$$a^2 = x^4y^2$$

This can be applied to negative and fractional powers as well. For example,

$$x^2 = 3y^4$$

If we raise both members to the -2 power, we get

$$(x^2)^{-2} = (3y^4)^{-2}$$

$$\frac{1}{(x^2)^2} = \frac{1}{(3y^4)^2}$$

$$\frac{1}{x^4} = \frac{1}{9y^8}$$

If we raise both members to the $\frac{1}{2}$ power, which is the same as taking the square root, we get:

$$(x^2)^{1/2} = (3y^4)^{1/2}$$
$$x = \sqrt{3}y^2$$

4. The **reciprocal** of both members of an equation is equivalent to the original equation. Note: The reciprocal of 0 is undefined.

$$\frac{2x+y}{z} = \frac{5}{2} \qquad \frac{z}{2x+y} = \frac{2}{5}$$

PROBLEM

Solve, justifying each step. $3x - 8 = 7x + 8$

Solution

$$3x - 8 = 7x + 8$$

Adding 8 to both sides, $\qquad 3x - 8 + 8 = 7x + 8 + 8$

Additive inverse property, $\qquad 3x + 0 = 7x + 16$

Additive identity property, $\qquad 3x = 7x + 16$

Adding $(-7x)$ to both sides, $\qquad 3x - 7x = 7x + 16 - 7x$

Commuting, $\qquad -4x = 7x - 7x + 16$

Additive inverse property, $\qquad -4x = 0 + 16$

Additive identity property, $\qquad -4x = 16$

Dividing both sides by -4, $\qquad x = {}^{16}/_{-4}$

$$x = -4$$

Check: Replacing x by -4 in the original equation:

$$3x - 8 = 7x + 8$$
$$3(-4) - 8 = 7(-4) + 8$$
$$-12 - 8 = -28 + 8$$
$$-20 = -20$$

Linear Equations

A linear equation with one unknown is one that can be put into the form $ax + b = 0$, where a and b are constants, $a \neq 0$.

To solve a linear equation means to transform it into the form $x = -b/a$.

1. If the equation has unknowns on both sides of the equality, it is convenient to put similar terms on the same sides. For example,

$$4x + 3 = 2x + 9$$

$$4x + 3 - 2x = 2x + 9 - 2x$$

$$(4x - 2x) + 3 = (2x - 2x) + 9$$

$$2x + 3 = 0 + 9$$

$$2x + 3 - 3 = 0 + 9 - 3$$

$$2x = 6$$

$$2x/2 = 6/2$$

$$x = 3$$

2. If the equation appears in fractional form, it is necessary to transform it, using cross multiplication, and then repeating the same procedure as in 1, we obtain:

$$\frac{3x + 4}{3} \diagup\!\!\!\!\diagdown \frac{7x + 2}{5}$$

By using cross multiplication we would obtain:

$$3(7x + 2) = 5(3x + 4).$$

This is equivalent to:

$$21x + 6 = 15x + 20,$$

which can be solved as in 1:

$$21x + 6 = 15x + 20$$

$$21x - 15x + 6 = 15x - 15x + 20$$

$$6x + 6 - 6 = 20 - 6$$

$$6x = 14$$

$$x = 14/6$$

$$x = 7/3$$

3. If there are radicals in the equation, it is necessary to square both sides and then apply 1:

$$\sqrt{3x+1} = 5$$

$$(\sqrt{3x+1})^2 = 5^2$$

$$3x + 1 = 25$$

$$3x + 1 - 1 = 25 - 1$$

$$3x = 24$$

$$x = {}^{24}/_3$$

$$x = 8$$

PROBLEM

Solve the equation $2(x + 3) = (3x + 5) - (x - 5)$.

Solution

We transform the given equation to an equivalent equation where we can easily recognize the solution set.

$$2(x + 3) = 3x + 5 - (x - 5)$$

Distribute, $\qquad 2x + 6 = 3x + 5 - x + 5$

Combine terms, $\qquad 2x + 6 = 2x + 10$

Subtract $2x$ from both sides, $\qquad 6 = 10$

Since $6 = 10$ is not a true statement, there is no real number which will make the original equation true. The equation is inconsistent and the solution set is ϕ, the empty set.

PROBLEM

Solve the equation $2(^2/_3y + 5) + 2(y + 5) = 130$.

Solution

The procedure for solving this equation is as follows:

$^4/_3y + 10 + 2y + 10 = 130,$ $\qquad$ Distributive property

$^4/_3y + 2y + 20 = 130,$ $\qquad$ Combining like terms

$^4/_3y + 2y = 110,$ $\qquad$ Subtracting 20 from both sides

$$^4/_3y + {}^6/_3y = 110, \qquad \text{Converting } 2y \text{ into a fraction with}$$
$$\text{denominator 3}$$

$$^{10}/_3y = 110, \qquad \text{Combining like terms}$$

$$y = 110 \times {}^3/_{10} = 33, \qquad \text{Dividing by } {}^{10}/_3$$

Check: Replace y by 33 in the original equation,

$$2(^2/_3(33) + 5) + 2(33 + 5) = 130$$
$$2(22 + 5) + 2(38) = 130$$
$$2(27) + 76 = 130$$
$$54 + 76 = 130$$
$$130 = 130$$

Therefore, the solution to the given equation is $y = 33$.

Drill 4: Linear Equations

DIRECTIONS: Solve for x.

1. $4x - 2 = 10$

   (A) -1 (B) 2

   (C) 3   (D) 4

   (E) 6

2. $7z + 1 - z = 2z - 7$

   (A) -2 (B) 0

   (C) 1   (D) 2

   (E) 3

3. $^1/_3b + 3 = {}^1/_2b$

   (A) $^1/_2$ (B) 2

   (C) $3^3/_5$ (D) 6

   (E) 18

4. $0.4p + 1 = 0.7p - 2$

    (A) 0.1   (B) 2

    (C) 5   (D) 10

    (E) 12

5. $4(3x + 2) - 11 = 3(3x - 2)$

    (A) -3 (B) -1

    (C) 2   (D) 3

    (E) 7

5. TWO LINEAR EQUATIONS

Equations of the form $ax + by = c$, where a, b, and c are constants and $a, b \neq 0$ are called **linear equations** with two unknown variables.

There are several ways to solve systems of linear equations in two variables:

Method 1:   **Addition or subtraction** – if necessary, multiply the equations by numbers that will make the coefficients of one unknown in the resulting equations numerically equal. If the signs of equal coefficients are the same, subtract the equation, otherwise add.

                The result is one equation with one unknown; we solve it and substitute the value into the other equations to find the unknown that we first eliminated.

Method 2:   **Substitution** – find the value of one unknown in terms of the other, substitute this value in the other equation and solve.

Method 3:   **Graph** – graph both equations. The point of intersection of the drawn lines is a simultaneous solution for the equations and its coordinates correspond to the answer that would be found analytically.

If the lines are parallel they have no simultaneous solution.

Dependent equations are equations that represent the same line; therefore, every point on the line of a dependent equation represents a solution. Since there is an infinite number of points on a line there is an infinite number of simultaneous solutions, for example

$$\begin{cases} 2x + y = 8 \\ 4x + 2y = 16 \end{cases}$$

The equations above are dependent, they represent the same line, all points that satisfy either of the equations are solutions of the system.

A system of linear equations is consistent if there is only one solution for the system.

A system of linear equations is inconsistent if it does not have any solutions.

Example of a consistent system. Find the point of intersection of the graphs of the equations as shown in the figure.

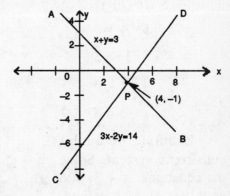

$$x + y = 3$$

$$3x - 2y = 14$$

To solve these linear equations, solve for y in terms of x. The equations will be in the form $y = mx + b$, where m is the slope and b is the intercept on the y-axis.

$x + y = 3$	
$y = 3 - x$	Subtract x from both sides.
$3x - 2y = 14$	Subtract $3x$ from both sides.
$-2y = 14 - 3x$	Divide by -2.
$y = -7 + {}^3/_2x$	

The graphs of the linear functions, $y = 3 - x$ and $y = -7 + {}^3/_2x$ can be determined by plotting only two points. For example, for $y = 3 - x$, let $x = 0$, then $y = 3$. Let $x = 1$, then $y = 2$. The two points on this first line are $(0, 3)$ and $(1, 2)$. For $y = -7 + {}^3/_2x$, let $x = 0$, then $y = -7$. Let $x = 1$, then $y = -5^1/_2$. The two points on this second line are $(0, -7)$ and $(1, -5^1/_2)$.

To find the point of intersection P of

$$x + y = 3 \quad \text{and} \quad 3x - 2y = 14,$$

solve them algebraically. Multiply the first equation by 2. Add these two equations to eliminate the variable y.

$$2x + 2y = 6$$
$$3x - 2y = 14$$

$$5x = 20$$

Solve for x to obtain $x = 4$. Substitute this into $y = 3 - x$ to get $y = 3 - 4 = -1$. P is $(4, -1)$. AB is the graph of the first equation, and CD is the graph of the second equation. The point of intersection P of the two graphs is the only point on both lines. The coordinates of P satisfy both equations and represent the desired solution of the problem. From the graph, P seems to be the point $(4, -1)$. These coordinates satisfy both equations, and hence are the exact coordinates of the point of intersection of the two lines.

To show that $(4, -1)$ satisfies both equations, substitute this point into both equations.

$x + y = 3$	$3x - 2y = 14$
$4 + (-1) = 3$	$3(4) - 2(-1) = 14$
$4 - 1 = 3$	$12 + 2 = 14$
$3 = 3$	$14 = 14$

Example of an inconsistent system. Solve the equations $2x + 3y = 6$ and $4x + 6y = 7$ simultaneously.

We have two equations in two unknowns,

$$2x + 3y = 6 \quad (1)$$

and

$$4x + 6y = 7 \quad (2)$$

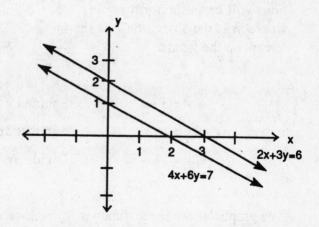

There are several methods to solve this problem. We have chosen to multiply each equation by a different number so that when the two equations are added, one of the variables drops out. Thus,

Multiplying equation (1) by 2: $\qquad 4x + 6y = 12 \qquad$ (3)

Multiplying equation (2) by -1: $\quad -4x - 6y = -7 \qquad$ (4)

Adding equations (3) and (4): $\qquad\qquad 0 = 5$

We obtain a peculiar result!

Actually, what we have shown in this case is that if there were a simultaneous solution to the given equations, then 0 would equal 5. But the conclusion is impossible; therefore, there can be no simultaneous solution to these two equations, hence no point satisfying both.

The straight lines which are the graphs of these equations must be parallel if they never intersect, but not identical, which can be seen from the graph of these equations (see the accompanying diagram).

Example of a dependent system. Solve the equations $2x + 3y = 6$ and $y = -(2x/3) + 2$ simultaneously.

We have two equations in two unknowns.

$$2x + 3y = 6 \tag{1}$$

and

$$y = -(2x/3) + 2 \tag{2}$$

There are several methods of solving for this problem. Since equation (2) already gives us an expression for y, we use the method of substitution. Substituting $-(2x/3) + 2$ for y in the first equation:

$$2x + 3(-2x/3 + 2) = 6$$

Distributing, $\quad 2x - 2x + 6 = 6$

$$6 = 6$$

Apparently we have gotten nowhere! The result $6 = 6$ is true, but indicates no solution. Actually, our work shows that no matter what real number x is, if y is determined by the second equation, then the first equation will always be satisfied.

The reason for this peculiarity may be seen if we take a closer look at the equation $y = -(2x/3) + 2$. It is equivalent to $3y = -2x + 6$, or $2x + 3y = 6$.

In other words, the two equations are equivalent. Any pair of values of x and y which satisfies one satisfies the other.

It is hardly necessary to verify that in this case the graphs of the given equations are identical lines, and that there are an infinite number of simultaneous solutions of these equations.

Two systems of linear equations are said to be equivalent if and only if they have the same solution set.

PROBLEM

Solve for x and y.

$$x + 2y = 8 \tag{1}$$

$$3x + 4y = 20 \tag{2}$$

Solution

Solve equation (1) for x in terms of y:

$$x = 8 - 2y \tag{3}$$

Substitute $(8 - 2y)$ for x in (2):

$$3(8 - 2y) + 4y = 20 \tag{4}$$

Solve (4) for y as follows:

Distribute: $24 - 6y + 4y = 20$

Combine like terms and then subtract 24 from both sides:

$$24 - 2y = 20$$

$$24 - 24 - 2y = 20 - 24$$

$$-2y = -4$$

Divide both sides by -2:

$$y = 2$$

Substitute 2 for y in equation (1):

$$x + 2(2) = 8$$

$$x = 4$$

Thus, our solution is $x = 4$, $y = 2$.

Check: Substitute $x = 4$, $y = 2$ in equations (1) and (2):

$$4 + 2(2) = 8$$

$$8 = 8$$

$$3(4) + 4(2) = 20$$

$$20 = 20$$

PROBLEM

Solve algebraically.

$$4x + 2y = -1 \tag{1}$$

$$5x - 3y = 7 \tag{2}$$

Solution

We arbitrarily choose to eliminate x first.

Multiply (1) by 5:	$20x + 10y = -5$	(3)
Multiply (2) by 4:	$20x - 12y = 28$	(4)
Subtract (3) $-$ (4):	$22y = -33$	(5)
Divide (5) by 22:	$y = -\,^{33}/_{22} = -\,^{3}/_{2}$	

To find x, substitute $y = -\,^{3}/_{2}$ in either of the original equations. If we use equation (1), we obtain $4x + 2(-\,^{3}/_{2}) = -1$, $4x - 3 = -1$, $4x = 2$, $x = \,^{1}/_{2}$.

The solution $(^{1}/_{2}, -^{3}/_{2})$ should be checked in both equations of the given system.

Replacing $(^{1}/_{2}, -^{3}/_{2})$ in equation (1):

$$4x + 2y = -1$$
$$4(^{1}/_{2}) + 2(-\,^{3}/_{2}) = -1$$
$$^{4}/_{2} - 3 = -1$$
$$2 - 3 = -1$$
$$-1 = -1$$

Replacing $(^{1}/_{2}, -^{3}/_{2})$ in equation (2):

$$5x - 3y = 7$$
$$5(^{1}/_{2}) - 3(-\,^{3}/_{2}) = 7$$
$$^{5}/_{2} + ^{9}/_{2} = 7$$
$$^{14}/_{2} = 7$$
$$7 = 7$$

(Instead of eliminating x from the two given equations, we could have eliminated y by multiplying equation (1) by 3, multiplying equation (2) by 2, and then adding the two derived equations.)

Drill 5: Two Linear Equations

DIRECTIONS: Find the solution set for each pair of equations.

1. $3x + 4y = -2$
   $x - 6y = -8$

   (A) $(2, -1)$ (B) $(1, -2)$

   (C) $(-2, -1)$ (D) $(1, 2)$

   (E) $(-2, 1)$

2. $2x + y = -10$
   $-2x - 4y = 4$

   (A) $(6, -2)$ (B) $(-6, 2)$

   (C) $(-2, 6)$ (D) $(2, 6)$

   (E) $(-6, -2)$

3. $6x + 5y = -4$
   $3x - 3y = 9$

   (A) $(1, -2)$ (B) $(1, 2)$

   (C) $(2, -1)$ (D) $(-2, 1)$

   (E) $(-1, 2)$

4. $4x + 3y = 9$
   $2x - 2y = 8$

   (A) $(-3, 1)$ (B) $(1, -3)$

   (C) $(3, 1)$ (D) $(3, -1)$

   (E) $(-1, 3)$

5. $x + y = 7$
   $x = y - 3$

   (A) $(5, 2)$ (B) $(-5, 2)$

   (C) $(2, 5)$ (D) $(-2, 5)$

   (E) $(2, -5)$

6. $5x + 6y = 4$
   $3x - 2y = 1$

   (A) $(3, 6)$ (B) $(^1/_2, {}^1/_4)$

   (C) $(-3, 6)$ (D) $(2, 4)$

   (E) $(^1/_3, {}^3/_2)$

7. $x - 2y = 7$
   $x + y = -2$

   (A) $(-2, 7)$ (B) $(3, -1)$

   (C) $(-7, 2)$ (D) $(1, -3)$

   (E) $(1, -2)$

8. $\quad 4x + 3y = 3$
   $-2x + 6y = 3$

   (A) $(^1/_2, {}^2/_3)$ (B) $(-0.3, 0.6)$

   (C) $(^2/_3, -1)$ (D) $(-0.2, 0.5)$

   (E) $(0.3, 0.6)$

9. $4x - 2y = -14$
   $8x + y = 7$

   (A) $(0, 7)$ (B) $(2, -7)$

   (C) $(7, 0)$ (D) $(-7, 2)$

   (E) $(0, 2)$

10. $\quad 6x - 3y = 1$
    $-9x + 5y = -1$

    (A) $(1, -1)$ (B) $(^2/_3, 1)$

    (C) $(1, {}^2/_3)$ (D) $(-1, 1)$

    (E) $(^2/_3, -1)$

6. QUADRATIC EQUATIONS

A second degree equation in x of the type $ax^2 + bx + c = 0$, $a \neq 0$, a, b, and c are real numbers, is called a **quadratic equation.**

To solve a quadratic equation is to find values of x which satisfy $ax^2 + bx + c = 0$. These values of x are called **solutions**, or **roots**, of the equation.

A quadratic equation has a maximum of two roots. Methods of solving quadratic equations:

1. **Direct solution**: Given $x^2 - 9 = 0$.

    We can solve directly by isolating the variable x:

    $$x^2 = 9$$

    $$x = \pm 3$$

2. **Factoring**: Given a quadratic equation $ax^2 + bx + c = 0$, a, b, and $c \neq 0$, to factor means to express it as the product $a(x - r_1)(x - r_2) = 0$, where r_1 and r_2 are the two roots.

    Some helpful hints to remember are:

    (a) $r_1 + r_2 = -{}^b/_a$

    (b) $r_1 r_2 = {}^c/_a$

Given $x^2 - 5x + 4 = 0$.

Since $r_1 + r_2 = -{}^b/_a = -{}^{(-5)}/_1 = 5$, so the possible solutions are $(3, 2)$, $(4, 1)$, and $(5, 0)$. Also $r_1 r_2 = {}^c/_a = {}^4/_1 = 4$; this equation is satisfied only by the second pair, so $r_1 = 4$, $r_2 = 1$ and the factored form is $(x - 4)(x - 1) = 0$.

If the coefficient of x^2 is not 1, it is necessary to divide the equation by this coefficient and then factor.

Given $2x^2 - 12x + 16 = 0$

Dividing by 2, we obtain:

$$x^2 - 6x + 8 = 0$$

Since $r_1 + r_2 = -{}^b/_a = 6$, the possible solutions are $(6, 0)$, $(5, 1)$, $(4, 2)$, and $(3, 3)$. Also $r_1 r_2 = 8$, so the only possible answer is $(4, 2)$ and the expression $x^2 - 6x + 8 = 0$ can be factored as $(x - 4)(x - 2)$.

PROBLEM

Solve the equation $x^2 + 8x + 15 = 0$.

Solution

Since $(x + a)(x + b) = x^2 + bx + ax + ab = x^2 + (a + b)x + ab$, we may factor the given equation, $0 = x^2 + 8x + 15$, replacing $a + b$ by 8 and ab by 15. Thus,

$$a + b = 8, \quad \text{and} \quad ab = 15.$$

We want the two numbers a and b whose sum is 8 and whose product is 15. We check all pairs of numbers whose product is 15:

(a) $1 \times 15 = 15$;   thus $a = 1$, $b = 15$, and $ab = 15$.

  $1 + 15 = 16$;   therefore we reject these values because $a + b \neq 8$.

(b) $3 \times 5 = 15$;   thus $a = 3$, $b = 5$, and $ab = 15$.

  $3 + 5 = 8$;   therefore $a + b = 8$, and we accept these values.

Hence, $x^2 + 8x + 15 = 0$ is equivalent to

$$0 = x^2 + (3 + 5)x + 3 \times 5 = (x + 3)(x + 5)$$

Hence, $x + 5 = 0$ or $x + 3 = 0$.

Since the product of these two numbers is 0, one of the numbers must be 0. Hence, $x = -5$, or $x = -3$, and the solution set is $x = \{-5, -3\}$.

The student should note that $x = -5$ or $x = -3$. We are certainly not making the statement that $x = -5$, and $x = -3$. Also, the student should check that both these numbers do actually satisfy the given equations and hence are solutions.

Check: Replacing x by (-5) in the original equation:

$$x^2 + 8x + 15 = 0$$

$$(-5)^2 + 8(-5) + 15 = 0$$

$$25 - 40 + 15 = 0$$

$$-15 + 15 = 0$$

$$0 = 0$$

Replacing x by (-3) in the original equation:

$$x^2 + 8x + 15 = 0$$

$$(-3)^2 + 8(-3) + 15 = 0$$
$$9 - 24 + 15 = 0$$
$$-15 + 15 = 0$$
$$0 = 0$$

PROBLEM

Solve the following equations by factoring.

(1) $2x^2 + 3x = 0$ (2) $y^2 - 2y - 3 = y - 3$

(3) $z^2 - 2z - 3 = 0$ (4) $2m^2 - 11m - 6 = 0$

Solution

(1) $2x^2 + 3x = 0$. Factoring out the common factor of x from the left side of the given equation,

$$x(2x + 3) = 0.$$

Whenever a product $ab = 0$, where a and b are any two numbers, either $a = 0$ or $b = 0$. Then, either

$$x = 0 \quad \text{or} \quad 2x + 3 = 0$$
$$2x = -3$$
$$x = -{}^3/_2$$

Hence, the solution set to the original equation $2x^2 + 3x = 0$ is $\{-{}^3/_2, 0\}$.

(2) $y^2 - 2y - 3 = y - 3$. Subtract $(y - 3)$ from both sides of the given equation:

$$y^2 - 2y - 3 - (y - 3) = y - 3 - (y - 3)$$
$$y^2 - 2y - 3 - y + 3 = y - 3 - y + 3$$
$$y^2 - 2y - 3 - y + 3 = y - 3 - y + 3$$
$$y^2 - 3y = 0$$

Factor out a common factor of y from the left side of this equation:

$$y(y - 3) = 0$$

Thus, $y = 0$ or $y - 3 = 0$, $y = 3$.

Therefore, the solution set to the original equation $y^2 - 2y - 3 = y - 3$ is $\{0, 3\}$.

(3) $z^2 - 2z - 3 = 0$. Factor the original equation into a product of two polynomials:

$$z^2 - 2z - 3 = (z - 3)(z + 1) = 0$$

Hence,

$$(z - 3)(z + 1) = 0; \text{ and } z - 3 = 0 \quad \text{or} \quad z + 1 = 0$$
$$z = 3 \qquad\qquad z = -1$$

Therefore, the solution set to the original equation $z^2 - 2z - 3 = 0$ is $\{-1, 3\}$.

(4) $2m^2 - 11m - 6 = 0$. Factor the original equation into a product of two polynomials:

$$2m^2 - 11m - 6 = (2m + 1)(m - 6) = 0$$

Thus,

$$2m + 1 = 0 \quad \text{or} \quad m - 6 = 0$$
$$2m = -1 \qquad\qquad m = 6$$
$$m = -^1/_2$$

Therefore, the solution set to the original equation $2m^2 - 11m - 6 = 0$ is $\{-^1/_2, 6\}$.

Drill 6: Quadratic Equations

DIRECTIONS: Solve for all values of x.

1. $x^2 - 2x - 8 = 0$

   (A) 4 and −2

   (B) 4 and 8

   (C) 4

   (D) −2 and 8

   (E) −2

2. $x^2 + 2x - 3 = 0$

   (A) −3 and 2

   (B) 2 and 1

   (C) 3 and 1

   (D) −3 and 1

   (E) −3

3. $x^2 - 7x = -10$

   (A) -3 and 5   (B) 2 and 5

   (C) 2   (D) -2 and -5

   (E) 5

4. $x^2 - 8x + 16 = 0$

   (A) 8 and 2   (B) 1 and 16

   (C) 4   (D) -2 and 4

   (E) 4 and -4

5. $3x^2 + 3x = 6$

   (A) 3 and -6 (B) 2 and 3

   (C) -3 and 2   (D) 1 and -3

   (E) 1 and -2

6. $x^2 + 7x = 0$

   (A) 7   (B) 0 and -7

   (C) -7 (D) 0 and 7

   (E) 0

7. $x^2 - 25 = 0$

   (A) 5   (B) 5 and -5

   (C) 15 and 10   (D) -5 and 10

   (E) -5

8. $2x^2 + 4x = 16$

   (A) 2 and -2 (B) 8 and -2

   (C) 4 and 8   (D) 2 and -4

   (E) 2 and 4

9. $6x^2 - x - 2 = 0$

   (A) 2 and 3   (B) $\frac{1}{2}$ and $\frac{1}{3}$

(C) $-\frac{1}{2}$ and $\frac{2}{3}$

(D) $\frac{2}{3}$ and 3

(E) 2 and $-\frac{1}{3}$

10. $12x^2 + 5x = 3$

(A) $\frac{1}{3}$ and $-\frac{1}{4}$

(B) 4 and -3

(C) 4 and $\frac{1}{6}$

(D) $\frac{1}{3}$ and -4

(E) $-\frac{3}{4}$ and $\frac{1}{3}$

7. INEQUALITIES

An inequality is a statement where the value of one quantity or expression is greater than (>), less than (<), greater than or equal to ($\geq$), less than or equal to ($\leq$), or not equal to ($\neq$) that of another.

EXAMPLE

$5 > 4$

The expression above means that the value of 5 is greater than the value of 4.

A **conditional inequality** is an inequality whose validity depends on the values of the variables in the sentence. That is, certain values of the variables will make the sentence true, and others will make it false. $3 - y > 3 + y$ is a conditional inequality for the set of real numbers, since it is true for any replacement less than 0 and false for all others.

$x + 5 > x + 2$ is an **absolute inequality** for the set of real numbers, meaning that for any real value x, the expression on the left is greater than the expression on the right.

The solution of a given inequality in one variable x consists of all values of x for which the inequality is true.

The graph of an inequality in one variable is represented by either a ray or a line segment on the real number line.

The endpoint is not a solution if the variable is strictly less than or greater than a particular value.

EXAMPLE

$x > 2$

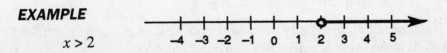

2 is not a solution and should be represented as shown.

The endpoint is a solution if the variable is either (1) less than or equal to or (2) greater than or equal to a particular value.

EXAMPLE

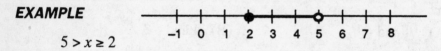

$5 > x \geq 2$

In this case 2 is the solution and should be represented as shown.

Properties of Inequalities

If x and y are real numbers then one and only one of the following statements is true.

$x > y, x = y,$ or $x < y$

This is the order property of real numbers.

If a, b, and c are real numbers:

A)   If $a < b$ and $b < c$, then $a < c$.

B)   If $a > b$ and $b > c$, then $a > c$.

This is the **transitive property of inequalities**.

If a, b, and c are real numbers and $a > b$, then $a + c > b + c$ and $a - c > b - c$. This is the **addition property of inequality**.

Two inequalities are said to have the same **sense** if their signs of inequality point in the same direction.

The sense of an inequality remains the same if both sides are multiplied or divided by the same positive real number.

EXAMPLE

$4 > 3$

If we multiply both sides by 5 we will obtain:

$4 \times 5 > 3 \times 5$

$20 > 15$

The sense of the inequality does not change.

The sense of an inequality becomes opposite if each side is multiplied or divided by the same negative real number.

EXAMPLE

$4 > 3$

If we multiply both sides by -5 we would obtain:

$4 \times -5 < 3 \times -5$

$-20 < -15$

The sense of the inequality becomes opposite.

If $a > b$ and a, b, and n are positive real numbers, then:

$a^n > b^n$ and $a^{-n} < b^{-n}$

If $x > y$ and $q > p$ then $x + q > y + p$.

If $x > y > 0$ and $q > p > 0$ then $xq > yp$.

Inequalities that have the same solution set are called **equivalent inequalities**.

PROBLEM

Solve the inequality $2x + 5 > 9$.

Solution

$2x + 5 + (-5) > 9 + (-5)$	Adding -5 to both sides
$2x + 0 > 9 + (-5)$	Additive inverse property
$2x > 9 + (-5)$	Additive identity property
$2x > 4$	Combining terms
$\frac{1}{2}(2x) > \frac{1}{2} \times 4$	Multiplying both sides by $\frac{1}{2}$
$x > 2$	

The solution set is

$X = \{x \mid 2x + 5 > 9\}$

$= \{x \mid x > 2\}$

(that is all x, such that x is greater than 2).

PROBLEM

Solve the inequality $4x + 3 < 6x + 8$.

Solution

In order to solve the inequality $4x + 3 < 6x + 8$, we must find all values of x which make it true. Thus, we wish to obtain x alone on one side of the inequality.

Add -3 to both sides:

$$
\begin{array}{r}
4x + 3 < 6x + 8 \\
\underline{-3 \qquad -3} \\
4x < 6x + 5
\end{array}
$$

Add $-6x$ to both sides:

$$
\begin{array}{r}
4x < 6x + 5 \\
\underline{-6x \quad -6x} \\
-2x < 5
\end{array}
$$

In order to obtain x alone we must divide both sides by (-2). Recall that dividing an inequality by a negative number reverses the inequality sign, hence

$$\frac{-2x}{-2} > \frac{5}{-2}.$$

Cancelling $-2/_{-2}$ we obtain, $x > -5/_2$.

Thus, our solution is $\{x \mid x > -5/_2\}$ (the set of all x such that x is greater than $-5/_2$).

Drill 7: Inequalities

DIRECTIONS: Find the solution set for each inequality.

1. $3m + 2 < 7$

    (A) $m \geq 5/_3$ (B) $m \leq 2$

    (C) $m < 2$ (D) $m > 2$

    (E) $m < 5/_3$

2. $1/_2 x - 3 \leq 1$

    (A) $-4 \leq x \leq 8$ (B) $x \geq -8$

(C) $x \leq 8$ (D) $2 \leq x \leq 8$

(E) $x \geq 8$

3. $-3p + 1 \geq 16$

(A) $p \geq -5$ (B) $p \geq \dfrac{-17}{3}$

(C) $p \leq \dfrac{-17}{3}$ (D) $p \leq -5$

(E) $p \geq 5$

4. $-6 < \frac{2}{3}r + 6 \leq 2$

(A) $-6 < r \leq -3$ (B) $-18 < r \leq -6$

(C) $r \geq -6$ (D) $-2 < r \leq -\frac{4}{3}$

(E) $r \leq -6$

5. $0 < 2 - y < 6$

(A) $-4 < y < 2$ (B) $-4 < y < 0$

(C) $-4 < y < -2$ (D) $-2 < y < 4$

(E) $0 < y < 4$

8. GRAPHS

Coordinate geometry refers to the study of geometric figures using algebraic principles.

The graph on the next page is called the Cartesian coordinate plane. The graph consists of a pair of perpendicular lines called **coordinate axes**. The **vertical axis** is the y-axis and the **horizontal axis** is the x-axis. The point of intersection of these two axes is called the **origin**; it is the zero point of both axes. Furthermore, points to the right of the origin on the x-axis and above the origin on the y-axis represent positive real numbers. Points to the left of the origin on the x-axis or below the origin on the y-axis represent negative real numbers.

The four regions cut off by the coordinate axes are, in counterclockwise direction from the top right, called the first, second, third, and fourth quadrant, respectively. The first quadrant contains all points with two positive coordinates.

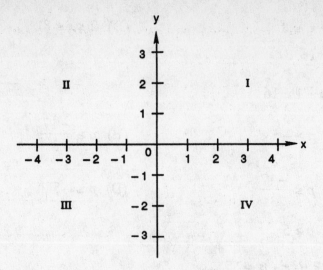

In the graph shown, two points are identified by the ordered pair (x, y) of numbers. The x-coordinate is the first number and the y-coordinate is the second number.

To plot a point on the graph when given the coordinates, draw perpendicular lines from the number-line coordinates to the point where the two lines intersect.

To find the coordinates of a given point on the graph, draw perpendicular lines from the point to the coordinates on the number line. The x-coordinate is written before the y-coordinate and a comma is used to separate the two.

In this case, point A has the coordinates (4, 2) and the coordinates of point B are (− 3, − 5).

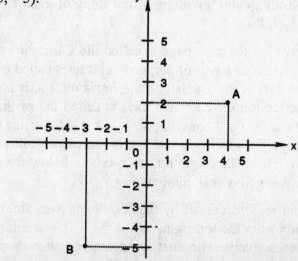

Graphing simple linear equations involves equations like

$$y = mx, y = b, \text{ or } x = b$$

where m and b are real numbers. Equations like $y = b$ and $x = b$ represent lines parallel to either the x- or y-axis.

EXAMPLE

$y = 3$

Since x does not appear in the equation, the value of x has no effect on y. To satisfy the equation y must always be 3.

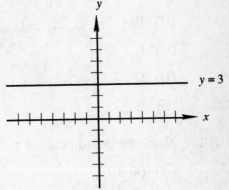

PROBLEM

Graph $y = 4x$.

Solution

Pick some values for x or y and substitute them in the equation to solve for the other variable. Try $y = 0$ and $y = 2$.

$$0 = 4x$$

$$0 = x$$

Therefore, $(0, 0)$ satisfies the equation.

$$2 = 4x$$

$$^1/_2 = x$$

$(^1/_2, 2)$ is another ordered pair which satisfies the equation.

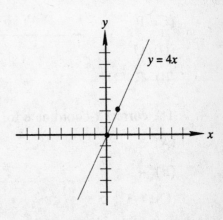

Drill 8: Graphs

1. Which point shown has the coordinates (− 3, 2)?

    (A) A

    (B) B

    (C) C

    (D) D

    (E) E

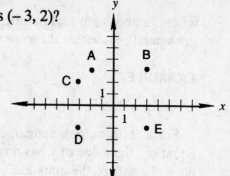

2. Name the coordinates of point A.

    (A) (4, 3)

    (B) (3, − 4)

    (C) (3, 4)

    (D) (− 4, 3)

    (E) (4, − 3)

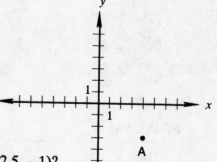

3. Which point shown has the coordinates (2.5, − 1)?

    (A) M

    (B) N

    (C) P

    (D) Q

    (E) R

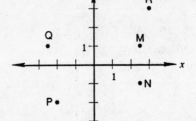

4. The correct *x*-coordinate for point H is what number?

    (A) 3

    (B) 4

    (C) − 3

    (D) − 4

    (E) − 5

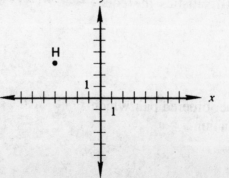

5. The correct *y*-coordinate for point R is what number?

(A) –7

(B) 2

(C) – 2

(D) 7

(E) 8

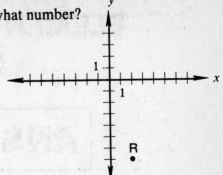

6. Which of the following is an equation of line 1?

(A) $x = 2$

(B) $y = 2$

(C) $x = 2y$

(D) $y = 2x$

(E) $x = y$

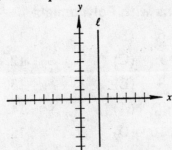

7. Which of the following equations gives a line parallel to the *x*-axis?

(A) $x = -y$ (B) $x = y$

(C) $y = 3x$ (D) $x + y = 0$

(E) $y = -6$

8. Which of the following is an equation of line *b*?

(A) $y = -1$

(B) $x = 2$

(C) $2y = x$

(D) $x + y = 2$

(E) $y = -2x$

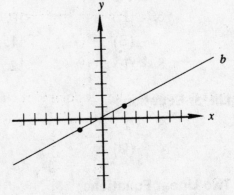

ELEMENTARY ALGEBRA DRILLS

ANSWER KEY

Drill 1 – Operations with Polynomials

1. (B)	6. (B)	11. (C)	16. (C)
2. (C)	7. (C)	12. (B)	17. (D)
3. (C)	8. (E)	13. (E)	18. (E)
4. (D)	9. (A)	14. (A)	19. (B)
5. (A)	10. (D)	15. (D)	20. (B)

Drill 2 – Simplifying Algebraic Expressions

1. (C)	4. (A)	7. (E)	10. (E)
2. (D)	5. (D)	8. (B)	
3. (B)	6. (B)	9. (A)	

Drill 3 – Rational Expressions

1. (B)	5. (A)	9. (C)	13. (A)
2. (C)	6. (D)	10. (A)	14. (A)
3. (A)	7. (B)	11. (C)	15. (D)
4. (E)	8. (E)	12. (E)	

Drill 4 – Linear Equations

1. (C)	3. (E)	5. (B)
2. (A)	4. (D)	

Drill 5 – Two Linear Equations

1. (E)	4. (D)	7. (D)	10. (B)
2. (B)	5. (C)	8. (E)	
3. (A)	6. (B)	9. (A)	

Drill 6 – Quadratic Equations

1. (A)	4. (C)	7. (B)	10. (E)
2. (D)	5. (E)	8. (D)	
3. (B)	6. (B)	9. (C)	

Drill 7 – Inequalities

1. (E)	3. (D)	5. (A)
2. (C)	4. (B)	

Drill 8 – Graphs

1. (C)	3. (B)	5. (A)	7. (E)
2. (E)	4. (D)	6. (A)	8. (C)

Entry Level Mathematics

Chapter 3
Geometry Review

GEOMETRY
DIAGNOSTIC TEST

16 Questions

(Answer sheets appear at the back of the book.)

DIRECTIONS: Each question has five multiple-choice answers. Select the single best answer.

1. What is the area of the parallelogram as shown in the figure below?

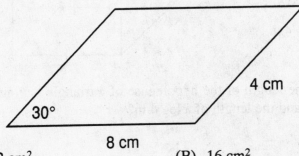

30°

4 cm

8 cm

(A) 32 cm² (B) 16 cm²

(C) 24 cm² (D) 28 cm²

(E) Not enough information is given.

2. Find the area of a regular hexagon formed from 6 equilateral triangles with sides of 8 inches.

(A) $16\sqrt{3}$ in²

(B) $96\sqrt{2}$ in²

(C) 64 in²

(D) 128 in²

(E) $96\sqrt{3}$ in²

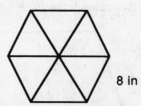

8 in

3. Which of the following are not complimentary or supplementary angles?

    (A) 45°, 45°   (B) 123°, 57°

    (C) 84°, 96°   (D) 39°, 51°

    (E) 73°, 117°

4. The box pictured has a square base with side x and a closed top. The surface area of the box is

    (A) $4x + h$.

    (B) $4x + 4h$.

    (C) hx^2.

    (D) $x^2 + 4xh$.

    (E) $2x^2 + 4xh$.

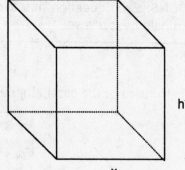

5. What is the length of the hypotenuse of a triangle having angles 45°, 45°, 90°, and the length of a leg 4 m?

    (A) 4 m

    (B) 16 m

    (C) $4\sqrt{3}$ m

    (D) $4\sqrt{2}$ m

    (E) 12 m

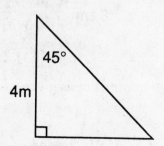

6. Find the area of the isosceles trapezoid.

    (A) $250\sqrt{3}$

    (B) 150

    (C) 250

    (D) $125\sqrt{3}$

    (E) Area cannot be found.

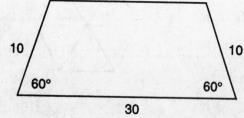

7. In rhombus *ABCD*, which of the following are true?

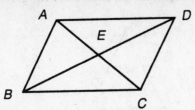

I.   ∠ *BAE* and ∠ *ECD* are congruent.

II.   ∠ *ADE* and ∠ *CDE* are congruent.

III. ∠ *ABE* and ∠ *ADE* are congruent.

(A) I only   (B) II only

(C) I and II only   (D) I and III only

(E) I, II, and III

8. If the angles of a triangle *ABC* are in the ratio of 3:5:7, then the triangle is

(A) acute.   (B) right.

(C) isosceles.   (D) obtuse.

(E) equilateral.

9. The area of this right-angled plane figure is

(A) 250.

(B) 162.

(C) 160.

(D) 150.

(E) 140.

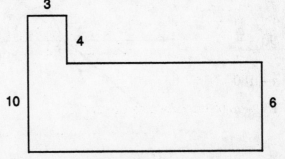

10. If the diameter of a circle is 14 m, find the area of the circle.

(A) 49π m^2 (B) 98π m^2

(C) 14π m^2 (D) 196π m^2

(E) 28π m^2

11. What is the height (altitude) of an equilateral triangle with the length of a side 6 centimeters?

(A) $3\sqrt{2}$ cm

(B) $3\sqrt{3}$ cm

(C) 6 cm

(D) 9 cm

(E) 3 cm

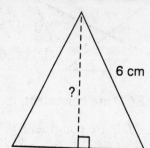

12. How long of a metal bar do you need to make a basketball hoop with a diameter of 48 cm?

(A) 24π cm   (B) 48π cm

(C) 96π cm   (D) 192π cm

(E) 12π cm

13. If lines l, m, and n intersect at point P, express $x + y$ in terms of a.

(A) $180 - \dfrac{a}{2}$

(B) $\dfrac{a}{2} - 180$

(C) $90 - \dfrac{a}{2}$

(D) $a - 180$

(E) $180 - a$

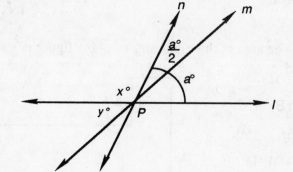

14. Find the area of a right triangle with a hypotenuse of 17 cm and a base of 8 cm.

(A) 45 cm^2 (B) 60 cm^2

(C) 68 cm^2 (D) 120 cm^2

(E) 138 cm^2

15. Find the area of a sector of a circle with a radius of 16 cm and a 45° arc.

    (A) 2π cm^2 (B) 32π cm^2

    (C) 720 cm^2 (D) 256π cm^2

    (E) 720π cm^2

16. In $\triangle ABC$, $AB = 6$, $BC = 4$, and $AC = 3$. What kind of triangle is it?

    (A) Right and scalene   (B) Obtuse and scalene

    (C) Acute and scalene   (D) Right and isosceles

    (E) Obtuse and isosceles

GEOMETRY
DIAGNOSTIC TEST

ANSWER KEY

1. (B)	5. (D)	9. (B)	13. (A)
2. (E)	6. (D)	10. (A)	14. (B)
3. (E)	7. (E)	11. (B)	15. (B)
4. (E)	8. (A)	12. (B)	16. (B)

DETERMINE YOUR STRENGTHS AND WEAKNESSES

GEOMETRY

Question Type	Question #	See Pages . . .
Points, Lines, and Angles	3, 7, 13	145–157
Triangles	1, 2, 5, 6, 7 8, 11, 14, 16	157–170
Quadrilaterals	1, 6, 7, 9	170–180
Circles	10, 12, 15	180–188
Solids	4	189–193

DETAILED EXPLANATIONS OF ANSWERS

GEOMETRY DIAGNOSTIC TEST

1. **(B)** The area of a parallelogram is

$$A = bh.$$

We know the base is 8 cm, but we must find the height. That is possible because we are given the measure of the angle. When the height is drawn in, we have a triangle with angles 30°–60°–90°. The hypotenuse of this is 4. Remember the relationship of the sides of a 30°–60°–90° triangle is $1 : \sqrt{3} : 2$. Since the hypotenuse is 4, the side opposite the 30° angle is 2. This is the height of the triangle and of the parallelogram. Now put this in the formula and get

$$A = (8)(2)$$

or the area is 16 cm².

2. **(E)** The area of the hexagon can be found by finding the area of one of the equilateral triangles. The height of one triangle can be found by using the Pythagorean Theorem.

$$h^2 + 4^2 = 8^2$$

$$h^2 + 16 = 64$$

$$h^2 = 48$$

$$h = 4\sqrt{3}$$

The area of one equilateral triangle

$$= \frac{1}{2}bh$$

$$= \frac{1}{2}(8)(4\sqrt{3})$$

$$A = 16\sqrt{3} \text{ in}^2$$

There are six triangles in the hexagon. The area of the hexagon

$$= 6(16\sqrt{3})$$

$$= 96\sqrt{3} \text{ in}^2$$

3.   **(E)**   Add the angles to see if the sum is 90° or 180°.

(A) 45° + 45° = 90°, complementary angle
(B) 123° + 57° = 180°, supplementary angle
(C) 84° + 96° = 180°, supplementary angle
(D) 39° + 51° = 90°, complementary angle
(E) 73° + 117° = 190°, not complementary or supplementary

4.   **(E)**   The surface area of the box equals the area of the base, plus the area of the top, plus the sum of the areas of the four faces. Hence, the surface area of the box

$$= 2x^2 + 4xh.$$

5.   **(D)**   The hypotenuse is the longest side of the triangle. It is the side opposite of the right angle. A special relationship exists between the lengths of sides of a 45°–45°–90°, or isosceles right, triangle. The hypotenuse is always $\sqrt{2}$ times the length of a leg. So this one is $\sqrt{2} \times 4$ or $4\sqrt{2}$. Another method may be used to find this. The Pythagorean Theorem for right triangles is

$$a^2 + b^2 = c^2,$$

where a and b are the legs, and c is the hypotenuse.

$$4^2 + 4^2 = c^2 \text{ or } 32^2 = c^2 \text{ or } \sqrt{32} = c$$

$$\sqrt{16} \times \sqrt{2} = c$$

Therefore, $4\sqrt{2} = c$.

6.   **(D)**   The height of the trapezoid must be drawn inside the figure in order to use the formula for the area of a trapezoid

$$= \frac{1}{2}h(a + b)$$

where a and b are the bases. When h is drawn, a 30°–60°–90° triangle is formed with the hypotenuse given as 10 (the side of the trapezoid). The side opposite the 30° angle is 5, making the height (the side opposite the 60° angle) $= 5\sqrt{3}$. Base $b = 30$ as given and base $a = 30 - 10 = 20$.

$$\text{Area} = \frac{1}{2}5\sqrt{3}\,(20 + 30) = 25(5\sqrt{3}) = 125\sqrt{3}$$

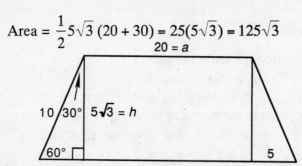

7.   (E)   All three statements are true. Since a rhombus is a parallelogram, sides BA and CD are parallel. Using AC as a transversal, $\angle BAE$ and $\angle ECD$ are alternate interior angles and are therefore congruent making I true. The diagonals of a rhombus bisect the angles and so $\angle ADE$ and $\angle CDE$ are congruent making II true. In a rhombus, all four sides are congruent so triangle ABD is isosceles with congruent sides AB and AD. The angles opposite those congruent sides are congruent, so $\angle ABE$ and $\angle ADE$ are congruent making III true.

8.   (A)   Note that the ratio (3:5:7) of the angles in the triangle ABC can be represented as three distinct angles, $3x$, $5x$, and $7x$. Since the total number of degrees in a triangle is 180°, write and solve the equation.

$$3x + 5x + 7x = 180°$$

$$15x = 180°$$

$$x = 12°$$

Thus, the measures of the angles in triangle ABC are:

$$3x = 3(12°) = 36°,$$

$$5x = 5(12°) = 60°, \text{ and}$$

$$7x = 7(12°) = 84°,$$

respectively. Since each of the three angles is less than 90°, then triangle ABC is an acute triangle.

9. **(B)** Complete the diagram as shown to get two rectangles. The smaller rectangle has sides 3 and 4 and the larger has sides 6 and 25. The area of the figure

$$= 3 \times 4 + 6 \times 25 = 162.$$

10. **(A)**

Area $= \pi r^2$

The diameter is 14, and the radius is one-half of the diameter, which is 7.
Substituting 7 for the radius,

$$A = \pi \times 7^2$$

$$A = \pi \times 49$$

$$A = 49\pi \ m^2$$

11. **(B)** All sides of an equilateral triangle are congruent, or have the same measure. The altitude is the perpendicular bisector of the base and the bisector of the vertex angle. So the altitude divides the triangle into two triangles that have angles of 30°–60°–90°. The sides of this kind of triangle have the special relationship $1:\sqrt{3}:2$. This makes the length of the altitude of the triangle $3\sqrt{3}$ cm.

12. **(B)** To find the circumference multiply π times the diameter.

$$c = \pi \times 48, \ c = 48\pi \ cm$$

13. **(A)** Since l, m, and n are lines intersecting at point P, adding $m \angle x$, $m \angle y$, and $m \angle {}^a/_2$ gives a straight angle, 180°.
Thus,

$$x + y + {}^a/_2 = 180$$

$$x + y = 180 - {}^a/_2$$

14. **(B)** The formula for finding the area of a triangle is

Area = $^1/_2$ × base × height.

The base is given, but to find the height use the Pythagorean Theorem,

$c^2 = a^2 + b^2$.

Since the hypotenuse, c, equals 17, and the base, b, equals 8,

$$17^2 = a^2 + 8^2$$

$$289 = a^2 + 64$$

$$a^2 = 225$$

Taking the square root of both sides,

$$a = 15$$

The area of a triangle = $^1/_2$ (base) (height), so substituting 8 cm for the base and 15 cm for the height,

Area = $^1/_2$ × 8 cm × 15 cm

Area = 60 cm^2

15. **(B)** The formula for finding the area of a sector

= (arc°/circle°) × π × radius squared.

Substituting the information given,

$$A = \frac{45}{360} \times \pi \times 16^2$$

$$A = \frac{1}{8} \times \pi \times 256$$

$$A = 32 \times \pi$$

$$A = 32\pi \text{ cm}^2$$

16. **(B)** Since all the sides are of different lengths, the triangle is scalene. A triangle with sides of lengths 3, 4, and 5 is a right triangle. Thus, a triangle with sides of lengths 3, 4, and 6 is an obtuse triangle.

GEOMETRY REVIEW

1. POINTS, LINES, AND ANGLES

Geometry is built upon a series of undefined terms. These terms are those which we accept as known in order to define other undefined terms.

(A) **Point**: A point has no size, thickness, or width.

(B) **Line**: A line is a series of adjacent points which extends indefinitely. A line can be either curved or straight; however, unless otherwise stated, the term "line" refers to a straight line.

(C) **Plane**: A plane is a two-dimensional flat object which extends indefinitely in all directions.

A line is referred to by one small letter, i.e., l; or two letters with the symbol — on top, i.e., $\overline{CD}$.

If A and B are two points on a line, then the **line segment** AB is the set of points on that line between A and B and including A and B, which are endpoints. The line segment is referred to as AB; or two letters with the symbol — on top, i.e., $\overline{AB}$.

A **ray** is a series of points that lie to one side of a single endpoint. A ray is referred to by two letters with the symbol → on top, i.e., $\overrightarrow{EF}$.

A **straight line** can be uniquely determined by two points.

PROBLEM

How many lines can be found that contain (a) one given point, (b) two given points, and (c) three given points?

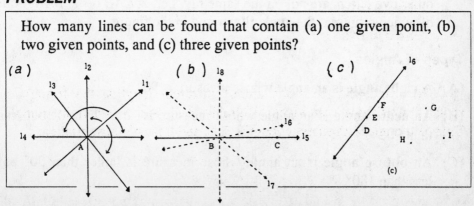

145

Solution

(a) *Given one point A*, there are an infinite number of distinct lines that contain the given point. To see this, consider line l_1 passing through point A. By rotating l_1 around A like the hands of a clock, we obtain different lines l_2, l_3, etc. Since we can rotate l_1 in infinitely many ways, there are infinitely many lines containing A.

(b) *Given two distinct points B and C*, there is one and only one distinct line. To see this, consider all the lines containing point B; l_5, l_6, l_7, and l_8. Only l_5 contains both points B and C. Thus, there is only one line containing both points B and C. Since there is always at least one line containing two distinct points and never more than one, the line passing through the two points is said to be determined by the two points.

(c) *Given three distinct points*, there may be one line or none. If a line exists that contains the three points, such as D, E, and F, then the points are said to be **colinear**. If no such line exists — as in the case of points G, H, and I, then the points are said to be **noncolinear**.

Intersecting Lines and Angles

An **angle** is a figure formed by two rays having the same endpoint. An angle such as the one illustrated below can be referred to in any of the following ways:

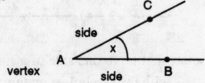

(A) by a capital letter which names its vertex, i.e., $\angle A$;

(B) by a lowercase letter or number placed inside the angle, i.e., $\angle x$;

(C) by three capital letters, where the middle letter is the vertex and the other two letters are not on the same ray, i.e., $\angle CAB$ or $\angle BAC$, both of which represent the angle illustrated in the figure.

Types of Angles

(A) A **right angle** is an angle whose measure is 90°.

(B) An **acute angle** is an angle whose measure is larger than 0° but less than 90°.

(C) An **obtuse angle** is an angle whose measure is larger than 90° but less than 180°.

(D) A **straight angle** is an angle whose measure is 180°. Such an angle is, in fact, a straight line.

(E) A **reflex angle** is an angle whose measure is greater than 180° but less than 360°.

(F) **Complementary angles** are two angles, the sum of the measures of which equals 90°.

(G) **Supplementary angles** are two angles, the sum of the measures of which equals 180°.

(H) **Congruent angles** are angles of equal measure.

(I) **Vertical angles** are formed when two lines intersect. These angles are equal.

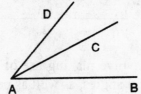

$$\angle a = \angle b$$

(J) **Adjacent angles** are two angles with a common vertex and a common side, but no common interior points. In the following figure, $\angle DAC$ and $\angle BAC$ are adjacent angles. $\angle DAB$ and $\angle BAC$ are not.

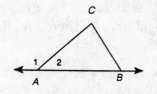

PROBLEM

In the figure, we are given $l\ AB$ and triangle ABC. We are told that the measure of $\angle 1$ is five times the measure of $\angle 2$. Determine the measures of $\angle 1$ and $\angle 2$.

Solution

Since $\angle 1$ and $\angle 2$ are adjacent angles whose non-common sides lie on a straight line, they are, by definition, supplementary. As supplements, their measures must sum to 180°.

If x = the measure of $\angle 2$, then $5x$ = the measure of $\angle 1$.

To determine the respective angle measures, set $x + 5x = 180°$ and solve for x. $6x = 180°$. Therefore, $x = 30°$ and $5x = 150°$.

Therefore, the measure of $\angle 1 = 150°$ and the measure of $\angle 2 = 30°$.

Perpendicular Lines

Two lines are said to be **perpendicular** if they intersect and form right angles. The symbol for perpendicular (or, is therefore perpendicular to) is $\perp$; l_1 is perpendicular to l_2 is written $l_1 \perp l_2$.

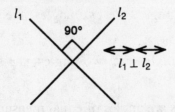

PROBLEM

We are given straight lines l_1 and l_2 intersecting at point P. $l_3 \perp l_1$ and the measure of $\angle APD$ is 170°. Find the measures of $\angle 1$, $\angle 2$, $\angle 3$, and $\angle 4$.

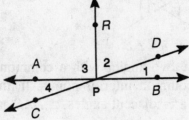

Solution

This problem will involve making use of several of the properties of supplementary and vertical angles, as well as perpendicular lines.

$\angle APD$ and $\angle 1$ are adjacent angles whose non-common sides lie on a straight line, l_1. Therefore, they are supplements and their measures sum to 180°.

$$m \angle APD + m \angle 1 = 180°.$$

We know $m \angle APD = 170°$. Therefore, by substitution, $170° + m \angle 1 = 180°$. This implies $m \angle 1 = 10°$.

$\angle 1$ and $\angle 4$ are vertical angles because they are formed by the intersection of two straight lines, l_2 and l_1, and their sides form two pairs of opposite rays. As vertical angles, they are, by theorem, of equal measure. Since $m \angle 1 = 10°$, then $m \angle 4 = 10°$.

Since $l_3 \perp l_1$, at their intersection the angles formed must be right angles. Therefore, $\angle 3$ is a right angle and its measure is 90°. $m \angle 3 = 90°$.

The figure shows us that $\angle APD$ is composed of $\angle 3$ and $\angle 2$. Since the measure of the whole must be equal to the sum of the measures of its parts, $m \angle APD = m \angle 3 + m \angle 2$. We know the $m \angle APD = 170°$ and $m \angle 3 = 90°$; therefore, by substitution, we can solve for $m \angle 2$, our last unknown.

$$170° = 90° + m \angle 2$$

$$80° = m \angle 2$$

Therefore, $\quad m \angle 1 = 10° \qquad\qquad m \angle 2 = 80°$

$$m \angle 3 = 90° \qquad\qquad m \angle 4 = 10°$$

PROBLEM

In the accompanying figure *SM* is the perpendicular bisector of *QR*, and *SN* is the perpendicular bisector of *QP*. Prove that *SR* = *SP*.

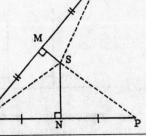

Solution

Every point on the perpendicular bisector of a segment is equidistant from the endpoints of the segment.

Since point *S* is on the perpendicular bisector of *QR*,

$$SR = SQ \tag{1}$$

Also, since point *S* is on the perpendicular bisector of *QP*,

$$SQ = SP \tag{2}$$

By the transitive property (quantities equal to the same quantity are equal), we have:

$$SR = SP \tag{3}$$

Parallel Lines

Two lines are called **parallel lines** if, and only if, they are in the same plane (coplanar) and do not intersect. The symbol for parallel, or is parallel to, is $\|$; l_1 is parallel to l_2 is written $l_1 \parallel l_2$.

The distance between two parallel lines is the length of the perpendicular segment from any point on one line to the other line.

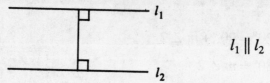

$$l_1 \parallel l_2$$

Given a line l and a point P not on line l, there is one and only one line through point P that is parallel to line l.

Two coplanar lines are either intersecting lines or parallel lines.

If two (or more) lines are perpendicular to the same line, then they are parallel to each other.

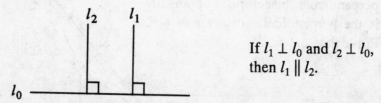

If $l_1 \perp l_0$ and $l_2 \perp l_0$, then $l_1 \parallel l_2$.

If two lines are cut by a transversal so that alternate interior angles are equal, the lines are parallel.

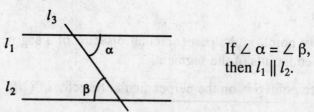

If $\angle \alpha = \angle \beta$, then $l_1 \parallel l_2$.

If two lines are parallel to the same line, then they are parallel to each other.

If $l_1 \parallel l_0$ and $l_2 \parallel l_0$, then $l_1 \parallel l_2$.

If a line is perpendicular to one of two parallel lines, then it is perpendicular to the other line, too.

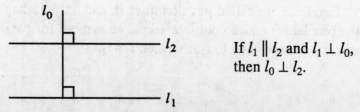

If $l_1 \parallel l_2$ and $l_1 \perp l_0$, then $l_0 \perp l_2$.

If two lines being cut by a transversal form congruent corresponding angles, then the two lines are parallel.

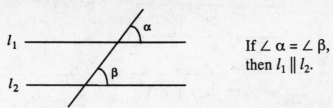

If $\angle \alpha = \angle \beta$, then $l_1 \parallel l_2$.

If two lines being cut by a transversal form interior angles on the same side of the transversal that are supplementary, then the two lines are parallel.

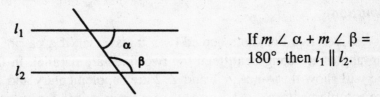

If $m \angle \alpha + m \angle \beta = 180°$, then $l_1 \parallel l_2$.

If a line is parallel to one of two parallel lines, it is also parallel to the other line.

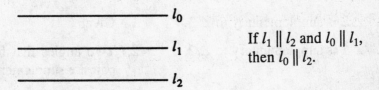

If $l_1 \parallel l_2$ and $l_0 \parallel l_1$, then $l_0 \parallel l_2$.

If two parallel lines are cut by a transversal, then:

(A) the alternate interior angles are congruent.

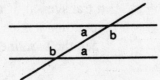

(B) the corresponding angles are congruent.

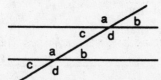

(C) the consecutive interior angles are supplementary.

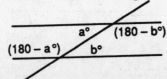

(D) the alternate exterior angles are congruent.

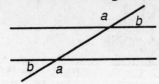

PROBLEM

Given: $\angle\,2$ is supplementary to $\angle\,3$.

Prove: $l_1 \parallel l_2$.

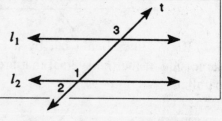

Solution

Given two lines intercepted by a transversal, if a pair of corresponding angles are congruent, then the two lines are parallel. In this problem, we will show that since $\angle\,1$ and $\angle\,2$ are supplementary and $\angle\,2$ and $\angle\,3$ are supplementary, $\angle\,1$ and $\angle\,3$ are congruent. Since corresponding angles are congruent, it follows $l_1 \parallel l_2$.

Statement	Reason
1. $\angle\,2$ is supplementary to $\angle\,3$.	1. Given.
2. $\angle\,1$ is supplementary to $\angle\,2$.	2. Two angles that form a linear pair are supplementary.
3. $\angle\,1 \cong \angle\,3$.	3. Angles supplementary to the same angle are congruent.
4. $l_1 \parallel l_2$.	4. Given two lines intercepted by a transversal, if a pair of corresponding angles are congruent, then the two lines are parallel.

PROBLEM

If line l_1 is parallel to line l_2 and line l_3 is parallel to line l_4, prove that $m \angle 1 = m \angle 2$.

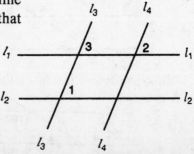

Solution

To show $\angle 1 \cong \angle 2$, we relate both to $\angle 3$. Because $l_3 \parallel l_4$, corresponding angles 1 and 3 are congruent. Since $l_1 \parallel l_2$, corresponding angles 3 and 2 are congruent. Because both $\angle 1$ and $\angle 2$ are congruent to the same angle, it follows that $\angle 1 \cong \angle 2$.

Statement	Reason
1. $l_3 \parallel l_4$.	1. Given.
2. $m \angle 1 = m \angle 3$.	2. If two parallel lines are cut by a transversal, corresponding angles are of equal measure.
3. $l_1 \parallel l_2$.	3. Given.
4. $m \angle 2 = m \angle 3$.	4. If two parallel lines are cut by a transversal, corresponding angles are equal in measure.
5. $m \angle 1 = m \angle 2$.	5. If two quantities are equal to the same quantity, they are equal to each other.

Drill 1: Points, Lines, and Angles

Intersecting Lines and Angles

1. Find a.

    (A) 38°

    (B) 68°

    (C) 78°

    (D) 90°

    (E) 112°

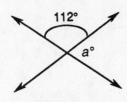

2. Find *c*.

   (A) 32°

   (B) 48°

   (C) 58°

   (D) 82°

   (E) 148°

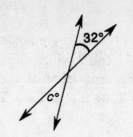

3. Determine *x*.

   (A) 21°

   (B) 23°

   (C) 51°

   (D) 102°

   (E) 153°

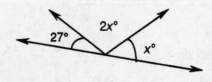

4. Find *x*.

   (A) 8

   (B) 11.75

   (C) 21

   (D) 23

   (E) 32

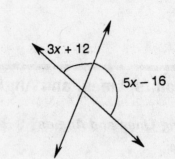

5. Find *z*.

   (A) 29°

   (B) 54°

   (C) 61°

   (D) 88°

   (E) 92°

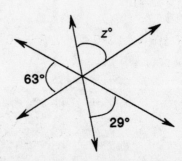

Perpendicular Lines

6. $\vec{BA} \perp \vec{BC}$ and $m \angle DBC = 53°$. Find $m \angle ABD$.

    (A) 27°

    (B) 33°

    (C) 37°

    (D) 53°

    (E) 90°

    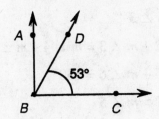

7. $m \angle 1 = 90°$. Find $m \angle 2$.

    (A) 80°

    (B) 90°

    (C) 100°

    (D) 135°

    (E) 180°

    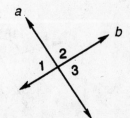

8. If $n \perp p$, which of the following statements is true?

    (A) $\angle 1 \cong \angle 2$

    (B) $\angle 4 \cong \angle 5$

    (C) $m \angle 4 + m \angle 5 > m \angle 1 + m \angle 2$

    (D) $m \angle 3 > m \angle 2$

    (E) $m \angle 4 = 90°$

    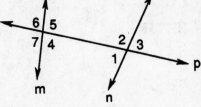

9. $CD \perp EF$. If $m \angle 1 = 2x$, $m \angle 2 = 30°$, and $m \angle 3 = x$, find x.

    (A) 5°

    (B) 10°

    (C) 12°

    (D) 20°

    (E) 25°

    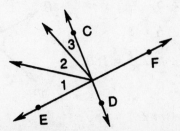

10. In the figure, $p \perp t$ and $q \perp t$. Which of the following statements is false?

    (A) $\angle 1 \cong \angle 4$

    (B) $\angle 2 \cong \angle 3$

    (C) $m \angle 2 + m \angle 3 = m \angle 4 + m \angle 6$

    (D) $m \angle 5 + m \angle 6 = 180°$

    (E) $m \angle 2 > m \angle 5$

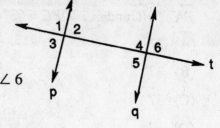

Parallel Lines

11. If $a \parallel b$, find z.

    (A) 26°

    (B) 32°

    (C) 64°

    (D) 86°

    (E) 116°

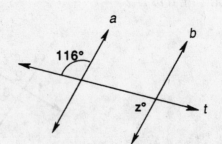

12. In the figure, $p \parallel q \parallel r$. Find $m \angle 7$.

    (A) 27°

    (B) 33°

    (C) 47°

    (D) 57°

    (E) 64°

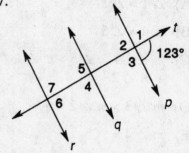

13. If $m \parallel n$, which of the following statements is false?

    (A) $\angle 2 \cong \angle 5$

    (B) $\angle 3 \cong \angle 6$

    (C) $m \angle 4 + m \angle 5 = 180°$

    (D) $\angle 1 \cong \angle 8$

    (E) $m \angle 7 + m \angle 1 = 180°$

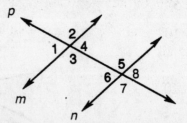

14. If $r \parallel s$, find $m \angle 2$.

    (A) 17°

    (B) 27°

    (C) 43°

    (D) 67°

    (E) 73°

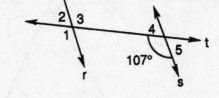

15. If $a \parallel b$ and $c \parallel d$, find $m \angle 5$.

    (A) 55°

    (B) 65°

    (C) 75°

    (D) 95°

    (E) 125°

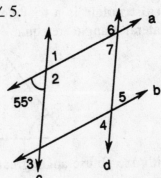

2. TRIANGLES

A closed three-sided geometric figure is called a **triangle**. The points of the intersection of the sides of a triangle are called the **vertices** of the triangle.

A side of a triangle is a line segment whose endpoints are the vertices of two angles of the triangle.

An interior angle of a triangle is an angle formed by two sides and includes the third side within its collection of points.

The sum of the interior angles of a triangle equals 180°.

The **perimeter** of a triangle is the sum of the measures of the sides of the triangle.

A triangle with no equal sides is called a **scalene triangle**.

A triangle having at least two equal sides is called an **isosceles triangle**. The third side is called the **base** of the triangle. The angles opposite the equal sides are equal.

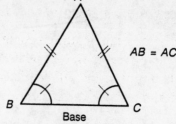

An **equilateral triangle** is a triangle having three equal sides. The angles of an equilateral triangle are equal.

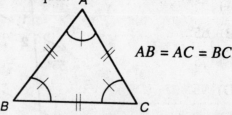

A triangle with one obtuse angle greater than 90° is called an **obtuse triangle**.

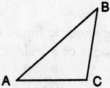

An **acute triangle** is a triangle with three acute angles (less than 90°).

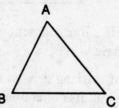

A triangle with a right angle is called a **right triangle**. The side opposite the right angle in a right triangle is called the **hypotenuse** of the right triangle. The other two sides are called **arms** or **legs** of the right triangle.

The **Pythagorean Theorem** is

$a^2 + b^2 = c^2$ in a right triangle.

a and b are the legs of the triangle and c is the hypotenuse.

In a 30°–60°–90° triangle, the hypotenuse is twice as long as the side opposite the 30° angle. The side opposite the 60° angle is equal to the length of the side opposite the 30° angle multiplied by $\sqrt{3}$. This gives a ratio of $1:\sqrt{3}:2$ for the sides of the triangle.

PROBLEM

Use the Pythagorean Theorem to show the special relationship in a 30°–60°–90° triangle.

Solution

Let the side opposite the 30° angle = 1. Then the hypotenuse = 2.

Using the Pythagorean Theorem,

$$a^2 + b^2 = c^2$$
$$1^2 + b^2 = 2^2$$
$$1 + b^2 = 4$$
$$b^2 = 4 - 1$$
$$b^2 = 3$$
$$b = \sqrt{3}$$

In a 45°–45°–90° triangle, the length of the hypotenuse is equal to the length of one of the legs multiplied by $\sqrt{2}$.

PROBLEM

Use the Pythagorean Theorem to show the special relationship in a 45°–45°–90° triangle.

Solution

Let the legs equal 1.

$$a^2 + b^2 = c^2$$
$$1^2 + 1^2 = c^2$$
$$1 + 1 = c^2$$

$$2 = c^2$$

$$\sqrt{2} = c$$

Two triangles are congruent if corresponding parts are congruent.

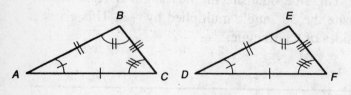

If $AB = DE$, $BC = EF$, $AC = DF$, $\angle A = \angle D$, $\angle B = \angle E$, and $\angle C = \angle F$, then $\triangle ABC \cong \triangle DEF$.

If two sides and the included angle of one triangle are equal respectively to two sides and the included angle of another triangle, then the two triangles are congruent. (S.A.S.)

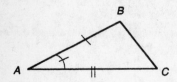 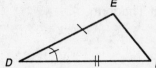

If $AB = DE$, $AC = DF$, and $\angle A = \angle D$, then $\triangle ABC \cong \triangle DEF$.

If two angles and the included side of one triangle are equal respectively to two sides and the included side of another triangle, then the two triangles are congruent. (A.S.A.)

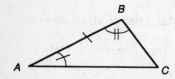 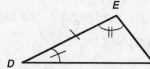

If $\angle A = \angle D$, $\angle B = \angle E$, and $AB = DE$, then $\triangle ABC \cong \triangle DEF$.

If three sides of one triangle are equal respectively to three sides of another triangle, then the triangles are congruent. (S.S.S.)

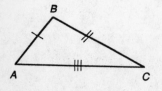 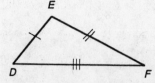

If $AB = DE$, $BC = EF$, and $AC = DF$, then $\triangle ABC \cong \triangle DEF$.

PROBLEM

Given figure *ABCDE* with straight line *ABCD*, *AB* = *CD*, *BE* = *CE*, and ∠ *EBA* = ∠ *ECD*, prove △*ABE* ≅ △*CED*.

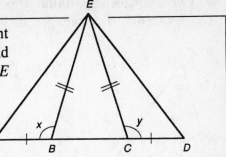

Solution

Given a triangle with two sides and an included angle equal to another triangle, then the triangles are congruent.

Statement	Reason
1. *AB* = *CD*.	1. Given.
2. *BE* = *CE*.	2. Given.
3. ∠ *EBA* = ∠ *ECD*.	3. Given.
4. ∴△*ABE* ≅ △*CED*.	4. S.A.S.

PROBLEM

Given figure *ABCD* with ∠ *x* = ∠ *y* and ∠ *r* = ∠ *s*, prove △*ABD* ≅ △*DBC*.

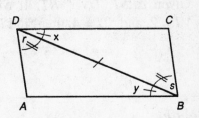

Solution

With the given information look for congruence between the triangles by having two angles and the included side equal.

Statement	Reason
1. ∠ *x* = ∠ *y*.	1. Given.
2. ∠ *r* = ∠ *s*.	2. Given.
3. *DB* = *DB*.	3. Any quantity equals itself (Identity).
4. ∴△*ABD* ≅ △*DBC*.	4. A.S.A.

Two triangles are **similar** if corresponding angles are congruent and the corresponding sides are proportional segments.

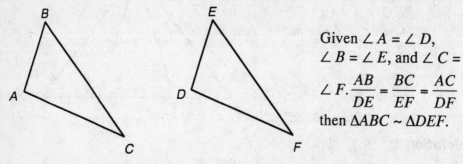

Given $\angle A = \angle D$, $\angle B = \angle E$, and $\angle C = \angle F$. $\dfrac{AB}{DE} = \dfrac{BC}{EF} = \dfrac{AC}{DF}$ then $\triangle ABC \sim \triangle DEF$.

A line parallel to one side of a triangle that intersects the other two sides divides these two sides into proportional segments.

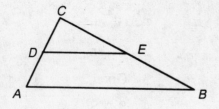

Given $\triangle ABC$ with $DE \parallel AB$, then $\dfrac{AD}{DC} = \dfrac{BE}{EC}$.

PROBLEM

Given $\triangle RST$, $UV \parallel RT$. If $SV = 3$, $VT = 2$, and $SU = 4$, then find UR.

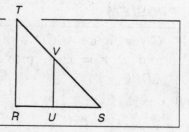

Solution

Given $\triangle RST$, with $UV \parallel RT$, then

$$\frac{VT}{VS} = \frac{RU}{SU}$$

$$\frac{2}{3} = \frac{UR}{4}$$

$$UR = \frac{8}{3}$$

An **altitude** of a triangle is a line segment from a vertex of the triangle perpendicular to the opposite side.

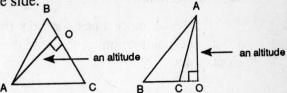

A line segment connecting a vertex of a triangle and the midpoint of the opposite side is called a **median** of the triangle.

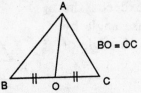

A line that bisects and is perpendicular to a side of a triangle is called a **perpendicular bisector** of that side.

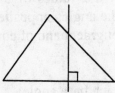

An **angle bisector** of a triangle is a line that bisects an angle and extends to the opposite side of the triangle.

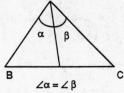

The line segment that joins the midpoints of two sides of a triangle is called a **midline** of the triangle.

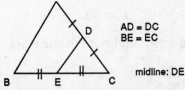

An **exterior angle** of a triangle is an angle formed outside a triangle by one side of the triangle and the extension of an adjacent side.

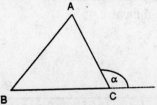

A triangle whose three interior angles have equal measure is said to be **equiangular**.

Three or more lines (or rays or segments) are concurrent if there exists one point common to all of them, that is, if they all intersect at the same point.

PROBLEM

The measure of the vertex angle of an isosceles triangle exceeds the measurement of each base angle by 30°. Find the value of each angle of the triangle.

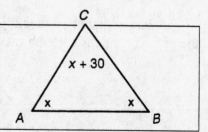

Solution

We know that the sum of the values of the angles of a triangle is 180°. In an isosceles triangle, the angles opposite the congruent sides (the base angles) are, themselves, congruent and of equal value.

Therefore,

(1)   Let x = the measure of each base angle.

(2)   Then $x + 30$ = the measure of the vertex angle.

We can solve for x algebraically by keeping in mind the sum of all the measures will be 180°.

$$x + x + (x + 30) = 180$$
$$3x + 30 = 180$$
$$3x = 150$$
$$x = 50$$

Therefore, the base angles each measure 50°, and the vertex angle measures 80°.

PROBLEM

Prove that the base angles of an isosceles right triangle measure 45°.

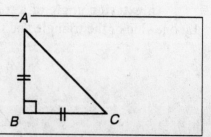

Solution

As drawn in the figure, $\triangle ABC$ is an isosceles right triangle with base angles BAC and BCA. The sum of the measures of the angles of any triangle is $180°$. For $\triangle ABC$, this means

$$m \angle BAC + m \angle BCA + m \angle ABC = 180° \qquad (1)$$

But $m \angle ABC = 90°$ because $\triangle ABC$ is a right triangle. Furthermore, $m \angle BCA = m \angle BAC$, since the base angles of an isosceles triangle are congruent. Using these facts in equation (1),

$$m \angle BAC + m \angle BCA + 90° = 180°$$

or $\qquad 2m \angle BAC = 2m \angle BCA = 90°$

or $\qquad m \angle BAC = m \angle BCA = 45°$

Therefore, the base angles of an isosceles right triangle measure $45°$.

The area of a triangle is given by the formula

$$A = {}^1\!/_2\, bh,$$

where b is the length of a base, which can be any side of the triangle and h is the corresponding height of the triangle, which is the perpendicular line segment that is drawn from the vertex opposite the base to the base itself.

$A = {}^1\!/_2\, bh$

$A = {}^1\!/_2\, (10)\, (3)$

$A = 15$

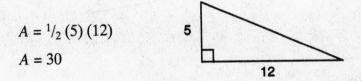

The area of a right triangle is found by taking ${}^1\!/_2$ the product of the lengths of its two arms.

$A = {}^1\!/_2\, (5)\, (12)$

$A = 30$

Drill 2: Triangles

Angle Measures

1. In $\triangle PQR$, $\angle Q$ is a right angle. Find $m \angle R$.

    (A) 27°

    (B) 33°

    (C) 54°

    (D) 67°

    (E) 157°

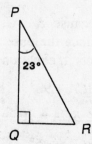

2. $\triangle MNO$ is an isosceles triangle. If the vertex angle, $\angle N$, has a measure of 96°, find the measure of $\angle M$.

    (A) 21°

    (B) 42°

    (C) 64°

    (D) 84°

    (E) 96°

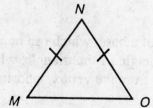

3. Find x.

    (A) 15°

    (B) 25°

    (C) 30°

    (D) 45°

    (E) 90°

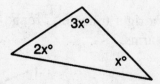

4. Find $m \angle 1$.

    (A) 40°

    (B) 66°

    (C) 74°

    (D) 114°

    (E) 140°

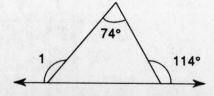

5. $\triangle ABC$ is a right triangle with a right angle at B. $\triangle BDC$ is a right triangle with right angle $\angle BDC$. If $m \angle C = 36°$. Find $m \angle A$.

    (A) 18°

    (B) 36°

    (C) 54°

    (D) 72°

    (E) 180°

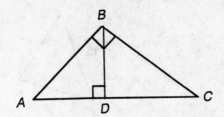

Similar Triangles

6. The two triangles shown are similar. Find b.

    (A) $2^2/_3$

    (B) 3

    (C) 4

    (D) 16

    (E) 24

7. The two triangles shown are similar. Find $m \angle 1$.

    (A) 48°

    (B) 53°

    (C) 74°

    (D) 127°

    (E) 180°

8. The two triangles shown are similar. Find a and b.

    (A) 5 and 10

    (B) 4 and 8

    (C) $4^2/_3$ and $7^1/_3$

    (D) 5 and 8

    (E) $5^1/_3$ and 8

9. The perimeter of △LXR is 45 and the perimeter of △ABC is 27. If LX = 15, find the length of AB.

   (A) 9

   (B) 15

   (C) 27

   (D) 45

   (E) 72

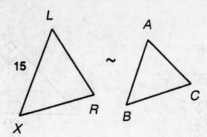

10. Find b.

    (A) 9

    (B) 15

    (C) 20

    (D) 45

    (E) 60

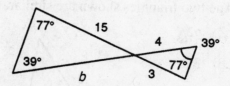

Area

11. Find the area of △MNO.

    (A) 22

    (B) 49

    (C) 56

    (D) 84

    (E) 112

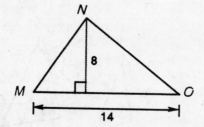

12. Find the area of △PQR.

    (A) 31.5

    (B) 38.5

    (C) 53

    (D) 77

    (E) 82.5

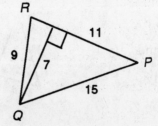

13. Find the area of △*STU*.

    (A) $4\sqrt{2}$

    (B) $8\sqrt{2}$

    (C) $12\sqrt{2}$

    (D) $16\sqrt{2}$

    (E) $32\sqrt{2}$

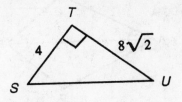

14. Find the area of △*ABC*.

    (A) 54 cm²

    (B) 81 cm²

    (C) 108 cm²

    (D) 135 cm²

    (E) 180 cm²

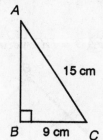

15. Find the area of △*XYZ*.

    (A) 20 cm²

    (B) 50 cm²

    (C) $50\sqrt{2}$ cm²

    (D) 100 cm²

    (E) 200 cm²

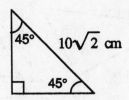

Congruent Triangles

DIRECTIONS: Determine whether or not the triangles are congruent and why. The answers are:

    (A) Congruent because of S.A.S.

    (B) Congruent because of A.S.A.

    (C) Congruent because of S.S.S.

    (D) Not congruent

16. Given △ADBC with ∠ x = ∠ y and ∠ r = ∠ s, is △ABC ≅ △ADB?

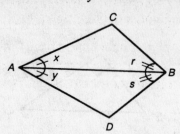

17. Given △ABC and △DEF with ∠ A = ∠ D, AC = DF, AB = DE, is △ABC ≅ △DEF?

18. Given △ABC and △DEF with ∠ A = ∠ E, BC = DF, and ∠ C = ∠ D, is △ABC ≅ △ADEF?

19. Given AB = BC and AD = DC, is △ABD ≅ △BCD?

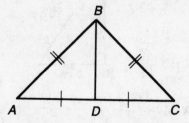

20. Given ∠ A = ∠ F, ∠ C = ∠ E, and CB = DE, is △ABC ≅ △DEF?

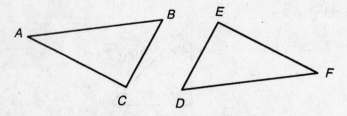

3. QUADRILATERALS

A **quadrilateral** is a polygon with four sides.

Parallelograms

A **parallelogram** is a quadrilateral whose opposite sides are parallel.

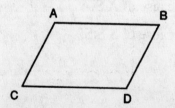

Two angles that have their vertices at the endpoints of the same side of a parallelogram are called **consecutive angles**.

The perpendicular segment connecting any point of a line containing one side of the parallelogram to the line containing the opposite side of the parallelogram is called the **altitude** of the parallelogram.

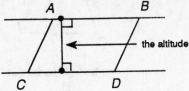

A diagonal of a polygon is a line segment joining any two non-consecutive vertices.

The area of a parallelogram is given by the formula $A = bh$, where b is the base and h is the height drawn perpendicular to that base. Note that the height equals the altitude of the parallelogram.

$A = bh$

$A = (10)(3)$

$A = 30$

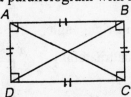

Rectangles

A **rectangle** is a parallelogram with right angles.

The diagonals of a rectangle are equal. ($AC = DB$)

If the diagonals of a parallelogram are equal, the parallelogram is a rectangle.

If a quadrilateral has four right angles, then it is a rectangle.

The area of a rectangle is given by the formula $A = lw$, where l is the length and w is the width.

$A = lw$

$A = (3)(10)$

$A = 30$

Rhombi

A **rhombus** is a parallelogram with two adjacent sides equal.

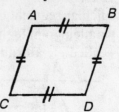

All sides of a rhombus are equal.

The diagonals of a rhombus are perpendicular to each other.

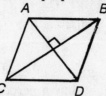

The diagonals of a rhombus bisect the angles of the rhombus.

If the diagonals of a parallelogram are perpendicular, the parallelogram is a rhombus.

If a quadrilateral has four equal sides, then it is a rhombus.

A parallelogram is a rhombus if either diagonal of the parallelogram bisects the angles of the vertices it joins.

Squares

A **square** is a rhombus with a right angle.

A square is an equilateral quadrilateral.

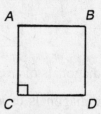

A square has all the properties of parallelograms and rectangles.

A rhombus is a square if one of its interior angles is a right angle.

In a square, the measure of either diagonal can be calculated by multiplying the length of any side by the square root of 2.

$$AD = AB \sqrt{2}$$

The area of a square is given by the formula $A = s^2$, where s is the side of the square. Since all sides of a square are equal, it does not matter which side is used.

$A = s^2$

$A = 6^2$ 6

$A = 36$

The area of a square can also be found by taking $^1/_2$ the product of the length of the diagonal squared.

$A = ^1/_2\, d^2$

$A = ^1/_2\, (8)^2$

$A = 32$ 8

Trapezoids

A **trapezoid** is a quadrilateral with two and only two sides parallel. The parallel sides of a trapezoid are called **bases**.

The **median** of a trapezoid is the line joining the midpoints of the non-parallel sides.

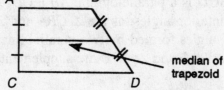

median of trapezoid

The perpendicular segment connecting any point in the line containing one base of the trapezoid to the line containing the other base is the **altitude** of the trapezoid.

altitude

An **isosceles trapezoid** is a trapezoid whose non-parallel sides are equal. A pair of angles including only one of the parallel sides is called **a pair of base angles**.

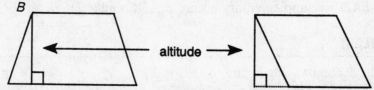

Pairs of base angles

The median of a trapezoid is parallel to the bases and equal to one-half their sum.

The base angles of an isosceles trapezoid are equal.

The diagonals of an isosceles trapezoid are equal.

The opposite angles of an isosceles trapezoid are supplementary.

PROBLEM

Prove that all pairs of consecutive angles of a parallelogram are supplementary.

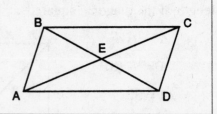

Solution

We must prove that the pairs of angles $\angle BAD$ and $\angle ADC$, $\angle ADC$ and $\angle DCB$, $\angle DCB$ and $\angle CBA$, and $\angle CBA$ and $\angle BAD$ are supplementary. (This means that the sum of their measures is 180°.)

Because $ABCD$ is a parallelogram, $AB \parallel CD$. Angles BAD and ADC are consecutive interior angles, as are $\angle CBA$ and $\angle DCB$. Since the consecutive interior angles formed by two parallel lines and a transversal are supplementary, $\angle BAD$ and $\angle ADC$ are supplementary, as are $\angle CBA$ and $\angle DCB$.

Similarly, $AD \parallel BC$. Angles ADC and DCB are consecutive interior angles, as are $\angle CBA$ and $\angle BAD$. Since the consecutive interior angles formed by two parallel lines and a transversal are supplementary, $\angle CBA$ and $\angle BAD$ are supplementary, as are $\angle ADC$ and $\angle DCB$.

PROBLEM

In the accompanying figure, $\triangle ABC$ is given to be an isosceles right triangle with $\angle ABC$ a right angle and $AB \cong BC$. Line segment BD, which bisects CA, is extended to E, so that $BD \cong DE$. Prove $BAEC$ is a square.

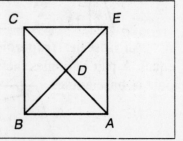

Solution

A square is a rectangle in which two consecutive sides are congruent. This definition will provide the framework for the proof in this problem. We will prove that *BAEC* is a parallelogram that is specifically a rectangle with consecutive sides congruent, namely a square.

Statement	Reason
1. $BD \cong DE$ and $AD \cong DC$.	1. Given (*BC* bisects *CA*).
2. *BAEC* is a parallelogram.	2. If diagonals of a quadrilateral bisect each other, then the quadrilateral is a parallelogram.
3. $\angle ABC$ is a right angle.	3. Given.
4. *BAEC* is a rectangle.	4. A parallelogram, one of whose angles is a right angle, is a rectangle.
5. $AB \cong BC$.	5. Given.
6. *BAEC* is a square.	6. If a rectangle has two congruent consecutive sides, then the rectangle is a square.

Drill 3: Quadrilaterals

Parallelograms, Rectangles, Rhombi, Squares, and Trapezoids

1. In parallelogram *wxyz*, $wx = 14$, $wz = 6$, $zy = 3x + 5$, and $xy = 2y - 4$. Find x and y.

   (A) 3 and 5

   (B) 4 and 5

   (C) 4 and 6

   (D) 6 and 10

   (E) 6 and 14

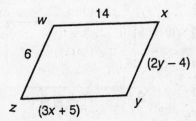

2. Quadrilateral *ABCD* is a parallelogram. If $m \angle B = (6x + 2)°$ and $m \angle D = 98°$, find *x*.

(A) 12

(B) 16

(C) $16\frac{2}{3}$

(D) 18

(E) 20

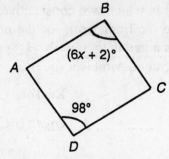

3. Find the area of parallelogram *STUV*.

(A) 56

(B) 90

(C) 108

(D) 162

(E) 180

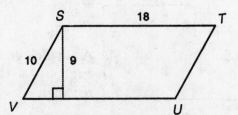

4. Find the area of parallelogram *MNOP*.

(A) 19

(B) 32

(C) $32\sqrt{3}$

(D) 44

(E) $44\sqrt{3}$

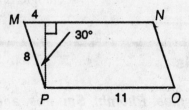

5. Find the perimeter of rectangle *PQRS*.

(A) 31 in

(B) 38 in

(C) 40 in

(D) 44 in

(E) 121 in

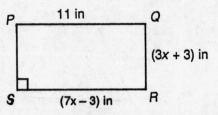

6. In rectangle *ABCD*, *AD* = 6 cm and *DC* = 8 cm. Find the length of the diagonal *AC*.

   (A) 10 cm

   (B) 12 cm

   (C) 20 cm

   (D) 28 cm

   (E) 48 cm

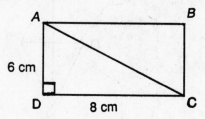

7. Find the area of rectangle *UVXY*.

   (A) 17 cm²

   (B) 34 cm²

   (C) 35 cm²

   (D) 70 cm²

   (E) 140 cm²

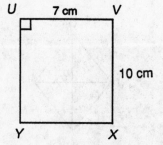

8. Find *x* in rectangle *BCDE* if the diagonal *EC* is 17 mm.

   (A) 6.55 mm

   (B) 8 mm

   (C) 8.5 mm

   (D) 17 mm

   (E) 34 mm

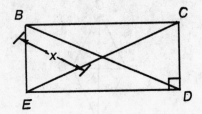

9. In rhombus *DEFG*, *DE* = 7 cm. Find the perimeter of the rhombus.

   (A) 14 cm

   (B) 28 cm

   (C) 42 cm

   (D) 49 cm

   (E) 56 cm

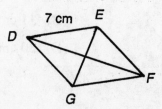

10. In rhombus *RHOM*, the diagonal *RO* is 8 cm and the diagonal *HM* is 12 cm. Find the area of the rhombus.

   (A) 20 cm²

   (B) 40 cm²

   (C) 48 cm²

   (D) 68 cm²

   (E) 96 cm²

11. In rhombus *GHIJ*, *GI* = 6 cm and *HJ* = 8 cm. Find the length of *GH*.

   (A) 3 cm

   (B) 4 cm

   (C) 5 cm

   (D) $4\sqrt{3}$ cm

   (E) 14 cm

12. In rhombus *CDEF*, *CD* is 13 mm and *DX* is 5 mm. Find the area of the rhombus.

   (A) 31 mm²

   (B) 60 mm²

   (C) 78 mm²

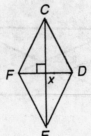

   (D) 120 mm²

   (E) 260 mm²

13. Quadrilateral *ATUV* is a square. If the perimeter of the square is 44 cm, find the length of *AT*.

   (A) 4 cm   (B) 11 cm

   (C) 22 cm   (D) 30 cm

   (E) 40 cm

14. The area of square *XYZW* is 196 cm². Find the perimeter of the square.

    (A) 28 cm

    (B) 42 cm

    (C) 56 cm

    (D) 98 cm

    (E) 196 cm

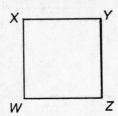

15. In square *MNOP*, *MN* is 6 cm. Find the length of diagonal *MO*.

    (A) 6 cm

    (B) $6\sqrt{2}$ cm

    (C) $6\sqrt{3}$ cm

    (D) $6\sqrt{6}$ cm

    (E) 12 cm

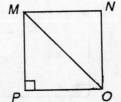

16. In square *ABCD*, *AB* = 3 cm. Find the area of the square.

    (A) 9 cm²

    (B) 12 cm²

    (C) 15 cm²

    (D) 18 cm²

    (E) 21 cm²

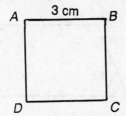

17. Find the area of trapezoid *RSTU*.

    (A) 80

    (B) 87.5

    (C) 140

    (D) 147

    (E) 175

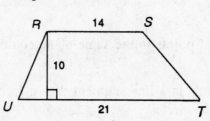

18. *ABCD* is an isosceles trapezoid. Find the perimeter.

    (A) 21 cm

    (B) 27 cm

    (C) 30 cm

    (D) 50 cm

    (E) 54 cm

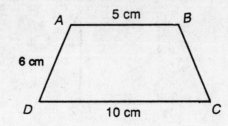

19. Find the area of trapezoid *MNOP*.

    (A) $(17 + 3\sqrt{3})$ mm^2

    (B) $^{33}/_2$ mm^2

    (C) $(33\sqrt{3})/2$ mm^2

    (D) 33 mm^2

    (E) $33\sqrt{3}$ mm^2

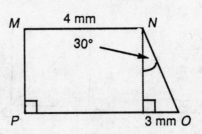

20. Trapezoid *XYZW* is isosceles. If $m \angle W = 58$ and $m \angle Z = (4x - 6)$, find x.

    (A) 8

    (B) 12

    (C) 13

    (D) 16

    (E) 58

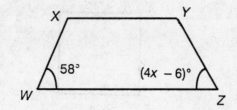

4. CIRCLES

A **circle** is a set of points in the same plane equidistant from a fixed point called its center.

A **radius** of a circle is a line segment drawn from the center of the circle to any point on the circle.

A portion of a circle is called an **arc** of the circle.

A line that intersects a circle in two points is called a **secant.**

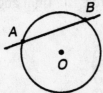

A line segment joining two points on a circle is called a **chord** of the circle.

A chord that passes through the center of the circle is called a **diameter** of the circle.

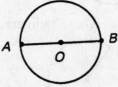

The line passing through the centers of two (or more) circles is called the **line of centers.**

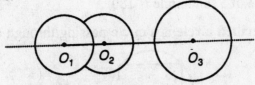

An angle whose vertex is on the circle and whose sides are chords of the circle is called an **inscribed angle.**

The measure of an inscribed angle is half the measure of its intercepted arc.

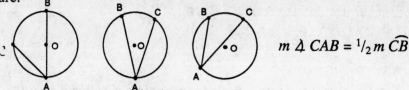

$$m \angle CAB = \frac{1}{2} m \, \widehat{CB}$$

An angle inscribed in a semicircle is a right angle.

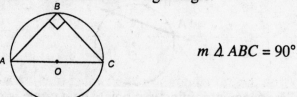

$$m \angle ABC = 90°$$

An angle whose vertex is at the center of a circle and whose sides are radii is called a **central angle.**

The measure of a minor arc is the measure of the central angle that intercepts that arc.

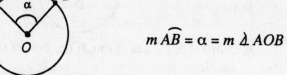

$$m \, \widehat{AB} = \alpha = m \angle AOB$$

Congruent circles are circles whose radii are congruent.

If $O_1A_1 \cong O_2A_2$, then $O_1 \cong O_2$.

The measure of a semicircle is 180°.

A **circumscribed circle** is a circle passing through all the vertices of a polygon.

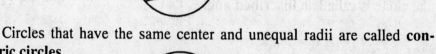

Circles that have the same center and unequal radii are called **concentric circles.**

Concentric Circles

PROBLEM

A and B are points on circle Q such that $\triangle AQB$ is equilateral. If the length of side AB = 12, find the length of $\overset{\frown}{AB}$.

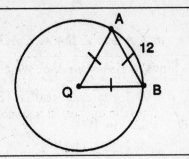

Solution

To find the arc length of $\overset{\frown}{AB}$, we must find the measure of the central angle $\angle AQB$ and the measure of the radius $\overline{QA}$. $\angle AQB$ is an interior angle of the equilateral triangle $\triangle AQB$. Therefore, $m \angle AQB = 60°$. Similarly, in the equilateral $\triangle AQB$,

$$AQ = AB = QB = 12.$$

Given the radius, r, and the central angle, n, the arc length is given by $n/360 \times 2\pi r$. Therefore, by substitution of $m \angle AQB$,

$$\frac{60}{360} \times 2\pi \times 12 = \frac{1}{6} \times 2\pi \times 12 = 4\pi.$$

Therefore, the length of $\overset{\frown}{AB} = 4\pi$.

PROBLEM

In circle O, the measure of $\overset{\frown}{AB}$ is 80°. Find the measure of $\angle A$.

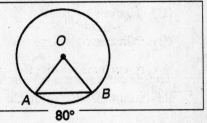

Solution

The accompanying figure shows that $\overset{\frown}{AB}$ is intercepted by central $\angle AOB$. By definition, we know that the measure of the central angle is the measure of its intercepted arc. In this case,

$$m \overset{\frown}{AB} = m \angle AOB = 80°.$$

Radius OA and radius OB are congruent and form two sides of $\triangle OAB$. By a theorem, the angles opposite these two congruent sides must, themselves, be congruent. Therefore, $m \angle A = m \angle B$.

The sum of the measures of the angles of a triangle is 180°. Therefore,

$$m \angle A + m \angle B + m \angle AOB = 180°.$$

Since $m \angle A = m \angle B$, we can write

$$m \angle A + m \angle A + 80° = 180°$$

or $\quad 2m \angle A = 100°$

or $\quad m \angle A = 50°.$

Therefore, the measure of $\angle A$ is 50°.

Drill 4: Circles

1. Find the circumference of circle A if its radius is 3 mm.

   (A) 3π mm   (B) 6π mm

   (C) 9π mm   (D) 12π mm

   (E) 15π mm

2. The circumference of circle H is 20π cm. Find the length of the radius.

   (A) 10 cm   (B) 20 cm

   (C) 10π cm   (D) 15π cm

   (E) 20π cm

3. The circumference of circle A is how many millimeters larger than the circumference of circle B?

   (A) 3

   (B) 6

   (C) 3π

   (D) 6π

   (E) 7π

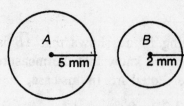

4. If the diameter of circle X is 9 cm, find the circumference of the circle.

   (A) 9 cm

   (B) 4.5π cm

   (C) 6π cm

   (D) 8π cm

   (E) 9π cm

5. Find the area of circle I.

   (A) 22 mm^2

   (B) 121 mm^2

   (C) 121π mm^2

   (D) 132 mm^2

   (E) 132π mm^2

6. The diameter of circle Z is 27 mm. Find the area of the circle.

   (A) 91.125 mm^2

   (B) 182.25 mm^2

   (C) 191.5π mm^2

   (D) 182.25π mm^2

   (E) 729 mm^2

7. The area of circle B is 225π cm^2. Find the length of the diameter of the circle.

   (A) 15 cm

   (B) 20 cm

   (C) 30 cm

   (D) 20π cm

   (E) 25π cm

8. The area of circle X is 144π mm^2 while the area of circle Y is 81π mm^2. Write the ratio of the radius of circle X to that of circle Y.

   (A) 3 : 4

   (B) 4 : 3

   (C) 9 : 12

   (D) 27 : 12

   (E) 18 : 24

9. The circumference of circle M is 18π cm. Find the area of the circle.

    (A) 18π cm^2 (B) 81 cm^2

    (C) 36 cm^2 (D) 36π cm^2

    (E) 81π cm^2

10. In two concentric circles, the smaller circle has a radius of 3 mm while the larger circle has a radius of 5 mm. Find the area of the shaded region.

    (A) 2π mm^2

    (B) 8π mm^2

    (C) 13π mm^2

    (D) 16π mm^2

    (E) 26π mm^2

11. The radius of the smaller of two concentric circles is 5 cm while the radius of the larger circle is 7 cm. Determine the area of the shaded region.

    (A) 7π cm^2

    (B) 24π cm^2

    (C) 25π cm^2

    (D) 36π cm^2

    (E) 49π cm^2

12. Find the measure of $\overset{\frown}{MN}$ if $m \angle MON = 62°$.

    (A) $16°$

    (B) $32°$

    (C) $59°$

    (D) $62°$

    (E) $124°$

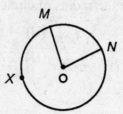

13. Find the measure of $\overset{\frown}{AXC}$.

    (A) 150°

    (B) 160°

    (C) 180°

    (D) 270°

    (E) 360°

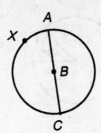

14. If $\overset{\frown}{MXP} = 236°$, find the measure of $\overset{\frown}{MP}$.

    (A) 62°

    (B) 124°

    (C) 236°

    (D) 270°

    (E) 360°

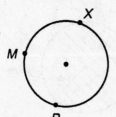

15. In circle S, major $\overset{\frown}{PQR}$ has a measure of 298°. Find the measure of the central $\angle\, PSR$.

    (A) 62°

    (B) 124°

    (C) 149°

    (D) 298°

    (E) 360°

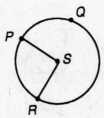

16. Find the measure of $\overset{\frown}{XY}$ in circle W.

    (A) 40°

    (B) 120°

    (C) 140°

    (D) 180°

    (E) 220°

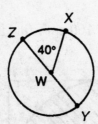

17. Find the area of the sector shown.

    (A) 4 cm²

    (B) 2π cm²

    (C) 16 cm²

    (D) 8π cm²

    (E) 16π cm²

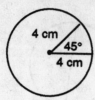

18. Find the area of the shaded region.

    (A) 10

    (B) 5π

    (C) 25

    (D) 20π

    (E) 25π

19. Find the area of the sector shown.

    (A) $\dfrac{9\pi \text{ mm}^2}{4}$

    (B) $\dfrac{9\pi \text{ mm}^2}{2}$

    (C) 18 mm²

    (D) 6π mm²

    (E) 9π mm²

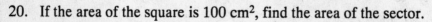

20. If the area of the square is 100 cm², find the area of the sector.

    (A) 10π cm²

    (B) 25 cm²

    (C) 25π cm²

    (D) 100 cm²

    (E) 100π cm²

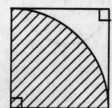

5. SOLIDS

Solid geometry is the study of figures which consist of points not all in the same plane.

Rectangular Solids

A solid with lateral faces and bases that are rectangles is called a **rectangular solid**.

The surface area of a rectangular solid is the sum of the areas of all the faces.

The volume of a rectangular solid is equal to the product of its length, width, and height.

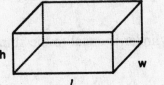

$$V = lwh$$

PROBLEM

What are the dimensions of a solid cube whose surface area is numerically equal to its volume?

Solution

The surface area of a cube of edge length a is equal to the sum of the areas of its 6 faces. Since a cube is a regular polygon, all 6 faces are congruent. Each face of a cube is a square of edge length a. Hence, the surface area of a cube of edge length a is

$$S = 6a^2.$$

The volume of a cube of edge length a is

$$V = a^3.$$

We require that $S = V$, or that

$$6a^2 = a^3 \quad \text{or} \quad a = 6$$

Hence, if a cube has edge length 6, its surface area will be numerically equal to its volume.

Cylinders

A solid with bases that are parallel circles and with cross sections parallel to the bases that are also circles is called a **circular cylinder** or a cylinder.

The altitude of a cylinder is the distance between two bases of the cylinder.

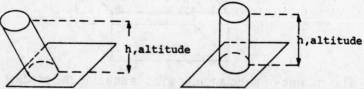

The lateral area of a cylinder is equal to the area of its curved cylindrical surface.

The total area of a cylinder is equal to the sum of its lateral area and the area of its bases.

The volume of any cylinder is the product of the area of its base and the altitude of its cylinder.

volume = (area of base) × (height)

$V = \pi r^2 h$

PROBLEM

Find, in terms of π, the volume of a right circular cylinder if the radius of its base measures 4 in. and its altitude measures 5 in.

Solution

If we picture the base of the cylinder having a depth of one unit of measure, we can then calculate the volume by determining the area of the base and multiplying it by the height of the cylinder. In effect, this multiplication amounts to stacking the bases up to the height of the cylinder.

Area of the bases = πr^2, where r is the radius of the circular base. Therefore, the volume is given by

$$V = \pi r^2 h.$$

By substitution,

$$V = \pi(4)^2 5 \text{ in}^3 = 80\pi \text{ in}^3.$$

Therefore, volume of the cylinder = 80π in^3.

Spheres

A **sphere** is the set of points in space at a given distance from a given point, called the center of the sphere.

The area of a sphere is equal to the area of its curved spherical surface.

The volume of a sphere is equal to one-third the product of its area and the measure of its radius.

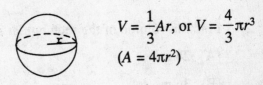

$$V = \frac{1}{3}Ar, \text{ or } V = \frac{4}{3}\pi r^3$$

$$(A = 4\pi r^2)$$

PROBLEM

A perfectly spherical planet Sandeep has a diameter of 6,000 km.

(a) Find its area.   (b) Find its volume.

Solution

(a) $d = 6,000$ km.

$$r = \frac{d}{2} = \frac{6,000}{2} = 3,000 \text{ km.}$$

$$= 3 \times 10^6 \text{ m}$$

Area $A = 4\pi r^2$

$$= 4\pi \, (3 \times 10^6)^2$$

$$A = 36 \times 10^{12}\pi \text{ m}^2$$

(b) Volume $V = \dfrac{4}{3}\pi r^3$

$$= \dfrac{4}{3}\pi\,(3 \times 10^6)^3$$

$$V = 36 \times 10^{18}\pi \text{ m}^3$$

Drill 5: Solids

1. Find the total area of the rectangular prism shown.

    (A) 138 cm²

    (B) 336 cm²

    (C) 381 cm²

    (D) 426 cm²

    (E) 540 cm²

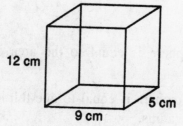

12 cm

9 cm

5 cm

2. Find the volume of the rectangular storage tank shown.

    (A) 24 m³

    (B) 36 m³

    (C) 38 m³

    (D) 42 m³

    (E) 45 m³

    1.5 m

    4 m

    6 m

3. The lateral area of a cube is 100 cm². Find the length of an edge of the cube.

    (A) 4 cm   (B) 5 cm

    (C) 10 cm   (D) 12 cm

    (E) 15 cm

4. Find the volume of a right circular cylinder of radius 4 inches and height 12 inches.

(A) 192π in^3 (B) 144π in^3

(C) 576π in^3 (D) 48π in^3

(E) 196 in^3

REFERENCE TABLE FOR GEOMETRY FORMULAS

Triangles

$$\text{Perimeter} = AB + BC + AC$$

$$\text{Area} = \frac{1}{2}bh$$

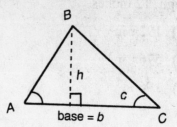

Right Triangles

Pythagorean
$$\text{Theorem} = a^2 + b^2 = c^2$$

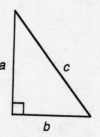

Quadrilaterals

$$\text{Perimeter} = AB + BC + CD + AD$$

$$\text{Area} = bh$$

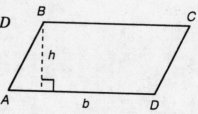

Rectangles

$$\text{Perimeter} = 2l + 2w$$

$$\text{Area} = lw$$

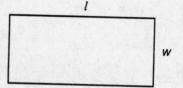

Squares

$$\text{Perimeter} = 4s$$

$$\text{Area} = s^2$$

Circles

Circumference = $2\pi r$

Area = πr^2

Diameter = $2r$

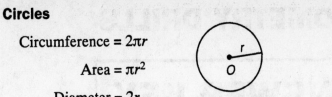

Solids

Rectangular Solids

Volume = lwh

Cylinders

Volume = $\pi r^2 h$

Spheres

Volume = $\dfrac{4}{3}\pi r^3$

GEOMETRY DRILLS

ANSWER KEY

Drill 1 – Points, Lines, and Angles

1. (B)	5. (D)	9. (D)	13. (B)
2. (A)	6. (C)	10. (E)	14. (E)
3. (C)	7. (B)	11. (C)	15. (A)
4. (D)	8. (A)	12. (D)	

Drill 2 – Triangles

1. (D)	6. (A)	11. (C)	16. (B)
2. (B)	7. (B)	12. (B)	17. (A)
3. (C)	8. (E)	13. (D)	18. (D)
4. (E)	9. (A)	14. (A)	19. (C)
5. (C)	10. (C)	15. (B)	20. (D)

Drill 3 – Quadrilaterals

1. (A)	6. (A)	11. (C)	16. (A)
2. (B)	7. (D)	12. (D)	17. (E)
3. (D)	8. (C)	13. (B)	18. (B)
4. (E)	9. (B)	14. (C)	19. (C)
5. (C)	10. (C)	15. (B)	20. (D)

Drill 4 – Circles

1. (B)	6. (D)	11. (B)	16. (C)
2. (A)	7. (C)	12. (D)	17. (B)
3. (D)	8. (B)	13. (C)	18. (D)
4. (E)	9. (E)	14. (B)	19. (A)
5. (C)	10. (D)	15. (A)	20. (C)

Drill 5 – Solids

1. (D)	2. (B)	3. (C)	4. (A)

ELM

Entry Level Mathematics

Chapter 4
Intermediate Algebra
Review

INTERMEDIATE ALGEBRA DIAGNOSTIC TEST

14 Questions

(Answer sheets appear at the back of the book.)

> **DIRECTIONS:** Each question has five multiple-choice answers. Select the single best answer.

1. If $x \neq 0$, then $(125^{2x})(5^x) =$

   (A) 5^{3x}. (B) 5^{4x}.

   (C) 5^{5x}. (D) 5^{7x}.

   (E) 5^{9x}.

2. If $\dfrac{5}{x-2} + \dfrac{2}{2x+1} = \dfrac{1}{x}$, then $x =$

   (A) $\dfrac{-1 \pm 2}{5}$. (B) $\dfrac{-2 \pm 2}{5}$.

   (C) $-1 \pm 2i$. (D) $-2 \pm 3i$.

   (E) $\dfrac{-1 \pm 2i}{5}$.

3. If a line contains the points $(2, 9)$ and $(-3, 1)$, then its y-intercept is

   (A) 1. (B) 2.

   (C) $\dfrac{19}{5}$. (D) $\dfrac{29}{5}$.

   (E) 8.

4. If $i^2 = -1$ and $y = 1 + 3i$, then $\dfrac{1}{y} =$

    (A) $\dfrac{1}{10} - \dfrac{3}{10}i.$ (B) $\dfrac{1}{4} - \dfrac{3}{4}i.$

    (C) $-\dfrac{1}{2} + \dfrac{3}{2}i.$ (D) $1 - 3i.$

    (E) $1 + 9i.$

5. What are the coordinates of the midpoint between the points $(-2, 3)$ and $(4, -5)$?

    (A) $(2, -1)$ (B) $(1, -1)$

    (C) $(0, -1)$ (D) $(1, 1)$

    (E) $(1, 2)$

6. If $f(x) = 3x - 1$ and $g(f(x)) = x$, then $g(x) =$

    (A) $x.$ (B) $\dfrac{x+1}{3}.$

    (C) $\dfrac{x-1}{3}.$ (D) $3x + 1.$

    (E) $3x + 2.$

7. Which of the following is the graph of the equation $y = 2x + 1$?

(A)
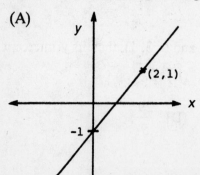

(B)
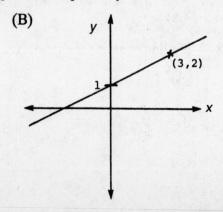

(C)

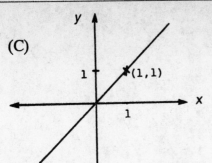

(D)

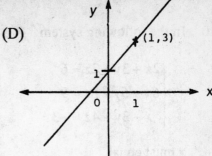

(E)

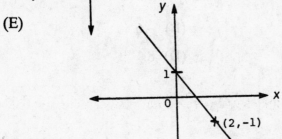

8. If $|2x - 5| = 3$, then

    (A) $x = -2\dfrac{1}{2}$ or 3.

    (B) $x = 2\dfrac{1}{2}$ or 4.

    (C) $x = 1$ or 3.

    (D) $x = 1$ or 4.

    (E) $x = 0$ or -3.

9. For the following sequence of numbers,

    $$\dfrac{1}{2}, \ \dfrac{1}{12}, \ \dfrac{1}{30}, \ \dots,$$

    the next number will be

    (A) $\dfrac{1}{36}$.

    (B) $\dfrac{1}{27}$.

    (C) $\dfrac{1}{48}$.

    (D) $\dfrac{1}{56}$.

    (E) $\dfrac{1}{72}$.

10. In the following system

$$\begin{cases} 2x + 3y + 2z = 6 \\ 6x + 5y + 8z = 9 \\ x - 3y + 4z = -3 \end{cases}$$

x must equal

(A) 2.   (B) -6.

(C) -7.   (D) 8.

(E) -10.

11. The first three terms of a progression are 3, 6, 12, ... What is the value of the tenth term?

(A) 1,200   (B) 2,468

(C) 188   (D) 1,536

(E) 3,272

12. If $\log_8 N = {}^2\!/_3$, what is the value of N?

(A) 2   (B) 4

(C) 8   (D) 10

(E) 12

13. In the equation $x^2 + 2x + 7 = 0$, the roots equal

(A) $-1 \pm i\sqrt{6}$.   (B) $-1 \pm \sqrt{6}$.

(C) $1 \pm i\sqrt{6}$.   (D) $-2 \pm \sqrt{6}$.

(E) $-2 \pm i\sqrt{6}$.

14. One solution to $x^3 - 16x = 0$ is

(A) -2.

(B) 2.

(C) 8.

(D) 4.

(E) $^1/_4$.

INTERMEDIATE ALGEBRA DIAGNOSTIC TEST

ANSWER KEY

1. (D)	5. (B)	9. (D)	13. (A)
2. (E)	6. (B)	10. (E)	14. (D)
3. (D)	7. (D)	11. (D)	
4. (A)	8. (D)	12. (B)	

DETERMINE YOUR STRENGTHS AND WEAKNESSES

INTERMEDIATE ALGEBRA

Question Type	Question #	See Pages . . .
Quadratic Equations	2, 13	212–217
Complex Numbers	4, 13, 2	218–220
Linear Equations and Rational Expressions	2, 10	221–225
Absolute Value Equations	8	225–228
Equations of Higher Degrees	14	228–231
Elementary Functions	6, 12	231–238
Fractional Exponents	1, 12	238–240
Sequences and Series	9, 11	240–242
Graphs	3, 5, 7	242–253

DETAILED EXPLANATIONS OF ANSWERS

INTERMEDIATE ALGEBRA
DIAGNOSTIC TEST

1. **(D)**

$$(125^{2x})(5^x) = (5^3)^{2x}\,(5^x)$$
$$= (5^{6x})\,(5^x)$$
$$= 5^{(6x + x)} = 5^{7x}$$

2. **(E)** Simplify the rational equation.

$$\frac{5}{x-2} + \frac{2}{2x+1} = \frac{1}{x}$$

$$\frac{5(2x+1) + 2(x-2)}{(x-2)(2x+1)} = \frac{1}{x}$$

$$\frac{10x + 5 + 2x - 4}{(x-2)(2x+1)} = \frac{1}{x}$$

$$\frac{12x+1}{(x-2)(2x+1)} = \frac{1}{x}$$

$$x(12x+1) = (x-2)(2x+1)$$

$$12x^2 + x = 2x^2 + x - 4x - 2$$

$$12x^2 + x = 2x^2 - 3x - 2$$

$$10x^2 + 4x + 2 = 0$$

$$5x^2 + 2x + 1 = 0$$

Use the quadratic formula to find the roots.

$$x = \frac{-2 \pm \sqrt{2^2 - 4(5)(1)}}{2(5)}$$

$$x = \frac{-2 \pm \sqrt{-16}}{2(5)}$$

$$x = \frac{-1 \pm \sqrt{-4}}{5}$$

$$x = \frac{-1 \pm 2i}{5}$$

3. **(D)** The equation of the line is obtained from the point-slope equation:

$$\frac{y-1}{x-(-3)} = \frac{9-1}{2-(-3)}$$

$$\frac{y-1}{x+3} = \frac{8}{5}$$

$$y - 1 = \frac{8}{5}(x+3)$$

$$y = \frac{8}{5}x + \frac{24}{5} + 1$$

$$y = \frac{8}{5}x + \frac{29}{5}$$

Therefore, the y-intercept is $\frac{29}{5}$.

4. **(A)** Multiply by complex conjugate to remove i from the denominator.

$$\frac{1}{y} = \frac{1}{1+3i} \times \frac{1-3i}{1-3i}$$

$$= \frac{1-3i}{1^2 - 3^2 i^2}$$

$$= \frac{1-3i}{10}$$

$$= \frac{1}{10} - \frac{3}{10}i$$

5.   **(B)**

$$x = \frac{x_1 + x_2}{2}$$

$$= \frac{-2 + 4}{2}$$

$$= 1$$

$$y = \frac{y_1 + y_2}{2}$$

$$= \frac{3 + (-5)}{2}$$

$$= -1$$

The coordinates of the midpoint are $(x, y) = (1, -1)$.

6.   **(B)**   Since $g(f(x)) = x$, $g(x)$ is the inverse function of $f(x)$. Let

$$y = f(x) = 3x - 1.$$

Interchange x and y to obtain the inverse of $f(x)$.

$$x = 3y - 1$$

$$3y = x + 1$$

$$y = \frac{x + 1}{3}$$

7.   **(D)**

$$y = 2x + 1 \rightarrow y\text{-intercept} = (0, 1), \quad \text{so we may eliminate (A) and (C).}$$

We may also eliminate (E) since the slope of y is 2 which is positive. Graph (B) indicates that the point $(3, 2)$ is on the graph but if we substitute these values into the given equation we find the statement false. The only possibility therefore is Graph (D).

8.　**(D)**

$$|2x - 5| = 3$$

$$2x - 5 = 3 \qquad\qquad 2x - 5 = -3$$

$$2x = 8 \qquad\qquad 2x = 2$$

$$x = 4 \qquad\qquad x = 1$$

Therefore, $x = 1$ or 4 is the solution to the given equation.

9.　**(D)**　To determine the next number, we look for a pattern among the previous terms. Only the denominators differ. We note by inspection that each denominator is equal to the product of two successive integers. For example, the first term:

$$\frac{1}{2} = \frac{1}{1 \times 2}$$

The second term:

$$\frac{1}{12} = \frac{1}{3 \times 4}$$

The third term:

$$\frac{1}{30} = \frac{1}{5 \times 6}$$

Thus, the next term in the sequence can be expected to be

$$\frac{1}{7 \times 8} \quad \text{or} \quad \frac{1}{56}.$$

10.　**(E)**　This is an example of a system of three equations in three unknowns. To solve for one unknown (x) we must eliminate the other two. We will first eliminate z. The given equations are:

$$2x + 3y + 2z = 6 \qquad\qquad (1)$$

$$6x + 5y + 8z = 9 \qquad\qquad (2)$$

$$x - 3y + 4z = -3 \qquad\qquad (3)$$

To eliminate z, we first multiply equation (1) by 4, and subtract from it equation (2):

$$4(2x + 3y + 2z = 6) = \quad 8x + 12y + 8z = 24$$
$$- (6x + 5y + 8z = 9)$$
$$\overline{\qquad\qquad 2x + 7y = 15} \qquad\qquad (4)$$

Next we multiply equation (1) by 2 and subtract from it equation (3):

$$2(2x + 3y + 2z = 6) = \quad 4x + 6y + 4z = 12$$
$$- (x - 3y + 4z = - 3)$$
$$\overline{\qquad\qquad 3x + 9y = 15} \qquad\qquad (5)$$

Thus, we are left with a system of two equations in two unknowns, namely equation (4) and equation (5). To find x, we must eliminate y. The best way to do this is to multiply equation (4) by 9 and equation (5) by 7, and then subtract the two equations:

$$9(2x + 7y = 15) = \quad 18x + 63y = 135$$
$$-(7 (3x + 9y = 15) = - (21x + 63y = 105)$$
$$\overline{\qquad\qquad - 3x = 30}$$

Solving for x: $x = - 10$.

11. **(D)** The progression given is a geometric progression. The expression for the nth term of a geometric progression is:

$$s_n = a_1 r^{n-1}$$

where a_1 is the first term and r is the common ratio between terms.

In the given sequence, the first term is 3. The common ratio is found to be:

$$\frac{6}{3} = \frac{12}{6} = 2.$$

Therefore, letting $n = 10$ (for the tenth term), we have:

$$s_{10} = 3(2)^{10 - 1} = 3(2)^9.$$

Since $\quad 2^9 = 512$

$$s_{10} = 3(512) = 1,536.$$

12. **(B)** To solve, the inverse of the logarithmic function must be used. This is stated as:

$$y = \log_a N$$
$$N = a^y.$$

Applying this to the given equation yields $N = 8^{2/3}$. So

$$N = \sqrt[3]{8^2} = \sqrt[3]{64} = 4.$$

13. **(A)** To solve this quadratic equation, use the quadratic formula:

$$x = \frac{-b \pm \sqrt{b^2 - 4ac}}{2a}$$

The equation is

$$x^2 + 2x + 7 = 0.$$

So $a = 1$, $b = 2$, and $c = 7$. Substituting into the formula:

$$x = \frac{-2 \pm \sqrt{2^2 - 4(1)(7)}}{2(1)}$$

$$= \frac{-2 \pm \sqrt{4 - 28}}{2}$$

$$= -1 \pm \sqrt{-6}$$

Since $i = \sqrt{-1}$, $x = -1 \pm i\sqrt{6}$.

14. **(D)**

$$x^3 - 16x = 0$$
$$x(x^2 - 16) = 0$$
$$x(x - 4)(x + 4) = 0$$

Factor the given equation. Find the solution set.

$$x = 0, \quad x - 4 = 0 \qquad \text{or} \qquad x + 4 = 0$$
$$x = 4 \qquad\qquad x = -4$$
$$x = \{-4, 0, 4\}$$

INTERMEDIATE ALGEBRA REVIEW

This section is a continuation of the algebra review. Basic operations are explained in the Elementary Algebra Review section.

1. QUADRATIC EQUATIONS

An equation in the form of

$$ax^2 + bx + c = 0,$$

where a, b, and c are real numbers and $a \neq 0$ is a **quadratic equation.** To solve a quadratic equation one can use several methods if factoring the equation is difficult and involves solutions that may not be whole numbers.

(A) **Completing the square** is one method that can be used. This method uses products based on

$$(x + a)^2 = x^2 + 2ax + a^2 \quad \text{and} \quad (x - a)^2 = x^2 - 2ax + a^2$$

1. Arrange the equation with the constant term on the right.

2. If the coefficient of x^2 is not 1, divide each term by the coefficient of x^2.

3. Complete the square:

   a. Find the x coefficient.

   b. Take one-half ($^1/_2$) of the coefficient and square it.

   c. Add the square to both sides of the equation.

4. Rewrite the left-hand terms as a perfect square.

5. Take the square root of both sides of the equation.

6. Solve the resulting equation.

7. Check in the original equation.

PROBLEM

Solve by completing the square, $x^2 - 6x + 8 = 0$.

Solution

$$x^2 - 6x = -8$$

Rearranging the constant term to the right-hand side of the equation.

$$(-6) \times (^1/_2) = -3$$

Taking one-half of the x coefficient.

$$(-3)^2 = 9$$

Squaring the coefficient.

$$x^2 - 6x + 9 = -8 + 9$$

Adding the square to both sides.

$$(x - 3)^2 = 1$$

$$x - 3 = \pm 1$$

Taking the square root of both sides.

$$x - 3 = 1 \qquad \text{and} \qquad x - 3 = -1$$

$$x = 4 \qquad\qquad\qquad x = 2$$

Check in the original equation.

$$4^2 - 6(4) + 8 = 0 \qquad \text{and} \qquad 2^2 - 6(2) + 8 = 0$$

$$16 - 24 + 8 = 0 \qquad\qquad\qquad 4 - 12 + 8 = 0$$

$$0 = 0 \qquad\qquad\qquad\qquad 0 = 0$$

(B) The **quadratic formula** is another way to solve quadratic equations that is faster than completing the square. Remember the general form of a quadratic equation is

$$ax^2 + bx + c = 0.$$

The quadratic formula is

$$\frac{-b \pm \sqrt{b^2 - 4ac}}{2a}$$

The expression $b^2 - 4ac$ under the square root symbol is called the **discriminant of the quadratic equation.** If the discriminant is 0, then both solutions or roots are the same.

If the discriminant is negative, then the roots are not real numbers; they are complex numbers. If the discriminant is positive, then there are two different real solutions.

PROBLEM

Solve by using the quadratic formula, $x^2 + 6x + 8 = 0$.

Solution

In this equation, $a = 1$, $b = 6$, and $c = 8$. Substitute into the quadratic formula.

$$x = \frac{-6 \pm \sqrt{6^2 - 4(1)(8)}}{2(1)}$$

$$= \frac{-6 \pm \sqrt{36 - 32}}{2}$$

$$= \frac{-6 \pm \sqrt{4}}{2}$$

$$= \frac{-6 \pm 2}{2}$$

$$x = \frac{-6 + 2}{2} \quad \text{or} \quad x = \frac{-6 - 2}{2}$$

$$= -2 \qquad\qquad\qquad = -4$$

Substitute in the original equation.

$$(-2)^2 + 6(-2) + 8 = 0 \qquad\qquad (-4)^2 + 6(-4) + 8 = 0$$

$$4 - 12 + 8 = 0 \qquad\qquad\qquad 16 - 24 + 8 = 0$$

$$0 = 0 \qquad\qquad\qquad\qquad 0 = 0$$

To solve quadratic inequalities the following steps can be used to find the solutions:

a. Put the inequality in a form where 0 is on one side.

b. Factor the quadratic equation.

c. Identify the critical points, the solutions to the factored equation.

d. Determine if the product of the two equations must be less than 0, greater than 0, or equal to or less/greater than 0.

(Remember that the product of two negative numbers or two positive numbers gives values greater than 0, and the product of a negative and positive number gives values less than 0.)

PROBLEM

Solve $x^2 - 5x + 4 \pounds 0$.

Solution

$$(x - 1)(x - 4) \le 0$$

Factor the quadratic equation. Since the product is negative, one of the factors can be positive and then the other must be negative.

Therefore, either

	$x - 1 \ge 0$	and	$x - 4 \le 0$	Case 1
or	$x - 1 \le 0$	and	$x - 4 \ge 0$	Case 2

Solving for x in each inequality:

	$x \ge 1$	and	$x \le 4$	Case 1
or	$x \le 1$	and	$x \ge 4$	Case 2

The solution to the equation is the set of all x, such that $x \ge 1$ and $x \le 4$, or $x \le 1$ and $x \ge 4$. Therefore, $1 \le x \le 4$ is the solution set.

Drill 1: Quadratic Equations

Completing the Squares

DIRECTIONS: Solve the following equations.

1. $5x^2 + 8x + 2 = 0$

(A) $(-4 \pm \sqrt{6})$ (B) $\frac{1}{5}(4 \pm \sqrt{6})$

(C) $\frac{1}{5}(-4 \pm \sqrt{6})$ (D) $5(4 \pm \sqrt{6})$

(E) $\frac{2}{5}(-4 \pm \sqrt{6})$

2. $2a^2 - a = 1$

(A) $1, 2$ (B) $-1, -\frac{1}{4}$

(C) $-\frac{1}{4}, 1$ (D) $1, -\frac{1}{2}$

(E) $-1, -\frac{1}{2}$

3. $2t^2 + 4t + 1 = 0$

   (A) $\pm \frac{1}{2}$

   (B) ± 1

   (C) $2 \pm \sqrt{2}$

   (D) $\dfrac{2 \pm \sqrt{2}}{2}$

   (E) $\dfrac{-2 \pm \sqrt{2}}{2}$

4. $6s^2 + 11s + 3 = 0$

   (A) $-\frac{3}{2}, -\frac{1}{3}$

   (B) $-\frac{3}{2}, -\frac{1}{4}$

   (C) $\frac{3}{2}, \frac{1}{3}$

   (D) $-\frac{3}{2}, \frac{1}{3}$

   (E) $\frac{3}{2}, -\frac{1}{2}$

5. $8r^2 + 6r = 9$

   (A) $-\frac{3}{4}, \frac{2}{3}$

   (B) $-\frac{3}{2}, \frac{3}{4}$

   (C) $\frac{2}{3}, \frac{3}{4}$

   (D) $\frac{3}{4}, -\frac{2}{3}$

   (E) $\frac{4}{3}, -\frac{2}{3}$

Quadratic Formula

DIRECTIONS: Use the quadratic formula to solve the following equations.

6. $8x = -4x^2 - 3$

   (A) $-\frac{7}{8}, -\frac{1}{4}$

   (B) $-\frac{1}{2}, -\frac{3}{2}$

   (C) $\frac{1}{2}, \frac{3}{2}$

   (D) $\frac{7}{8}, \frac{1}{4}$

   (E) $-2, -\frac{2}{3}$

7. $3w^2 - 4w = \frac{5}{3}$

   (A) $-\frac{5}{3}, -\frac{1}{3}$

   (B) $-\frac{5}{3}, \frac{1}{3}$

   (C) $\frac{5}{3}, -\frac{1}{3}$

   (D) $3, -\frac{3}{5}$

   (E) $-1, \frac{1}{3}$

8. $3x^2 + 7x + 2 = 0$

   (A) $-2, -\frac{1}{3}$

   (B) $2, \frac{1}{3}$

    (C) $3, {}^{1}/_{2}$ (D) $-3, -{}^{1}/_{2}$

    (E) $-2, {}^{1}/_{2}$

9. $2m^2 - 5m = 3$

    (A) $1, {}^{3}/_{2}$ (B) $-1, -{}^{3}/_{2}$

    (C) $3, -{}^{1}/_{2}$ (D) $-3, {}^{1}/_{2}$

    (E) $-3, -{}^{1}/_{2}$

10. $2n^2 - 7n + 6 = 0$

    (A) $-2, -{}^{3}/_{2}$ (B) $3, {}^{1}/_{2}$

    (C) $-3, -{}^{1}/_{2}$ (D) $2, {}^{3}/_{2}$

    (E) $-2, -{}^{2}/_{3}$

Quadratic Inequalities

DIRECTIONS: Solve the following inequalities.

11. $x^2 - 7x + 12 < 0$

    (A) $3 < x < 4$ (B) $2 < x < 6$

    (C) $x = 3$ or $x = 4$ (D) $x < 3$ or $x > 4$

    (E) $3 \le x \le 4$

12. $x^2 + 5x + 6 < 0$

    (A) $-3 < x$ or $x > -2$ (B) $2 < x < 3$

    (C) $-6 < x < -1$ (D) $-3 \le x \le -2$

    (E) $-3 < x < -2$

13. $x^2 - 5x + 6 \ge 0$

    (A) $2 \le x \le 3$ (B) $x < 2$ or $x > 3$

    (C) $x \le 2$ or $x \ge 3$ (D) $1 < x < 6$

    (E) $x < 1$ or $x > 6$

2. COMPLEX NUMBERS

A **complex number** is a number that can be written in the form $a + bi$, where a and b are real numbers and $i = \sqrt{-1}$. The number a is the **real part**, and the number b is the **imaginary part** of the complex number.

To add, subtract, or multiply complex numbers, compute in the usual way, replace i^2 with -1 and simplify.

$$(a + bi) + (c + di) = (a + c) + (b + d)i$$

$$(a + bi) - (c + di) = (a - c) + (b - d)i$$

$$(a + bi)(c + di) = ac + adi + bci + bdi^2 = ac - bd + (ad + bc)i$$

PROBLEM

Simplify the following $(3 + i)(2 + i)$.

Solution

$$(3 + i)(2 + i) = 3(2 + i) + i(2 + i)$$

$$= 6 + 3i + 2i + i^2$$

$$= 6 + (3 + 2)i + (-1)$$

$$= 5 + 5i$$

Complex numbers, $a + bi$, may be obtained when using the quadratic formula to solve quadratic equations.

PROBLEM

Solve the equation $x^2 - x + 1 = 0$.

Solution

In this equation, $a = 1$, $b = -1$, and $c = 1$. Substitute into the quadratic formula.

$$x = \frac{-(-1) \pm \sqrt{(-1)^2 - 4(1)(1)}}{2(1)}$$

$$= \frac{1 \pm \sqrt{1 - 4}}{2}$$

$$= \frac{1 \pm \sqrt{-3}}{2}$$

$$= \frac{1 \pm \sqrt{3}i}{2}$$

$$x = \frac{1 + \sqrt{3}i}{2} \quad \text{or} \quad x = \frac{1 - \sqrt{3}i}{2}$$

Drill 2: Complex Numbers

DIRECTIONS: Simplify the following.

1. $3i^3 =$

    (A) $-3i$　　　　　　　　　(B) $3i$

    (C) $9i$　　　　　　　　　(D) $-i$

    (E) 3

2. $2i^7 =$

    (A) $-128i$　　　　　　　　(B) $2i$

    (C) $14i$　　　　　　　　　(D) $-14i$

    (E) $-2i$

3. $-4i^4 =$

    (A) 4　　　　　　　　　(B) -4

    (C) $4i$　　　　　　　　　(D) $-4i$

    (E) -14

4. $-5i^6 =$

    (A) -5　　　　　　　　　(B) $-5i$

    (C) $-i$　　　　　　　　　(D) $30i$

    (E) 5

5. $(3 + 2i)(2 + 3i) =$

    (A) $12 + 13i$　　　　　　　(B) $-12 - 13i$

(C) $13i$

(D) $-13i$

(E) $-i$

6. $(2-i)(2+i) =$

(A) -5

(B) $5i$

(C) $-5i$

(D) 5

(E) 3

7. $(5-4i)^2 =$

(A) $9-40i$

(B) $-9-40i$

(C) $41-40i$

(D) $9+40i$

(E) $-9+40i$

DIRECTIONS: Solve the following equations.

8. $x^2 + 16 = 0$

(A) ± 4

(B) $\pm 4i$

(C) $4 \pm i$

(D) $-4 \pm i$

(E) $i \pm 4$

9. $4y^2 + 1 = 0$

(A) $\pm \frac{1}{2}$

(B) $i \pm \frac{1}{2}$

(C) $-i \pm \frac{1}{2}$

(D) $\frac{1}{2} \pm i$

(E) $\pm \frac{1}{2}i$

10. $x^2 - 4x + 13 = 0$

(A) $3 \pm 2i$

(B) $\pm 6i$

(C) $\pm 5i$

(D) $2 \pm 3i$

(E) $-2 \pm 3i$

3. LINEAR EQUATIONS AND RATIONAL EXPRESSIONS

A system of three linear equations in three unknowns is solved by eliminating one unknown from any two of the three equations and solving them. After finding two unknowns substitute them in any of the equations to find the third unknown.

PROBLEM

Solve the system.

$$2x + 3y - 4z = -8 \tag{1}$$

$$x + y - 2z = -5 \tag{2}$$

$$7x - 2y + 5z = 4 \tag{3}$$

Solution

We cannot eliminate any variable from two pairs of equations by a single multiplication. However, both x and z may be eliminated from equations (1) and (2) by multiplying equation (2) by -2. Then

$$2x + 3y - 4z = -8 \tag{1}$$

$$\underline{-2x - 2y + 4z = 10} \tag{4}$$

$$y = 2$$

Although we may now eliminate either x or z from another pair of equations, we can more conveniently substitute $y = 2$ in equations (2) and (3) to get two equations in two variables. Thus, making the substitution $y = 2$ in equations (2) and (3), we have

$$x - 2z = -7 \tag{5}$$

$$7x + 5z = 8 \tag{6}$$

Multiply equation (5) by 5 and multiply equation (6) by 2. Then add the two new equations. Then $x = -1$. Substitute x in either equation (5) or (6) to find z.

$$5x - 10z = -35 \tag{7}$$

$$\underline{14x + 10z = 16} \tag{8}$$

$$19x = -19 \tag{9}$$

$$x = -1$$

Substitute x into equation (5).

$$-1 - 2z = -7$$
$$-2z = -6$$
$$z = 3$$

The solution of the system is $x = -1$, $y = 2$, and $z = 3$. Check by substitution.

A system of equations, as shown below, that has all constant terms, $b_1, b_2, ..., b_n$ equal to 0 is said to be a homogeneous system:

$$\begin{cases} a_{11}x_1 + a_{12}x_2 + ... + a_{1n}x_m = b_1 \\ a_{21}x_1 + a_{22}x_2 + ... + a_{2n}x_m = b_2 \\ \quad M \qquad\quad M \qquad\qquad\quad M \qquad M \\ a_{n1}x_1 + a_{n2}x_2 + ... + a_{nn}x_m = b_n \end{cases}$$

A homogeneous system always has at least one solution which is called the trivial solution that is

$$x_1 = 0, x_2 = 0, ..., x_m = 0.$$

For any given homogeneous system of equations, in which the number of variables is greater than or equal to the number of equations, there are non-trivial solutions.

Equations with Rational Expressions

Rational equations contain fractions that have numerators and denominators that are polynomials. Solving rational equations uses the same rules as linear and quadratic equations. Start by clearing the equation of fractions, usually using the lowest common denominator of the fractions that appear in the equation.

PROBLEM

Solve the following equation.

$$\frac{x+1}{5} - 2 = -\frac{4}{x} \quad (x \neq 0)$$

Solution

$$\frac{x+1}{5} - 2 = -\frac{4}{x} \quad (x \neq 0)$$

Multiply both sides by $5x$.

$$x(x + 1) - 5x(2) = -4(5)$$

$$x^2 + x - 10x = -20$$

Combine terms and add 20 to both sides.

$$x^2 - 9x + 20 = 0$$

Factor the quadratic equation.

$$(x - 4)(x - 5) = 0$$

Solve for x.

$$x - 4 = 0 \quad \text{or} \quad x - 5 = 0$$

$$x = 4 \qquad\qquad x = 5$$

Multiplying both sides of an equation by a quantity that contains a variable sometimes leads to a false solution or an **extraneous solution**. This happens if the solution would make one of the denominators equal to 0. Any value that would cause the denominator of a rational expression to equal 0 is excluded from the solution set.

Drill 3: Linear Equations and Rational Expressions

DIRECTIONS: Solve the following systems of equations.

1. $x + y + z = 4$
    $2x + y - z = 1$
    $2x - 3y + z = 1$
    Find the value of z.

    (A) -1 (B) 1

    (C) 0   (D) 2

    (E) -2

2. $x + y + 2z = 7$
    $x + 2y + z = 8$
    $2x + y + z = 9$
    Find the value of x.

    (A) 1   (B) 2

    (C) -3 (D) 3

    (E) -1

3. $2x - y + 3z = 9$
   $x + y + 2z = 4$
   $y + z = 1$
   Find the value of y.

   (A) -1 (B) 0

   (C) 1 (D) 2

   (E) No solution

4. $2x + y - z = 1$
   $x + 2y + 2z = 2$
   $4x + 5y + 3z = 3$
   Find the value of x.

   (A) -1 (B) 1

   (C) 2 (D) 3

   (E) No solution

Equations Containing Rational Expressions

DIRECTIONS: Solve the following equations.

5. $\dfrac{a+2}{a+1} = \dfrac{a-4}{a-3}$ Solve for a.

   (A) -2 (B) 4

   (C) 1 (D) -1

   (E) 0

6. $\dfrac{x+4}{x+7} - \dfrac{x}{x+3} = \dfrac{3}{8}$ Solve for x.

   (A) $-1, 11$ (B) $-11, 1$

   (C) $3, 8$ (D) $1, 5$

   (E) $2, 1$

7. $\dfrac{3}{x+1} - \dfrac{x-2}{2} = \dfrac{x-2}{x+1}$ Solve for x.

(A) 2, 0   (B) − 3, 4

(C) 3, 2   (D) − 4, 3

(E) No solution

8. $\dfrac{5}{x+4} + \dfrac{1}{x+4} = x - 1$ Solve for x.

(A) − 2, 5   (B) 1, 0

(C) − 5, 2   (D) − 5, − 2

(E) No solution

4. ABSOLUTE VALUE EQUATIONS

The absolute value of a, $|a|$, is defined as:

$|a| = a$ when $a > 0$,

$|a| = -a$ when $a < 0$,

$|a| = 0$ when $a = 0$.

When the definition of absolute value is applied to an equation, the quantity within the absolute value symbol is considered to have two values. This value can be either positive or negative before the absolute value is taken. As a result, each absolute value equation actually contains two separate equations.

When evaluating equations containing absolute values, proceed as follows.

EXAMPLE

$|5 - 3x| = 7$ is valid if either

$$5 - 3x = 7 \qquad \text{or} \qquad 5 - 3x = -7$$
$$-3x = 2 \qquad\qquad\qquad -3x = -12$$
$$x = -2/3 \qquad\qquad\qquad x = 4$$

The solution set is therefore $x = (-2/3, 4)$.

Remember, the absolute value of a number cannot be negative. So, for the equation $|5x + 4| = -3$, there would be no solution.

EXAMPLE

Solve for x in $|2x - 6| = |4 - 5x|$

There are four possibilities here. $2x - 6$ and $4 - 5x$ can be either positive or negative. Therefore,

$$2x - 6 = 4 - 5x \tag{1}$$

$$-(2x - 6) = 4 - 5x \tag{2}$$

$$2x - 6 = -(4 - 5x) \tag{3}$$

$$-(2x - 6) = -(4 - 5x) \tag{4}$$

Equations (2) and (3) result in the same solution, as do equations (1) and (4). Therefore, it is necessary to solve only for equations (1) and (2). This gives:

$$2x - 6 = 4 - 5x \quad \text{or} \quad -(2x - 6) = 4 - 5x$$
$$7x = 10 \qquad\qquad -2x + 6 = 4 - 5x$$
$$x = {}^{10}/_7 \qquad\qquad\qquad x = -{}^2/_3$$

The solution set is therefore $({}^{10}/_7, -{}^2/_3)$.

Absolute value inequalities have the following relationship:

a. $|x| < k$ is equal to $-k < x < k$.

b. $|x| > k$ is equal to $x < -k$ or $x > k$.

If the value of k is included in the interval depends on if the symbol greater than, less than, or equal to is used.

PROBLEM

Solve $|2 - 3x| \geq 8$.

Solution

Write as two separate inequalities and solve each one for x.

$$2 - 3x \leq -8 \quad \text{or} \quad 2 - 3x \geq 8$$

Add (-2) to both sides.

$$-3x \leq -10 \qquad\qquad -3x \geq 6$$

Multiply both sides by (-1). (Note inequalities reverse when multiplied or divided by a negative number.)

$$3x \geq 10 \qquad\qquad 3x \leq -6$$

Divide both sides by 3.

$$x \geq {}^{10}/_3 \qquad \text{or} \qquad x \leq -2$$

Drill 4: Absolute Value Equations

DIRECTIONS: Solve the equations.

1. $|4x - 2| = 6$

   (A) -2 and -1 (B) -1 and 2

   (C) 2 (D) $^1/_2$ and -2

   (E) No solution

2. $|3 - {}^y/_2| = -7$

   (A) -8 and 20 (B) 8 and -20

   (C) 2 and -5 (D) 4 and -2

   (E) No solution

3. $2|x + 7| = 12$

   (A) -13 and -1 (B) -6 and 6

   (C) -1 and 13 (D) 6 and -13

   (E) No solution

4. $|5x| - 7 = 3$

   (A) 2 and 4 (B) $^4/_5$ and 3

   (C) -2 and 2 (D) 2

   (E) No solution

5. $\left|\dfrac{3m}{4}\right| = 9$

   (A) 24 and -16 (B) $^4/_{27}$ and $-^4/_3$

   (C) $^4/_3$ and 12 (D) -12 and 12

   (E) No solution

DIRECTIONS: Solve each inequality.

6. $|3x + 2| > 14$

  (A) $x > 4$ or $x < -\,{}^{16}/_3$ (B) $-\,{}^{16}/_3 < x < 4$

  (C) $x < 4$ (D) $x > {}^{14}/_3$ or $x < -\,{}^{14}/_3$

  (E) $x > 4$ or $x < -4$

7. $3|2x + 5| \geq 9$

  (A) $-4 < x < -1$ (B) $1 < x < 4$

  (C) $x \geq -1$ or $x \leq -4$ (D) $x \geq -3$ or $x \leq -12$

  (E) $x > -1$ or $x < -4$

8. $|3 - 2x| < 7$

  (A) $x < -2$ or $x > 5$ (B) $-2 < x < 5$

  (C) $-\,{}^{7}/_2 < x < {}^{7}/_2$ (D) $-10 < x < 4$

  (E) $-4 < x < 10$

9. $|8x - 2| > 0$

  (A) $x > 4$ or $x < 4$ (B) $x > 2$ or $x < -2$

  (C) $x > {}^{1}/_4$ or $x < -\,{}^{1}/_4$ (D) $x > {}^{1}/_4$ or $x < {}^{1}/_4$

  (E) $-\,{}^{1}/_4 < x < {}^{1}/_4$

5. EQUATIONS OF HIGHER DEGREES

Polynomial equations of $n \geq 1$ have n roots (although some roots may be the same). Let polynomial equation

$$a_n x^n + a_{n-1} x^{n-1} + \ldots + a_1 x + a_0 = 0$$

have integral coefficients. If the equation has a rational root $p/_q$ (where p and q are integers with no common factor other than ± 1), then p is a factor of a_0 and q is a factor of a_n. If no such root exists the roots of the equation are irrational or imaginary.

PROBLEM

Find the roots of $x^3 - 3x^2 - 10x = 0$.

Solution

$$x^3 - 3x^2 - 10x = 0$$

Factor x.

$$x(x^2 - 3x - 10) = 0$$

Factor $(x^2 - 3x - 10)$.

$$x(x - 5)(x + 2) = 0$$

$$x = 0 \qquad x - 5 = 0 \qquad x + 2 = 0$$

$$x = 5 \qquad x = -2$$

The roots are 0, 5, and –2.

Binomial Theorem

The **binomial theorem** expands $(a + b)^n$ as follows:

$$(a + b)^n = a^n + \frac{n!}{1!(n-1)!}a^{n-1}b + \frac{n!}{2!(n-2)!}a^{n-2}b^2$$

$$+ \dots + \frac{n!}{r!(n-r)!}a^{n-r}b^r + \dots + b^n$$

$n!$ is **factorial notation** which is defined as

$$n! = n(n-1)(n-2)(n-3)\dots(3)(2)(1).$$

Note that by definition $0! = 1$.

EXAMPLE

$$3! = (3)(2)(1) = 6$$

PROBLEM

Use the binomial theorem to expand $(2x - y)^3$.

Solution

Let $a = 2x$, $b = -y$, and $n = 3$.

$$(a + b)^3 = a^3 + \frac{3!}{1!(3-1)!}a^2b + \frac{3!}{2!(3-2)!}ab^2 + b^3$$

$$= a^3 + \frac{3 \times 2!}{2!}a^2b + \frac{3 \times 2!}{2!}ab^2 + b^3$$

$$= a^3 + 3a^2b + 3ab^2 + b^3$$
$$= (2x)^3 + 3(2x)^2(-y) + 3(2x)(-y)^2 + (-y)^3$$
$$= 8x^3 - 3(4)x^2y + 6xy^2 - y^3$$
$$= 8x^3 - 12x^2y + 6xy^2 - y^3$$

Drill 5: Equations of Higher Degrees

DIRECTIONS: Find a root to the following equations.

1. $x^3 - 5x^2 - x + 5 = 0$

   (A) -5 (B) 0

   (C) $-\frac{1}{5}$ (D) $\frac{1}{5}$

   (E) -1

2. $x^3 - 2x^2 - 9x + 18 = 0$

   (A) 9 (B) 2

   (C) 0 (D) -6

   (E) 6

3. $x^4 - 6x^3 + 8x^2 = 0$

   (A) 0 (B) -2

   (C) -4 (D) 1

   (E) -1

DIRECTIONS: Use the binomial theorem to expand each binomial.

4. $(a + b)^4 =$

   (A) $a^4 + 3a^3b + 2a^2b^2 + 3ab^4 + b^5$

   (B) $a^4 + 2a^2b^2 + b^4$

   (C) $a^4 + 12a^3b + 8a^2b^2 + 12ab^4 + b^5$

   (D) $a^4 - 4a^3b + 6a^2b^2 - 4ab^3 + b^5$

   (E) $a^4 + 4a^3b + 6a^2b^2 + 4ab^3 + b^5$

5. $(x + 1)^5 =$

    (A) $x^5 + 10x^4 + 20x^3 + 1$

    (B) $x^5 + 6x^4 + 12x^3 + 13x^2 + 9x + 1$

    (C) $x^5 + 5x^4 + 10x^3 + 10x^2 + 5x + 1$

    (D) $x^5 + 10x^4 + 5x^3 + 5x^2 + 10x + 1$

    (E) $x^5 + 5x^4 + 10x^2 + 1$

6. $(x - y)^3 =$

    (A) $x^3 - 3x^2y + 3xy^2 - y^3$

    (B) $x^3 + 3x^2y + 3xy + y^3$

    (C) $x^3 - y^3$

    (D) $x^3 - 2xy - y^3$

    (E) $x^3 - 6x^2y + 6xy^2 - y^3$

6. ELEMENTARY FUNCTIONS

A **function** is any process that assigns a single value to y to each number of x. Because the value of x determines the value of y, y is called the **dependent variable** and x is called the **independent variable**. The set of all the values of x which the function is defined is called the **domain** of the function. The set of corresponding values of y is called the **range** of the function.

PROBLEM

Is $y^2 = x$ a function?

Solution

Graph the equation. Note that x can have two values of y. Therefore $y^2 = x$ is not a function.

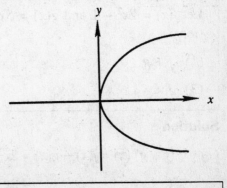

PROBLEM

Find the domain and range for $y = 5 - x^2$.

Solution

First determine if there are any values that would make the function undefined (i.e., dividing by 0). There are none. The domain is the set of real numbers. The range can be found by putting some values in for x.

x	2	1	0	-1	-2
y	1	4	5	4	1

The range is the set of real numbers less than or equal to 5.

PROBLEM

Evaluate $f(1)$ for $y = f(x) = 5x + 2$.

Solution

$$f(x) = 5x + 2$$
$$f(1) = 5(1) + 2$$
$$= 5 + 2$$
$$= 7$$

Functions can be added, subtracted, multiplied, or divided to form new functions.

a. $(f + g)(x) = f(x) + g(x)$

b. $(f - g)(x) = f(x) - g(x)$

c. $(f \cdot g)(x) = f(x)\, g(x)$

d. $(f / g)(x) = f(x) / g(x)$

PROBLEM

Let $f(x) = 2x^2 - 1$ and $g(x) = 5x + 3$. Determine the following functions:

(1) $f + g$ (2) $f - g$

(3) $f \times g$ (4) f / g

Solution

(1) $(f + g)(x) = f(x) + g(x) = 2x^2 - 1 + 5x + 3$
$$= 2x^2 + 5x + 2$$

(2) $(f - g)(x) = f(x) - g(x) = 2x^2 - 1 - (5x + 3)$

$$= 2x^2 - 1 - 5x - 3$$

$$= 2x^2 - 5x - 4$$

(3) $(f \times g)(x) = f(x)\,g(x) = (2x^2 - 1)(5x + 3)$

$$= 10x^3 + 6x^2 - 5x - 3$$

(4) $(f / g)(x) = f(x) / g(x) = (2x^2 - 1) / (5x + 3)$

Note the domain of (d) is for all real numbers except $- ^3/_5$

The **composite function** $f \circ g$ is defined $(f \circ g)(x) = f(g(x))$.

PROBLEM

Given $f(x) = 3x$ and $g(x) = 4x + 2$.

Find $(f \circ g)(x)$ and $(g \circ f)(x)$.

Solution

$$(f \circ g)(x) = f(g(x)) = 3(4x + 2)$$

$$= 12x + 6$$

$$(g \circ f)(x) = g(f(x)) = 4(3x) + 2$$

$$= 12x + 2$$

Note that $(f \circ g)(x) \neq (g \circ f)(x)$.

PROBLEM

Find $(f \circ g)(2)$ if

$f(x) = x^2 - 3$ and $g(x) = 3x + 1$

Solution

$$(f \circ g)(2) = f(g(2))$$

$$g(x) = 3x + 1$$

Substitute the value of x.

$$g(2) = 3(2) + 1$$

$$= 7$$

$$f(x) = x^2 - 3$$

Substitute the value of $g(2)$ in $f(x)$.

$$f(7) = (7)^2 - 3$$
$$= 49 - 3$$
$$= 46$$

The **inverse** of a function, f^{-1}, is obtained from f by interchanging the x and y and then solving for y.

Two functions f and g are inverses of one another if $g \circ f = x$ and $f \circ g = x$. To find g when f is given, interchange x and g in the equation $y = f(x)$ and solve for $y = g(x)$.

PROBLEM

Find the inverse of the functions

(1) $f(x) = 3x + 2$ (2) $f(x) = x^2 - 3$

Solution

(1) $f(x) = y = 3x + 2$

To find $f^{-1}(x)$, interchange x and y.

$$x = 3y + 2$$
$$3y = x - 2$$

Solve for y.

$$y = \frac{x-2}{3}$$

(2) $f(x) = y = x^2 - 3$.

To find $f^{-1}(x)$, interchange x and y.

$$x = y^2 - 3$$
$$y^2 = x + 3$$

Solve for y.

$$y = \sqrt{x+3}$$

Logarithms and Exponential Functions and Equations

An equation

$$y = b^x$$

(with $b > 0$ and $b \neq 1$) is called an **exponential function**. The exponential function with base b can be written as

$$y = f(x) = b^x.$$

The inverse of an exponential function is the **logarithmic function**,

$$f^{-1}(x) = \log_b x.$$

PROBLEM

Write the following equations in logarithmic form:

$3^4 = 81$ and $M^k = 5$.

Solution

The expression $y = b^x$ is equivalent to the logarithmic expression $\log_b y = x$. Therefore, $3^4 = 81$ is equivalent to the logarithmic expression

$$\log_3 81 = 4$$

and $M^k = 5$ is equivalent to the logarithmic expression

$$\log_M 5 = k.$$

PROBLEM

Find the value of $\log_5 25$ and $\log_4 x = 2$.

Solution

$\log_5 25$ is equivalent to $5^x = 25$. Thus $x = 2$, since $5^2 = 25$.

$\log_4 x = 2$ is equivalent to $4^2 = x.$ $x = 16$.

Logarithm Properties

If M, N, p, and b are positive numbers and $b = 1$, then

a. $\log_b 1 = 0$

b. $\log_b b = 1$

c. $\log_b b^x = x$

d. $\log_b M\,N = \log_b M + \log_b N$

e. $\log_b M\,/\,N = \log_b M - \log_b N$

f. $\log_b M^p = p\,\log_b M$

PROBLEM

If $\log_{10}3 = .4771$ and $\log_{10}4 = .6021$, find $\log_{10}12$.

Solution

Since $\quad 12 = 4(3)$, $\log_{10}12 = \log_{10}(4)\,(3)$

Remember

$$\log_b M\,N = \log_b M + \log_b N.$$

Therefore

$$\log_{10}12 = \log_{10}4 + \log_{10}3$$

$$= .6021 + .4771$$

$$= 1.0792$$

Drill 6: Elementary Functions

Logarithms and Exponentials

DIRECTIONS: Find the value of *x*.

1. $\log_7 1 = x$

    (A) 1   (B) 7

    (C) $^1/_7$ (D) 0

    (E) .1

2. $\log_2 8 = x$

    (A) 2   (B) 3

    (C) 4   (D) 16

    (E) 64

3. $\log_x 16 = 4$

    (A) 2   (B) 4

    (C) $1/4$ (D) 16

    (E) 64

4. $\log_3 x = 2$

    (A) $2/3$ (B) $3/2$

    (C) 6   (D) 8

    (E) 9

5. Given $\log_{10} 2 = 0.3010$ and $\log_{10} 3 = 0.4771$, find $\log_{10} 6 = x$.

    (A) 0.1761   (B) 0.1436

    (C) 0.6020   (D) 0.7781

    (E) 0.9542

DIRECTIONS: Evaluate each expression when $f(x) = 2x + 1$ and $g(x) = x^2 - 1$.

6. $(f \circ g)(2)$

    (A) 7   (B) 8

    (C) 10   (D) 15

    (E) 24

7. $(g \circ f)(-3)$

    (A) -40 (B) 3

    (C) 13   (D) 17

    (E) 24

8. $(g + f)(2)$

    (A) -2 (B) 2

    (C) 7   (D) 8

    (E) 15

9. $f^{-1}(x)$

    (A) $1 - 2x$ (B) $(x - 1)/2$

    (C) $x - \frac{1}{2}$ (D) x^2

    (E) $x/2$

10. $g^{-1}(x)$

    (A) $\sqrt{x}$ (B) $1 - x^2$

    (C) $x + 1$ (D) $(x + 1)^{1/2}$

    (E) $(x + 1)^2$

7. FRACTIONAL EXPONENTS

The properties that govern integral exponents extend to fractional exponents.

$$a^p a^q = a^{p + q}$$

$$(a^p)^q = a^{pq}$$

$$\frac{a^p}{a^q} = a^{p - q}$$

$$(ab)^p = a^p b^p$$

$$\left(\frac{a}{b}\right)^p = \frac{a^p}{b^p}$$

$$a^0 = 1, \text{ if } a \neq 0$$

$$a^{-n} = \frac{1}{a^n}$$

$$a^{m/n} = \sqrt[n]{a^m}$$

A **fractional exponent** is defined as

$$a^{1/n} = \sqrt[n]{a}$$

where $n > 1$ and a is a real number (non-negative if n is even), i.e.,

$$3^{1/2} = \sqrt{3}.$$

PROBLEM

Reduce $16^{3/4}$.

Solution

$$16^{3/4} = \sqrt[4]{16^3}$$
$$= \sqrt[4]{4,096}$$
$$= 8$$

Note $\quad 16 = 2 \times 2 \times 2 \times 2 = 2^4$

so $\quad (2^4)^{3/4} = 2^3 = 8$.

Drill 7: Fractional Exponents

DIRECTIONS: Simplify the following.

1. $4^{1/2}$

   (A) 16   (B) 2

   (C) 4   (D) 8

   (E) 6

2. $(4^{1/5})^3$

   (A) $12^{1/5}$ (B) $4^{2/5}$

   (C) $4^{4/5}$ (D) $4^{3/5}$

   (E) $4^{1/15}$

3. $\dfrac{x^{a/4}}{x^{a/3}}$

   (A) $\dfrac{1}{x^{a/12}}$ (B) $x^{a/12}$

   (C) $x^{2a/7}$ (D) $x^{1/4}$

   (E) x^a

4. $16^{-3/2}$

    (A) 64   (B) 4

    (C) $^1\!/_{64}$ (D) $^1\!/_4$

    (E) $^1\!/_{16}$

8. SEQUENCES AND SERIES

A **sequence** is a set of numbers in order, i.e.,

$$2, 4, 6, \ldots, 2n, \ldots.$$

Two important types of sequences are the arithmetic sequence and geometric sequence.

Arithmetic progression is a sequence of the form

$$a, a + d, a + 2d, a + 3d, \ldots, a + (n-1)d, \ldots$$

where a is the first term, $a + (n-1)d$ is the nth term, and d is the common difference.

The formula to find the sum of the first n terms is

$$S_n = \frac{n(a+l)}{2}$$

n is the number of terms, a is the first term, and l is the last (n^{th}) term.

PROBLEM

Find the sum of the first 20 terms in the series, 3, 8, 13, ...

Solution

To use the formula find the values for a, n, d, and l.

The number of terms $n = 20$ and the first term $a = 3$.

The difference

$$d = 8 - 3 = 5.$$

The last term

$$l = a + (n-1)d = 3 + (20-1)5 = 98.$$

Substitute into the formula

$$S_{20} = \frac{(20(3 + 98))}{2}$$

$$= 10(101) = 1{,}010$$

Geometric progression is a sequence of the form

$$a, \, ar, \, ar^2, \, ar^3, \, \ldots, \, ar^{n-1}, \, \ldots$$

where a is the first term and r is the common ratio. The formula to find the sum of the first n terms is

$$S_n = \frac{a - ar^n}{1 - r}, \quad r \neq 1$$

and n is the number of terms, a is the first term, and r is the common ratio.

PROBLEM

Find the sum of the first six terms of the geometric progression $1 + \frac{1}{2} + \frac{1}{4} + \ldots$

Solution

$$a = 1, \, n = 6, \text{ and } r = \frac{1}{2}$$

Substitute into the formula to obtain

$$S_6 = \frac{(1 - 1(\frac{1}{2})^6)}{(1 - \frac{1}{2})}$$

$$= \frac{(1 - \frac{1}{64})}{(\frac{1}{2})}$$

$$= \frac{63}{32}$$

Drill 8: Sequences and Series

1. Find the sum of the first 100 positive odd numbers.

    (A) 10,100   (B) 10,000

    (C) 5,050   (D) 9,900

    (E) 100,000

2. Find the sum of the first 20 terms for the series – 10, 10, 30, ...

(A) 4,000 (B) 1,700

(C) 2,100 (D) 3,600

(E) 3,900

3. Find the sum of the first six terms of the series 8, 4, 2, ...

(A) $^{63}/_4$ (B) $^{63}/_8$

(C) $^{126}/_8$ (D) 16

(E) $^{31}/_2$

4. Find the sum of the first five terms of the series 4, 8, 16, ...

(A) 128 (B) 64

(C) 124 (D) 62

(E) 120

9. GRAPHS

This section is a continuation of the review started in the Elementary Algebra Review section. Graphs and number lines illustrate answers that were solved by algebraic means. Information about two points can be obtained and an equation connecting the points can be found.

(A) The distance from A to B with coordinates (x_A, y_A) and (x_B, y_B), respectively, is:

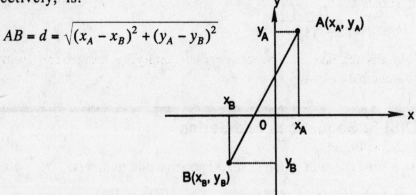

$$AB = d = \sqrt{(x_A - x_B)^2 + (y_A - y_B)^2}$$

This is known as the **distance formula**.

PROBLEM

Find the distance between the point $A(1, 3)$ and $B(5, 3)$.

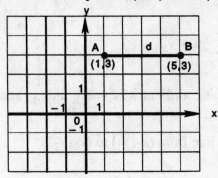

Solution

In this case, where the ordinate of both points is the same, the distance between the two points is given by the absolute value of the difference between the two abscissas. In fact, this case reduces to merely counting boxes as the figure shows.

Let,

x_1 = abscissa of A $\qquad\qquad$ y_1 = ordinate of A

x_2 = abscissa of B $\qquad\qquad$ y_2 = ordinate of B

d = the distance

Therefore,

$$d = |x_1 - x_2|.$$

By substitution,

$$d = |1 - 5| = |-4| = 4.$$

This answer can also be obtained by applying the general formula for distance between any two points

$$d = \sqrt{(x_1 - x_2)^2 + (y_1 - y_2)^2}$$

By substitution,

$$d = \sqrt{(1 - 5)^2 + (3 - 3)^2}$$

$$= \sqrt{(-4)^2 + (0)^2}$$

$$= \sqrt{16}$$

$$= 4$$

The distance is 4.

To find the **midpoint** of a segment between the two given endpoints, use the formula

$$MP = \left(\frac{x_1 + x_2}{2}, \frac{y_1 + y_2}{2} \right)$$

where x_1 and y_1 are the coordinates of one point; x_2 and y_2 are the coordinates of the other point.

The **slope** of the line from (x_1, y_1) to (x_2, y_2) is

$$m = \frac{y_2 - y_1}{x_2 - x_1}.$$

The equation of the line from (x_1, y_1) to (x_2, y_2) is

$$y - y_1 = m(x - x_1)$$

where m is the slope. This reduces to a form of

$$y = mx + b$$

with slope = m and y-intercept = b.

Lines are parallel if the slopes of each line are equal. Lines are perpendicular if their slopes are negative reciprocals.

PROBLEM

Find the slope and the y-intercept of the line with equation

$$2(x - 3) = -3(y + 5).$$

Solution

Write the equation in the form

$$y = mx + b$$

to find the slope, m, and y-intercept, b.

$$2(x - 3) = -3(y + 5)$$
$$2x - 6 = -3y - 15$$
$$3y = -2x + 6 - 15$$

Simplify.

$$3y = -2x - 9$$

Divide both sides by 3.

$$y = -\frac{2}{3}x - 3$$

$$m = -\frac{2}{3} \text{ and } b = -3$$

Inequalities can be represented on number lines and graphs. Solve for the unknown and graph.

The results can be **bounded intervals** between two numbers.

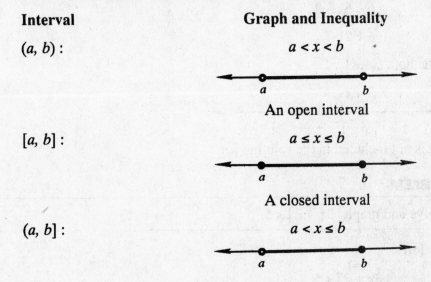

Interval	Graph and Inequality
(a, b) :	$a < x < b$
	An open interval
$[a, b]$:	$a \leq x \leq b$
	A closed interval
$(a, b]$:	$a < x \leq b$
	A half-open or half-closed interval

Note that a parenthesis in $(a, b]$ means a is not included in the interval and a bracket means b is included in the interval. In the three examples the numbers a and b are the boundaries for the values of x.

The results can be **unbounded intervals**. The results can be numbers less than or greater than a certain number.

Interval	Graph and Inequality
(a, ∞) :	$a < x$
	An open unbounded interval
$(-\infty, b]$:	$x \leq b$
	A closed unbounded interval

PROBLEM

Solve $3(x + 2) < 5x$ and graph.

Solution

$$3(x + 2) < 5x$$

$$3x + 6 < 5x$$

Add $(-3x)$ to both sides.

$$6 < 5x - 3x$$

$$6 < 2x$$

Divide both sides by 2.

$$3 < x$$

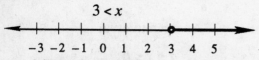

$x = 3$ is not included in the solution set.

PROBLEM

Solve and graph $|3x + 2| \leq 5$.

Solution

$$|3x + 2| \leq 5$$

Rewrite without absolute signs.

$$-5 \leq 3x + 2 \leq 5$$

Add -2 to all sides.

$$-7 \leq 3x \leq 3$$

Divide all sides by 3.

$$-\tfrac{7}{3} \leq x \leq 1$$

The solution set includes both $-\tfrac{7}{3}$ and 1.

A graph of a linear inequality, graphs all ordered pairs (x, y) that satisfy the inequality. A broken line means that the ordered pair that satisfies the linear equation is not included in the solution.

PROBLEM

Solve and graph $2x - 3y \geq 6$.

Solution

The $\geq$ sign means that the graph includes

$$2x - 3y = 6$$

and values

$$2x - 3y > 6.$$

Find the x-intercept. Set $y = 0$.

$$2x - 3y = 6$$

$$2x = 6$$

$$x = 3 \text{ or } \{3, 0\}$$

Find the y-intercept. Set $x = 0$.

$$-3y = 6$$

$$y = -2 \text{ or } \{0, -2\}$$

Determine the region for which

$$2x - 3y > 6$$

is true. Try two points on either side of the line. Try the points (0, 0) and (5, 1).

For (0, 0)	For (5, 1)
$2x - 3y > 6$	$2x - 3y > 6$
$2(0) - 3(0) > 6$	$2(5) - 3(1) > 6$
$0 - 0 > 6$	$10 - 3 > 6$
$0 > 6$	$7 > 6$
False	True

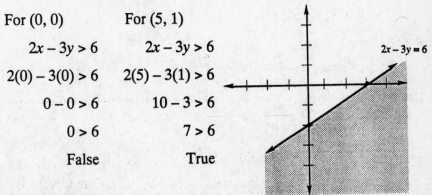

The shaded region represents the solution to the inequality.

Graphs of quadratic equations are parabolas. The graph of

$$y = a(x - h)^2 + k$$

is a parabola with vertex (h, k). The parabola opens upward when $a > 0$ and downward when $a < 0$. The axis of symmetry is the line $x = h$. The graph of

$$y = ax^2 + bx + c$$

has vertex coordinates of

$$\left(-\frac{b}{2a}, c - \frac{b^2}{4a}\right).$$

PROBLEM

Graph $y = -x^2 + 2x + 1$.

Solution

The vertex $= \left(-\dfrac{b}{2a}, c - \dfrac{b^2}{4a}\right).$

$a = -1, b = 2, c = 1$

$$-\frac{b}{2a} = -\frac{2}{2(-1)}$$

$$= \frac{-2}{-2} = 1$$

$$c - \frac{b^2}{4a} = 1 - \frac{2^2}{4(-1)}$$

$$= 1 - \frac{4}{(-4)}$$

$$= 1 + 1 = 2$$

The vertex is $(1, 2)$ and the parabola points downward since $a = -1$.

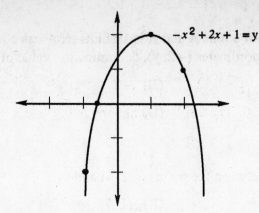

x	y
-1	-2
0	1
1	2
2	1

Drill 9: Graphs

1. Find the distance between $(4, -7)$ and $(-2, -7)$.

    (A) 4   (B) 6

    (C) 7   (D) 14

    (E) 15

2. Find the distance between $(3, 8)$ and $(5, 11)$.

    (A) 2   (B) 3

    (C) $\sqrt{13}$ (D) $\sqrt{15}$

    (E) $3\sqrt{3}$

3. How far from the origin is point $(3, 4)$?

    (A) 3   (B) 4

    (C) 5   (D) $5\sqrt{3}$

    (E) $4\sqrt{5}$

4. Find the distance between the points $(-4, 2)$ and $(3, -5)$.

    (A) 3   (B) $3\sqrt{3}$

    (C) 7   (D) $7\sqrt{2}$

    (E) $7\sqrt{3}$

5. The distance between points A and B is 10 units. If A has coordinates $(4, -6)$ and B has coordinates $(-2, y)$, determine the value of y.

   (A) -6 (B) -2

   (C) 0 (D) 1

   (E) 2

6. Find the midpoint between the points $(-2, 6)$ and $(4, 8)$.

   (A) $(3, 7)$ (B) $(1, 7)$

   (C) $(3, 1)$ (D) $(1, 1)$

   (E) $(-3, 7)$

7. Find the coordinates of the midpoint between the points $(-5, 7)$ and $(3, -1)$.

   (A) $(-4, 4)$ (B) $(3, -1)$

   (C) $(1, -3)$ (D) $(-1, 3)$

   (E) $(4, -4)$

8. The y-coordinate of the midpoint of segment AB if A has coordinates $(-3, 7)$ and B has coordinates $(-3, -2)$ is what value?

   (A) $5/2$ (B) 3

   (C) $7/2$ (D) 5

   (E) $15/2$

9. One endpoint of a line segment is $(5, -3)$. The midpoint is $(-1, 6)$. What is the other endpoint?

   (A) $(7, 3)$ (B) $(2, 1.5)$

   (C) $(-7, 15)$ (D) $(-2, 1.5)$

   (E) $(-7, 12)$

10. The point $(-2, 6)$ is the midpoint for which of the following pair of points?

    (A) $(1, 4)$ and $(-3, 8)$ (B) $(-1, -3)$ and $(5, 9)$

    (C) $(1, 4)$ and $(5, 9)$ (D) $(-1, 4)$ and $(3, -8)$

    (E) $(1, 3)$ and $(-5, 9)$

11. Which line is parallel to $y = 3x + 4$?

(A) $y = 4x - 3$ (B) $y = 3x - 7$

(C) $y = 7x + 4$ (D) $y = -\frac{1}{3}x + 8$

(E) $3y = x + 4$

12. What is the slope of the line through $(3, 4)$ and $(0, -3)$?

(A) $\frac{3}{7}$ (B) -1

(C) $\frac{3}{4}$ (D) 3

(E) $\frac{7}{3}$

13. What is the y-intercept of the line determined by $3x - 2y = 8$?

(A) -4 (B) 8

(C) -8 (D) 4

(E) 3

14. What is the equation that has $m = -3$ and passes through $(2, -4)$?

(A) $y = -3x$ (B) $y = -3x - 10$

(C) $y = -3x + 2$ (D) $y = -3x - 4$

(E) $y = -3x + 6$

15. What is the slope of the line through $(5, 2)$ and $(-1, 1)$?

(A) $-\frac{1}{6}$ (B) $-\frac{1}{5}$

(C) $\frac{1}{2}$ (D) $\frac{1}{6}$

(E) 6

16. Solve for x and graph $x + 4 < 0$.

(A)

(B)

(C)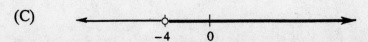

(D)

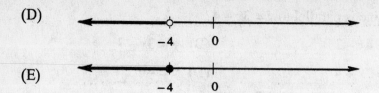

(E)

17. Solve for x and graph $2x + 7 \leq 5 - 6x$.

(A)

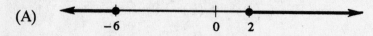

(B)

(C)

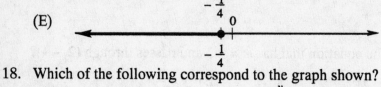

(D)

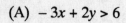

(E)

18. Which of the following correspond to the graph shown?

(A) $-3x + 2y > 6$

(B) $3x - 2y > 6$

(C) $3x + 2y > 6$

(D) $3x + 2y \geq 6$

(E) $3x + 2y < 6$

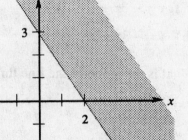

19. Graph the solution set to $|2 - 3x| \geq 8$.

(A)

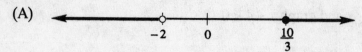

(B)

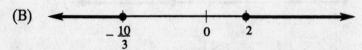

(C)

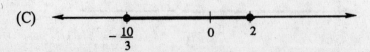

(D)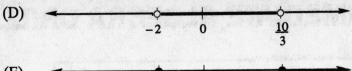

$-2 \qquad 0 \qquad \dfrac{10}{3}$

(E)

$-2 \qquad 0 \qquad \dfrac{10}{3}$

20. The graph of $y = x^2 + 1$ might look like which of the following?

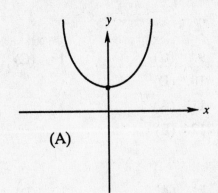

(A)

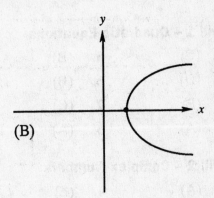

(B)

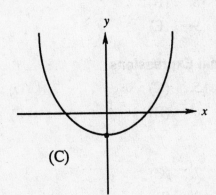

(C)

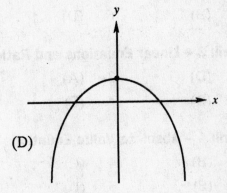

(D)

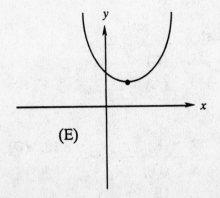

(E)

INTERMEDIATE ALGEBRA DRILLS

ANSWER KEY

Drill 1 – Quadratic Equations

1.	(C)	5.	(B)	9.	(C)	13.	(C)
2.	(D)	6.	(B)	10.	(D)		
3.	(E)	7.	(C)	11.	(A)		
4.	(A)	8.	(A)	12.	(E)		

Drill 2 – Complex Numbers

1.	(A)	4.	(E)	7.	(A)	10.	(D)
2.	(E)	5.	(C)	8.	(B)		
3.	(B)	6.	(D)	9.	(E)		

Drill 3 – Linear Equations and Rational Expressions

1.	(D)	3.	(A)	5.	(C)	7.	(D)
2.	(D)	4.	(E)	6.	(B)	8.	(C)

Drill 4 – Absolute Value Equations

1.	(B)	4.	(C)	7.	(C)
2.	(E)	5.	(D)	8.	(B)
3.	(A)	6.	(A)	9.	(D)

Drill 5 – Equations of Higher Degrees

1.	(E)	3.	(A)	5.	(C)
2.	(B)	4.	(E)	6.	(A)

Drill 6 – Elementary Functions

1.	(D)	4.	(E)	7.	(E)	10.	(D)
2.	(B)	5.	(D)	8.	(D)		
3.	(A)	6.	(A)	9.	(B)		

Drill 7 – Fractional Exponents

1.	(B)	2.	(D)	3.	(A)	4.	(C)

Drill 8 – Sequences and Series

1.	(B)	2.	(D)	3.	(A)	4.	(C)

Drill 9 – Graphs

1.	(B)	6.	(B)	11.	(B)	16.	(D)
2.	(C)	7.	(D)	12.	(E)	17.	(E)
3.	(C)	8.	(A)	13.	(A)	18.	(C)
4.	(D)	9.	(C)	14.	(C)	19.	(E)
5.	(E)	10.	(E)	15.	(D)	20.	(A)

ELM

Entry Level Mathematics

Chapter 5
Word Problems
Review

WORD PROBLEMS
DIAGNOSTIC TEST

14 Questions

(Answer sheets appear in the back of the book.)

> **DIRECTIONS:** Each question has five multiple-choice answers. Select the single best answer.

1. John bought a $250 radio. The salesman gave him a 10% discount. How much did he pay for the radio?

   (A) $25   (B) $125

   (C) $175   (D) $225

   (E) $275

2. An airplane travels 1,800 miles in 3 hours flying with the wind. On the return trip, flying against the wind, it takes 4 hours to travel 2,000 miles. Find the rate of the plane in still air.

   (A) 425 mph   (B) 500 mph

   (C) 542 mph   (D) 550 mph

   (E) 600 mph

3. After taking 5 tests, John had an average of 80. On the next test, John got an 86. What is his average for all 6 tests?

   (A) 80   (B) 81

   (C) 82   (D) 83

   (E) 84

4. How long must a rectangular bin be to hold 1,800 cubic meters, if the width is 10 meters, and the height is 6 meters?

(A) 30 m (B) 45 m

(C) 60 m (D) 10,800 m

(E) Cannot be determined

5. Lynsey is 5 years older than Gretta. The sum of their ages is 95. How old is Lynsey?

(A) 5 (B) 40

(C) 45 (D) 50

(E) 55

6. In the Daly Auto Factory, robots assemble cars. If 3 robots assemble 17 cars in 10 minutes, how many cars can 14 robots assemble in 45 minutes if all robots work at the same rate all the time?

(A) 357 (B) 340

(C) 705 (D) 150

(E) 272

7. John wishes to contribute $2,500 to his favorite charities A and B in the ratio of 2 to 3. The amount he should contribute to charity A is

(A) $500. (B) $1,000.

(C) $1,250. (D) $1,500.

(E) $2,000.

8. How much time is left on the parking meter pictured below?

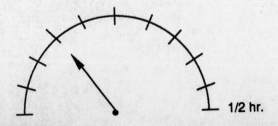

1/2 hr.

(A) 8 minutes   (B) 9 minutes

(C) 10 minutes   (D) 12 minutes

(E) 15 minutes

9. Emile receives a flat weekly salary of $240 plus 12% commission of the total volume of all sales he makes. What must his dollar volume be in a week if he is to make a total weekly salary of $540?

(A) $2,880   (B) $3,600

(C) $6,480   (D) $2,500

(E) $2,000

Table 1 — Amount of money spent on textbooks in August

	Freshman	Sophomore	Junior	Senior	Graduate
	$180	$158	$179	$166	$116
	195	191	194	189	153
	168	202	210	190	98
	184	173	203	157	121
	205	187	183	203	92
	208	212	177	171	118
	184	197	192	180	126
	178	181	169	164	114
	193	166	198	188	119
	196	180	204	170	96
Total	$1,891	$1,847	$1,909	$1,778	$1,153

10. Which of the following is the best approximation (to the nearest dollar) of the average amount of money spent on textbooks by any senior class student in the school's bookstore in August?

(A) $193   (B) $168

(C) $183   (D) $178

(E) $173

11. Ms. Jones received a 10% salary increase each of the last two years. If her annual salary this year is $41,745, what was her annual salary two years ago?

(A) $34,500

(B) $33,813.45

(C) $33,396

(D) $34,000

(E) $34,750

12. A man has $20,000 to invest. He invests $5,000 at 5% and $7,000 at 7%. In order to have a yearly income of $1,500, he must invest the remainder at

(A) 8%.

(B) 8.5%.

(C) 9%.

(D) 9.5%.

(E) 10%.

13. A doctor has 44 cc of 2% tincture of iodine. If the iodine is boiled, alcohol is evaporated away and the strength of tincture is raised. How much alcohol must be boiled away in order to raise the strength of the tincture to 8%?

(A) 33 cc

(B) 32 cc

(C) 30 cc

(D) 24 cc

(E) 10 cc

14. If the cost of five apples is $3.25, and if the cost of an orange and one of these apples together is $1.05, what is the cost of an orange alone?

(A) $0.35

(B) $0.40

(C) $0.45

(D) $0.50

(E) $0.55

WORD PROBLEMS
DIAGNOSTIC TEST

ANSWER KEY

1.	(D)	5.	(D)	9.	(D)	13.	(A)
2.	(D)	6.	(A)	10.	(D)	14.	(B)
3.	(B)	7.	(B)	11.	(A)		
4.	(A)	8.	(B)	12.	(D)		

DETERMINE YOUR STRENGTHS AND WEAKNESSES

WORD PROBLEMS

Question Type	Question #	See Pages . . .
Algebraic	5, 14	271–272
Rate	2	273–274
Work	6	275–276
Mixture	13, 14	276–278
Interest	11, 12	278–280
Discount	1	281–282
Profit	9	282–284
Ratios and Proportions	6, 7	284–286
Geometry	4	287–288
Averages	3, 10	289–290
Data Interpretation	8, 10	290–294

DETAILED EXPLANATIONS OF ANSWERS

WORD PROBLEMS DIAGNOSTIC TEST

1.   **(D)**   Since the salesman has given John a discount, we need to figure out the amount of money deducted from John's bill. Ten percent of the cost of the radio must be subtracted from the original cost to compute the new cost. ten percent of $250 is .10 × 250 or $25. Subtracting the $25 discount from the original $250 price yields $225.

2.   **(D)**   Using the formula

$$\text{Distance} = \text{Rate} \times \text{Time},$$

which can be rewritten as

$$\text{Rate} = \frac{\text{Distance}}{\text{Time}} = \text{Speed}$$

(Actual speed of plane in still air)

= (Apparent speed of plane) – (wind speed)

Traveling *with* the wind produces a *positive* wind speed, while traveling *against* the wind produces a *negative* wind speed. Therefore,

Let w = wind speed

x = actual speed of plane in still air

$$x = \left(\frac{1{,}800 \text{ mi}}{3 \text{ hr}}\right) - (w) \text{ with the wind}$$

$$x = \left(\frac{2{,}000 \text{ mi}}{4 \text{ hr}}\right) - (-w) \text{ against the wind}$$

Setting these equations equal,

$$(600 \text{ mi/hr}) - (w) = (500 \text{ mi/hr}) - (-w)$$

$$600 \text{ mi/hr} - w = 500 \text{ mi/hr} + w$$

Solving for w,

$$2w = 100 \text{ mi/hr.}$$

$$w = 50 \text{ mi/hr.}$$

Substituting this into either initial equation gives

$$x = (600 \text{ mi/hr} - 50 \text{ mi/hr}) = (500 \text{ mi/hr} + 50 \text{ mi/hr}) = 550 \text{ mi/hr.}$$

3.   **(B)**   Note that the new average is *not* found by just averaging 80 and the new score; it is *not*

$$(80 + 86)/2 = 166/2 = 83.$$

John's 5-test average of 80 means that the total points earned is 5 times 80 or 400 points. Adding the new score of 86 and dividing by six tests we get

$$(400 + 86)/6 = 486/6 = 81.$$

John's new average is 81.

4.   **(A)**   The formula for the volume is $v = lwh$. Substitute 1,800 for the volume, v, l for the length, 10 for the width, w, and 6 for the height, h.

$$1,800 = l \times 10 \times 6$$

$$1,800 = 60l$$

$$30 = l$$

The length is 30 meters.

5.   **(D)**   Set up an algebraic relationship. Let x = Gretta's age, and $(x + 5)$ = Lynsey's age, since Lynsey is 5 years older.
The sum of their ages is 95, so

$$(x) + (x + 5) = 95$$

$$2x + 5 = 95$$

$$2x = 90$$

$$x = 45$$

Since x = Gretta's age which is 45, and Lynsey is 5 years older, Lynsey is 45 + 5, or 50 years old.

6.   (A)   One method for attacking this problem is to let x be the number of cars that 14 robots can assemble in 45 minutes. Because the robots work at the same rate all the time, we can express this rate by using the information that 3 robots can assemble 17 cars in 10 minutes.

Now, if 3 robots can assemble 17 cars in 10 minutes, then 3 robots can assemble $17/10$ cars in 1 minute. Consequently, 1 robot assembles

$$\frac{1}{3}\left(\frac{17}{10}\right) \text{ or } \frac{17}{30}$$

of a car in 1 minute.

Similarly, if 14 robots assemble x cars in 45 minutes, then the 14 robots assemble $x/45$ cars in 1 minute. Thus, 1 robot assembles

$$\frac{1}{14}\left(\frac{x}{45}\right), \text{ or } \frac{x}{14(45)}$$

of a car in 1 minute. Because the rates are equal, we have the proportion

$$\frac{x}{14(45)} = \frac{17}{30}$$

$$\frac{x}{630} = \frac{17}{30}$$

Solving this proportion for x yields,

$$30x = (630)(17)$$

$$30x = 10,710$$

$$x = \frac{10,710}{30} = 357$$

7.   (B)   If John contributes $2X$ to A and $3X$ to B, then his contributions to A and B will be in the ratio of 2 to 3. Then

$$2X + 3X = 2,500, \text{ or } X = 500.$$

Therefore, he should contribute 2(500) = $1,000 to charity A.

8. **(B)** The meter shows that $3/10$ of the total time on the meter is left. However, this is a $1/2$-hour meter. Since

$$\frac{3}{10} \times \frac{1}{2} = \frac{3}{20},$$

this means that there is $3/20$ of an hour left on the meter, and $3/20$ of an hour is 9 minutes.

There are 10 calibrations for a half hour or 30 minutes. Each calibration is therefore $30/10 = 3$ minutes. Since the arrow is on the 3rd calibration, $3 \times 3 = 9$ minutes left.

9. **(D)** Since we do not know Emile's dollar volume during the week in question, we can assign this amount the value of x.

Now, Emile's total salary of $540 can be divided into two parts; one part is his flat salary of $240, and the other part is his salary from commissions which amounts to $540 − $240 = $300. This part of his salary is equal to 12% of his dollar volume, x. Thus, 12% of x = $300. This means

$$(0.12)x = 300$$

$$x = 300/0.12 = \$2,500.$$

10. **(D)** The average (arithmetic mean), $\bar{x}$, of a set of numbers is equal to the sum of the numbers divided by the number of numbers, n. That is,

$$\bar{x} = \frac{\text{sum of numbers}}{n}$$

Thus, this question can be answered by calculating the average of the amounts of money spent in the school's bookstore on textbooks only. These amounts are listed in the column headed "Senior" in Table 1. They are:

$$166, 189, 190, 157, 203, 171, 180, 164, 188, \text{ and } 170.$$

The sum of these numbers is also given in Table 1 as 1,778. Since there are 10 numbers, it follows that,

$$\bar{x} = \frac{1,778}{10} = 177.8$$

Thus, the best approximation of the average amount of money spent by any senior class student is $178.

11. (A) Let x be Ms. Jone's salary two years ago. Then $x + 10\%x$ was her salary last year and

$$(x + 10\%x) + 10\%(x + 10\%x)$$

is an expression for her salary this year.

$$(x + 10\%x) + 10\%(x + 10\%x) = 41{,}745$$

$$1.1x + .11x = 41{,}745$$

$$1.21x = 41{,}745$$

$$x = 34{,}500$$

12. (D) Of the $20,000 he has to invest, the man invests $5,000 at 5% giving him

$$\$5{,}000(0.5) = \$250$$

in interest. He invests $7,000 at 7% giving him

$$\$7{,}000(0.7) = \$490$$

in interest. The remaining amount of interest needed to reach $1,500 a year is, therefore,

$$\$1{,}500 - \$740 = \$760.$$

The remaining amount of principal is

$$\$20{,}000 - \$12{,}000 = \$8{,}000.$$

Letting x be the rate of interest, we have

$$8{,}000x = 760 \text{ or } 760/8{,}000 = .095 = 9.5\%.$$

13. (A)

Solution	Amount	%	Amount of Iodine
Original Amount	44	.02	44(0.2)
Boiled Away	x	0	0
New Solution	$(44 - x)$	.08	$(44 - x)\,(0.8)$

The amount of iodine in the original solution less the amount of iodine in the alcohol evaporated (which is 0) equals the amount of iodine in the new solution.

$$.02(44) - 0 = .08(44 - x)$$

Solve for x.

$$.88 - 0 = 3.52 - .08x$$
$$.08x = 3.52 - .88$$
$$.08x = 2.64$$
$$x = 33$$

14. **(B)** Cost of an apple

$$= \frac{\$3.25}{5} = \$0.65.$$

Cost of an orange

$$= \$1.05 - \$0.65 = \$0.40.$$

WORD PROBLEMS REVIEW

One of the main problems students have in mathematics involves solving word problems. The secret to solving these problems is being able to convert words into numbers and variables in the form of an algebraic equation.

The easiest way to approach a word problem is to read the question and ask yourself what you are trying to find. This unknown quantity can be represented by a variable.

Next, determine how the variable relates to the other quantities in the problem. More than likely, these quantities can be explained in terms of the original variable. If not, a separate variable may have to be used to represent a quantity.

Using these variables and the relationships determined among them, an equation can be written. Solve for a particular variable and then substitute this number in for each relationship that involves this variable in order to find any unknown quantities.

Lastly, re-read the problem to be sure that you have answered the questions correctly and fully.

1. ALGEBRAIC

The following illustrates how to formulate an equation and solve the problem.

PROBLEM

Find two consecutive odd integers whose sum is 36.

Solution

Let x = the first odd integer

Let $x + 2$ = the second odd integer

The sum of the two numbers is 36. Therefore,

$$x + (x + 2) = 36.$$

Simplifying,

$$2x + 2 = 36$$
$$2x + 2 + (-2) = 36 + (-2)$$
$$2x = 34$$
$$x = 17$$

Substituting 17 in for x, we find the second odd integer =

$$(x + 2) = (17 + 2) = 19.$$

Therefore, we find that the two consecutive odd integers whose sum is 36 are 17 and 19, respectively.

Drill 1: Algebraic

1. The sum of two numbers is 41. One number is one less than twice the other. Find the larger of the two numbers.

   (A) 13   (B) 14

   (C) 21   (D) 27

   (E) 41

2. The sum of two consecutive integers is 111. Three times the larger integer less two times the smaller integer is 58. Find the value of the smaller integer.

   (A) 55   (B) 56

   (C) 58   (D) 111

   (E) 112

3. The difference between two integers is 12. The sum of the two integers is 2. Find both integers.

   (A) 7 and 5   (B) 7 and −5

   (C) −7 and 5   (D) 2 and 12

   (E) −2 and 12

2. RATE

One of the formulas you will use for rate problems will be

Rate × Time = Distance

PROBLEM

If a plane travels five hours from New York to California at a speed of 600 miles per hour, how many miles does the plane travel?

Solution

Using the formula rate × time = distance, multiply

600 mph × 5 hours = 3,000 miles.

The average rate at which an object travels can be solved by dividing the total distance traveled by the total amount of time.

PROBLEM

On a 40-mile bicycle trip, Cathy rode half the distance at 20 mph and the other half at 10 mph. What was Cathy's average speed on the bike trip?

Solution

First you need to break down the problem. On half of the trip which would be 20 miles, Cathy rode 20 mph. Using the rate formula,

$$\frac{distance}{rate} = time,$$

you would compute,

$$\frac{20 \text{ miles}}{20 \text{ miles per hour}} = 1 \text{ hour}$$

to travel the first 20 miles. During the second 20 miles, Cathy traveled at 10 miles per hour, which would be

$$\frac{20 \text{ miles}}{10 \text{ miles per hour}} = 2 \text{ hours}.$$

Thus, the average speed Cathy traveled would be $^{40}/_3 = 13.34$ miles per hour.

In solving for some rate problems you can use cross multiplication involving ratios to solve for x.

PROBLEM

If two pairs of shoes cost $52, then what is the cost of 10 pairs of shoes at this rate?

Solution

$$\frac{2}{52} = \frac{10}{x}, 2x = 52 \times 10, x = \frac{520}{2}, x = \$260.$$

Drill 2: Rate

1. Two towns are 420 miles apart. A car leaves the first town traveling toward the second town at 55 mph. At the same time, a second car leaves the other town and heads toward the first town at 65 mph. How long will it take for the two cars to meet?

    (A) 2 hr   (B) 3 hr

    (C) 3.5 hr   (D) 4 hr

    (E) 4.25 hr

2. A camper leaves the campsite walking due east at a rate of 3.5 mph. Another camper leaves the campsite at the same time but travels due west. In two hours the two campers will be 15 miles apart. What is the walking rate of the second camper?

    (A) 2.5 mph   (B) 3 mph

    (C) 3.25 mph   (D) 3.5 mph

    (E) 4 mph

3. A bicycle racer covers a 75 mile training route to prepare for an upcoming race. If the racer could increase his speed by 5 mph, he could complete the same course in 3/4 of the time. Find his average rate of speed.

    (A) 15 mph   (B) 15.5 mph

    (C) 16 mph   (D) 18 mph

    (E) 20 mph

3. WORK

In work problems, one of the basic formulas is

$$\frac{1}{x} + \frac{1}{y} = \frac{1}{z}$$

where x and y represent the number of hours it takes two objects or people to complete the work and z is the total number of hours when both are working together.

PROBLEM

Otis can seal and stamp 400 envelopes in 2 hours while Elizabeth seals and stamps 400 envelopes in 1 hour. In how many hours can Otis and Elizabeth, working together, complete a 400-piece mailing at these rates?

Solution

$$\frac{1}{2} + \frac{1}{1} = \frac{1}{z}, \quad \frac{1}{2} + \frac{2}{2} = \frac{3}{2}, \quad \frac{3}{2} = \frac{1}{z}, \quad 3z = 2$$

$z = \frac{2}{3}$ of an hour or 40 minutes. Working together, Otis and Elizabeth can seal and stamp 400 envelopes in 40 minutes.

Drill 3: Work

1. It takes Marty 3 hours to type the address labels for his club's newsletter. It only takes Pat $2\frac{1}{4}$ hours to type the same amount of labels. How long would it take them working together to complete the address labels?

    (A) $\frac{7}{9}$ hr   (B) $1\frac{2}{7}$ hr

    (C) $1\frac{4}{5}$ hr   (D) $2\frac{5}{8}$ hr

    (E) $5\frac{1}{4}$ hr

2. It takes Troy 3 hours to mow his family's large lawn. With his little brother's help, he can finish the job in only 2 hours. How long would it take the little brother to mow the entire lawn alone?

    (A) 4 hr   (B) 5 hr

(C) 5.5 hr   (D) 6 hr

(E) 6.75 hr

3. A tank can be filled by one inlet pipe in 15 minutes. It takes an outlet pipe 75 minutes to drain the tank. If the outlet pipe is left open by accident, how long would it take to fill the tank?

(A) 15.5 min   (B) 15.9 min

(C) 16.8 min   (D) 18.75 min

(E) 19.3 min

4. MIXTURE

Mixture problems present the combination of different products and ask you to solve for different parts of the mixture.

PROBLEM

A chemist has an 18% solution and a 45% solution of a disinfectant. How many ounces of each should be used to make 12 ounces of a 36% solution?

Solution

Let x = Number of ounces from the 18% solution, and

y = Number of ounces from the 45% solution.

$$x + y = 12 \qquad\qquad (1)$$

$$.18x + .45y = .36(12) \qquad\qquad (2)$$

Note that .18 of the first solution is pure disinfectant and that .45 of the second solution is pure disinfectant. When the proper quantities are drawn from each mixture the result is 12 ounces of mixture which is .36 pure disinfectant.

The second equation cannot be solved with two unknowns. Therefore, write one variable in terms of the other and substitute it into the second equation.

$$x = 12 - y \qquad\qquad (1)$$

$$.18(12 - y) + .45y = .36(12) \qquad\qquad (2)$$

Simplifying,

$$2.16 - .18y + .45y = 4.32$$
$$.27y = 4.32 - 2.16$$
$$.27y = 2.16$$
$$y = 8$$

Substituting 8 in for y in the first equation,

$$x + 8 = 12$$
$$x = 4$$

Therefore, 4 ounces of the first and 8 ounces of the second solution should be used.

PROBLEM

Clark pays $2.00 per pound for 3 pounds of peanut butter chocolates and then decides to buy 2 pounds of chocolate covered raisins at $2.50 per pound. If Clark mixes both together, what is the cost per pound of the mixture?

Solution

The total mixture is 5 pounds and the total value of the chocolates is

$$3(\$2.00) + 2(\$2.50) = \$11.00$$

The price per pound of the chocolates is

$$\frac{\$11.00}{5 \text{ pounds}} = \$2.20.$$

Drill 4: Mixture

1. How many liters of a 20% alcohol solution must be added to 80 liters of a 50% alcohol solution to form a 45% solution?

    (A) 4   (B) 8

    (C) 16   (D) 20

    (E) 32

2. How many kilograms of water must be evaporated from 50 kg of a 10% salt solution to obtain a 15% salt solution?

    (A) 15   (B) 15.75

    (C) 16   (D) 16.$\overline{66}$

    (E) 16.75

3. If 1.5 pounds of coffee A at $3.00 a pound are mixed with 2.5 pounds of coffee B at $4.20 a pound, what is the cost per pound of the mixture?

    (A) $2.95   (B) $3.45

    (C) $3.60   (D) $3.75

    (E) $5.00

5. INTEREST

If the problem calls for computing simple interest, the interest is computed on the principal alone. If the problem involves compounded interest, then the interest on the principal is taken into account in addition to the interest earned before.

PROBLEM

How much interest will Jerry pay on his loan of $400 for 60 days at 6% per year?

Solution

Use the formula:

Interest = Principal × Rate × Time ($I = P \times R \times T$).

$400 × 6%/year × 60 days

$$= \$400 \times .06 \times \frac{60}{365}$$

$$= \$400 \times 0.00986 = \$3.94$$

Jerry will pay $3.94.

PROBLEM

Mr. Smith wishes to find out how much interest he will receive on $300 if the rate is three percent compounded annually for three years.

Solution

Compound interest is interest computed on both the principal and the interest it has previously earned. The interest is added to the principal at the end of every year. The interest on the first year is found by multiplying the rate by the principal. Hence, the interest for the first year is

$$3\% \times \$300 = .03 \times \$300 = \$9.00.$$

The principal for the second year is now $309, the old principal ($300) plus the interest ($9). The interest for the second year is found by multiplying the rate by the new principal. Hence, the interest for the second year is

$$3\% \times \$309 = .03 \times \$309 = \$9.27.$$

The principal now becomes $309 + $9.27 = $318.27.

The interest for the third year is found using this new principal. It is

$$3\% \times \$318.27 = .03 \times \$318.27 = \$9.55.$$

At the end of the third year his principal is $318.27 + 9.55 = $327.82. To find how much interest was earned, we subtract his starting principal ($300) from his ending principal ($327.82) to obtain

$$\$327.82 - \$300.00 = \$27.82.$$

To find the total amount with compound interest:

$$A = P(1 + r)^{nt}$$

where P = the principal

   r = interest rate as a decimal

   t = compounding period

   n = the number of compounding periods

In the example above, to find the amount earned after three years

   $P = \$300$

   $r = .03$

   $t = 1$ year

$$n = 3$$

$$A = \$300(1 + .03)^{3(1)}$$

$$= \$300(1.03)^3$$

$$= \$327.82$$

Drill 5: Interest

1. A man invests $3,000, part in a 12-month certificate of deposit pay-
    ing 8% and the rest in municipal bonds that pay 7% a year. If the
    yearly return from both investments is $220, how much was invested
    in bonds?

    (A) $80   (B) $140

    (C) $220   (D) $1,000

    (E) $2,000

2. A sum of money was invested at 11% a year. Four times that amount
    was invested at 7.5%. How much was invested at 11% if the total
    annual return was $1,025?

    (A) $112.75   (B) $1,025

    (C) $2,500   (D) $3,400

    (E) $10,000

3. One bank pays 6.5% a year simple interest on a savings account
    while a credit union pays 7.2% a year. If you had $1,500 to invest for
    three years, how much more would you earn by putting the money in
    the credit union than in the bank?

    (A) $10.50   (B) $31.50

    (C) $97.50   (D) $108

    (E) $1,500

6. DISCOUNT

If the discount problem asks to find the final price after the discount, first multiply the original price by the percent of discount. Then subtract this result from the original price.

If the problem asks to find the original price when only the percent of discount and the discounted price are given, simply subtract the percent of discount from 100% and divide this percent into the sale price. This will give you the original price.

PROBLEM

A popular bookstore gives a 10% discount to students. What does a student actually pay for a book costing $24?

Solution

10% of $24 is $2.40 and hence the student pays $24 − $2.40 = $21.60.

PROBLEM

Eugene paid $100 for a business suit. The suit's price included a 25% discount. What was the original price of the suit?

Solution

Let x represent the original price of the suit and take the complement of .25 (discount price) which is .75.

$$.75x = \$100 \text{ or } x = 133.34.$$

So, the original price of the suit was $133.34.

Drill 6: Discount

1. A man bought a coat marked 20% off for $156. How much had the coat cost originally?

    (A) $136   (B) $156

    (C) $175   (D) $195

    (E) $205

2. A woman saved $225 on the new sofa which was on sale for 30% off. What was the original price of the sofa?

(A) $25   (B) $200

(C) $225   (D) $525

(E) $750

3. At an office supply store, customers are given a discount if they pay in cash. If a customer is given a discount of $9.66 on a total order of $276, what is the percent of discount?

(A) 2%   (B) 3.5%

(C) 4.5%   (D) 9.66%

(E) 276%

7. PROFIT

The formula used for the profit problems is

Profit = Revenue − Cost   or

Profit = Selling Price − Expenses

PROBLEM

Four high school and college friends started a business of remodeling and selling old automobiles during the summer. For this purpose they paid $600 to rent an empty barn for the summer. They obtained the cars from a dealer for $250 each, and it takes an average of $410 in materials to remodel each car. How many automobiles must the students sell at $1,440 each to obtain a gross profit of $7,000?

Solution

Total − Total Cost = Gross Profit

Revenue − [Variable Cost + Fixed Cost] = Gross Profit

Let a = number of cars

Revenue = $1,440a$

Variable Cost = ($250 + 410)a$

Fixed Cost = $600

The desired gross profit is $7,000.

Using the equation for the gross profit,

$$1{,}440a - [660a + 600] = 7{,}000$$

$$1{,}440a - 660a - 600 = 7{,}000$$

$$780a = 7{,}000 + 600$$

$$780a = 7{,}600$$

$$a = 9.74$$

or to the nearest car, $a = 10$.

PROBLEM

A glass vase sells for $25. The net profit is 7%, and the operating expenses are 39%. Find the gross profit on the vase.

Solution

The gross profit is equal to the net profit plus the operating expenses. The net profit is 7% of the selling cost; thus it is equal to

$$7\% \times \$25 = .07 \times \$25 = \$1.75.$$

The operating expenses are 39% of the selling price, thus equal to

$$39\% \times \$25 = .30 \times \$25 = \$9.75.$$

$1.75	net profit
+ $9.75	operating expenses
$11.50	gross profit

Drill 7: Profit

1. An item cost a store owner $50. She marked it up 40% and advertised it at that price. How much profit did she make if she later sold it at 15% off the advertised price?

    (A) $7.50   (B) $9.50

    (C) $10.50   (D) $39.50

    (E) $50

2. An antique dealer made a profit of 115% on the sale of an oak desk. If the desk cost her $200, how much profit did she make on the sale?

(A) $230   (B) $315

(C) $430   (D) $445

(E) $475

3. As a graduation gift, a young man was given 100 shares of stock worth $27.50 apiece. Within a year the price of the stock had risen by 8%. How much more were the stocks worth at the end of the first year than when they were given to the young man?

(A) $110   (B) $220

(C) $1,220   (D) $2,750

(E) $2,970

8. RATIOS AND PROPORTIONS

The ratio of two numbers x and y written $x:y$ is the fraction x/y where $y \neq 0$. A ratio compares x to y by dividing one by the other. Therefore, in order to compare ratios, simply compare the fractions.

A proportion is an equality of two ratios. The laws of proportion are listed below:

If $a/b = c/d$, then

(A) $ad = bc$

(B) $b/a = d/c$

(C) $a/c = b/d$

(D) $(a + b)/b = (c + d)/d$

(E) $(a - b)/b = (c - d)/d$

Given a proportion $a:b = c:d$, then a and d are called extremes, b and c are called the means, and d is called the fourth proportion to a, b, and c.

PROBLEM

Solve the proportion $\dfrac{x+1}{4} = \dfrac{15}{12}$.

Solution

Cross multiply to determine x; that is, multiply the numerator of the first fraction by the denominator of the second, and equate this to the product of the numerator of the second and the denominator of the first.

$$(x + 1)12 = 4 \times 15$$

$$12x + 12 = 60$$

$$x = 4$$

PROBLEM

If a car gets 24 miles per gallon of gasoline, how many gallons of gasoline are needed for a trip of 252 miles?

Solution

Given the car uses 1 gallon : 24 miles, let x = number of gallons of gas needed. Set up the proportion

$$\frac{1 \text{ gallon}}{24 \text{ miles}} = \frac{x}{252 \text{ miles}}.$$

Cross multiply to determine x.

$$252 = 24x$$

$$x = 10.5 \text{ gallons}$$

PROBLEM

U is inversely proportional with V. If U is 8 when V is 6, how much will U be if V is 24?

Solution

Given that

$$U = \frac{K}{V}, \quad K = \text{constant}$$

$$8 = \frac{K}{6}$$

$$K = 48$$

To find the value of U put in the values of K and V.

$$U = \frac{48}{24}$$

$$U = 2$$

Note: Since U is *inversely proportional* to V, as V increases U decreases.

Drill 8: Ratios and Proportions

1. Four out of every five students at West High take a mathematics course. If the enrollment at West High is 785, how many students take mathematics?

   (A) 628   (B) 157

   (C) 705   (D) 655

   (E) 247

2. A summer league softball team won 28 out of the 32 games they played. What is the ratio of games won to games played?

   (A) 4:5   (B) 3:4

   (C) 7:8   (D) 2:3

   (E) 1:8

3. A class of 24 students contains 16 males. What is the ratio of females to males?

   (A) 1:2   (B) 2:1

   (C) 2:3   (D) 3:1

   (E) 3:2

9. GEOMETRY

PROBLEM

A boy knows that his height is 6 ft. and his shadow is 4 ft. long. At the same time of day, a tree's shadow is 24 ft. long. How high is the tree? (See following figure.)

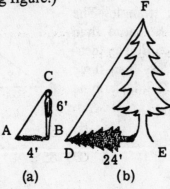

(a) (b)

Solution

Show that $\triangle ABC \sim \triangle DEF$, and then set up a proportion between the known sides AB and DE, and the sides BC and EF.

First, assume that both the boy and the tree are $\perp$ to the earth. Then, $BC \perp BA$ and $EF \perp E\Delta$. Hence,

$\angle ABC \cong \angle DEF$.

Since it is the same time of day, the rays of light from the sun are incident on both the tree and the boy at the same angle, relative to the earth's surface. Therefore,

$\angle BAC \cong \angle EDF$.

We have shown, so far, that 2 pairs of corresponding angles are congruent. Since the sum of the angles of any triangle is 180°, the third pair of corresponding angles is congruent (i.e., $\angle ACB \cong \angle DFE$). By the Angle Angle Angle (A.A.A.) Theorem

$\angle ABC \sim \angle DEF$.

By definition of similarity,

$$\frac{FE}{CB} = \frac{ED}{BA}.$$

$CB = 6'$, $ED = 24'$, and $BA = 4'$. Therefore,

$$FE = (6') (24'/4') = 36'.$$

Drill 9: Geometry

1. $\triangle PQR$ is a scalene triangle. The measure of $\angle P$ is 8° more than twice the measure of $\angle R$. The measure of $\angle Q$ is two less than three times the measure of $\angle R$. Determine the measure of $\angle Q$.

    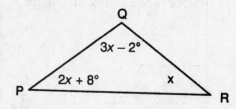

    (A) 29°   (B) 53°

    (C) 60°   (D) 85°

    (E) 174°

2. Angle A and angle B are supplementary. The measure of angle B is 50 more than four times the measure of angle A. Find the measure of angle B.

    (A) 35°   (B) 125°

    (C) 140°   (D) 145°

    (E) 155°

3. Triangle RUS is isosceles with base $\overline{SU}$. Each leg is 3 less than 5 times the length of the base. If the perimeter of the triangle is 60 cm, find the length of a leg.

    (A) 6   (B) 12

    (C) 27   (D) 30

    (E) 33

4. A glass is 4 inches in diameter and 6 inches tall. If the glass is $1/4$ full, how much more liquid is needed to fill the glass?

    (A) 6π (B) 12π

    (C) 18π (D) 20π

    (E) 24π

10. AVERAGES

Mean

The mean is the arithmetic average. It is the sum of the variables divided by the total number of variables. For example:

$$\frac{4+3+8}{3} = 5.$$

PROBLEM

Find the mean salary for four company employees who make $5/hr, $8/hr, $12/hr, and $15/hr.

Solution

The mean salary range is the average.

$$\frac{\$5 + \$8 + \$12 + \$15}{4} = \frac{\$40}{4} = \$10/hr$$

PROBLEM

Find the mean length of five fish with lengths of 7.5 in, 7.75 in, 8.5 in, 8.5 in, and 8.25 in.

Solution

The mean length is the average length.

$$\frac{7.5 + 7.75 + 8.5 + 8.5 + 8.25}{5} = \frac{40.5}{5} = 8.1 \text{ in}$$

Drill 10: Averages

1. The heights of four boys on a little league team are 97 cm, 102 cm, 116 cm, and 137 cm. What is the average height of the players?

    (A) 40 cm (B) 102 cm

    (C) 109 cm (D) 113 cm

    (E) 116 cm

2. Three people apply to work at summer camp. Their ages are 18, 25, and 32. What is the average age of the applicants?

    (A) 3 (B) 25

    (C) 50 (D) 75

    (E) 150

3. Sam received the following grades on his geometry tests: 85, 90, 94, and 82. He took one more test. What did he get if his final average was 88?

    (A) 87.75 (B) 87.8

    (C) 88 (D) 89

    (E) 70.2

11. DATA INTERPRETATION

Some of the problems test ability to apply information given in graphs and tables.

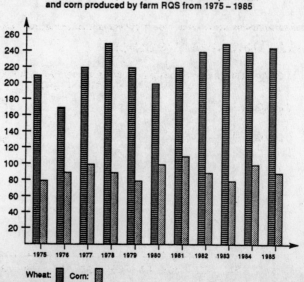

Number of bushels (to the nearest 5 bushels) of wheat and corn produced by farm RQS from 1975 – 1985

Wheat: ▐ Corn: ▐

PROBLEM

In which year was the least number of bushels of wheat produced? (See figure on previous page.)

Solution

By inspection of the graph, we find that the shortest bar representing wheat production is the one representing the wheat production for 1976. Thus, the least number of bushels of wheat was produced in 1976.

PROBLEM

What was the ratio of wheat production in 1985 to that of 1975?

Solution

From the graph representing wheat production, the number of bushels of wheat produced in 1975 is equal to 210 bushels. This number can be found by locating the bar on the graph representing wheat production in 1975 and then drawing a horizontal line from the top of that bar to the vertical axis. The point where this horizontal line meets the vertical axis represents the number of bushels of wheat produced in 1975. This number on the vertical axis is 210. Similarly, the graph indicates that the number of bushels of wheat produced in 1985 is equal to 245 bushels.

Thus, the ratio of wheat production in 1985 to that of 1975 is 245 to 210, which can be written as $245/210$. Simplifying this ratio to its simplest form yields

$$\frac{245}{210} = \frac{5 \times 7 \times 7}{2 \times 3 \times 5 \times 7} = \frac{7}{2 \times 3} = \frac{7}{6} \text{ or } 7{:}6.$$

Drill 11: Data Interpretation

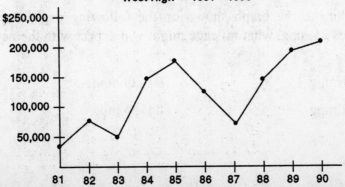

Amount of Scholarship Money Awarded to Graduating Seniors
West High — 1981 – 1990

1. What was the approximate amount of scholarship money awarded in 1985?

    (A) $150,000   (B) $155,000

    (C) $165,000   (D) $175,000

    (E) $190,000

2. By how much did the scholarship money increase between 1987 and 1988?

    (A) $25,000   (B) $30,000

    (C) $50,000   (D) $55,000

    (E) $75,000

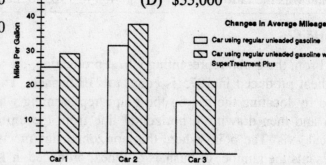

3. By how much did the mileage increase for Car 2 when the new product was used?

    (A) 5 mpg   (B) 6 mpg

    (C) 7 mpg   (D) 10 mpg

    (E) 12 mpg

4. Which car's mileage increased the most in this test?

    (A) Car 1   (B) Car 2

    (C) Car 3   (D) Cars 1 and 2

    (E) Cars 2 and 3

5. According to the graph shown on the following page, if your car averages 25 mpg, what mileage might you expect with the new product?

    (A) 21 mpg   (B) 29 mpg

    (C) 31 mpg   (D) 35 mpg

    (E) 37 mpg

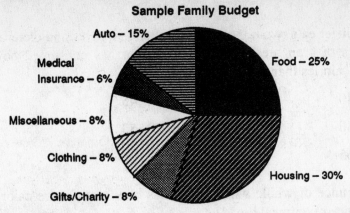

Sample Family Budget

6. Using the budget shown, a family with an income of $1,500 a month would plan to spend what amount on housing?

(A) $300   (B) $375

(C) $450   (D) $490

(E) $520

7. In this sample family budget, how does the amount spent on an automobile compare to the amount spent on housing?

(A) $1/3$ (B) $1/2$

(C) $2/3$ (D) $1^{1}/2$

(E) 2

8. A family with a monthly income of $1,240 spends $125 a month on clothing. By what amount do they exceed the sample budget?

(A) $1.00   (B) $5.20

(C) $10.00   (D) $25.80

(E) $31.75

CALORIE CHART — BREADS

Bread	Amount	Calories
French Bread	2 oz	140
Bran Bread	1 oz	95
Whole Wheat Bread	1 oz	115
Oatmeal Bread	0.5 oz	55
Raisin Bread	1 oz	125

9. One dieter eats two ounces of French bread. A second dieter eats two ounces of bran bread. The second dieter has consumed how many more calories than the first dieter?

(A) 40   (B) 45

(C) 50   (D) 55

(E) 65

10. One ounce of whole wheat bread has how many more calories than an ounce of oatmeal bread?

(A) 5   (B) 15

(C) 60   (D) 75

(E) 125

WORD PROBLEM DRILLS

ANSWER KEY

Drill 1 – Algebraic
1. (D) 2. (A) 3. (B)

Drill 2 – Rate
1. (C) 2. (E) 3. (A)

Drill 3 – Work
1. (B) 2. (D) 3. (D)

Drill 4 – Mixture
1. (C) 2. (D) 3. (D)

Drill 5 – Interest
1. (E) 2. (C) 3. (B)

Drill 6 – Discount
1. (D) 2. (E) 3. (B)

Drill 7 – Profit
1. (B) 2. (A) 3. (B)

Drill 8 – Ratios and Proportions
1. (A) 2. (C) 3. (A)

Drill 9 – Geometry
1. (D) 2. (D) 3. (C) 4. (C)

Drill 10 – Averages
1. (D) 2. (B) 3. (D)

Drill 11 – Data Interpretation
1. (D) 4. (E) 7. (B) 10. (A)
2. (E) 5. (B) 8. (D)
3. (B) 6. (C) 9. (C)

DETAILED EXPLANATIONS OF ANSWERS

WORD PROBLEMS REVIEW

Drill 1 – Algebraic

1. **(D)** Let x and y represent the two numbers. Since their sum is 41, one equation is $x + y = 41$.

Then if one of the two numbers, say x, is one less than twice the other, the second equation can be written $x = 2y - 1$.

So the two equations are

$$x + y = 41$$

and $\quad x = 2y - 1.$

Solve the first equation for x:

$$x = 41 - y.$$

Substitute $(41 - y)$ for x in the second equation:

$$41 - y = 2y - 1.$$

Solve for y:

$$41 - y = 2y - 1$$
$$42 - y = 2y$$
$$42 = 3y$$
$$14 = y$$

Then if $y = 14$ and $x + y = 41$, $x = 27$.

Check: $\quad 27 + 14 = 41 \qquad 27 = 2(14) - 1$

$\qquad\qquad\quad 41 = 41 \qquad\quad 27 = 28 - 1$

$\qquad\qquad\qquad\qquad\qquad\quad 27 = 27$

2.   (A) If a represents the smaller integer, then its consecutive integer is represented by $a + 1$. So the first equation becomes

$$a + (a + 1) = 111.$$

Three times the larger integer is $3(a + 1)$ while two times the smaller integer is $2a$. "Less" indicates subtraction, so the second equation becomes

$$3(a + 1) - 2a = 58.$$

Solve this equation for a:

$$3(a + 1) - 2a = 58$$

$$3a + 3 - 2a = 58$$

$$a + 3 = 58$$

$$a = 55$$

Since a represented the smaller integer, we have answered the question.

Check: $55 + (55 + 1) = 111$ $3(55 + 1) - 2(55) = 58$

$\qquad\qquad\quad 55 + 56 = 111$ $168 - 110 = 58$

$\qquad\qquad\qquad\quad 111 = 111$ $58 = 58$

3.   (B) Let X and Y represent two integers.

"Difference" indicates subtraction, so the first equation can be written as $X - Y = 12$.

"Sum" indicates addition, so the second equation is $X + Y = 2$.

Solve these two equations simultaneously by adding them together. (The Y's are eliminated.)

$$X - Y = 12$$

$$\underline{X + Y = 2}$$

$$2X = 14$$

Solve for X by dividing both sides by 2.

$$X = 7$$

Then substitute X into either one of the two original equations to find Y.

$$7 - Y = 12$$

$$-Y = 5$$

$$Y = -5$$

Check: $7 - (-5) = 12$ $7 + (-5) = 2$

           $7 + 5 = 12$ $2 = 2$

           $12 = 12$

Drill 2 – Rate

1.   (C)   For a problem such as this, a diagram, a chart, and the formula $D = RT$ are helpful.

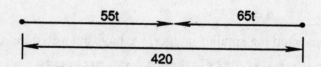

As the diagram indicates, this is an addition problem. The distance covered by the first car must be added to the distance covered by the second car to obtain the distance between the two cities.

The chart uses the three parts of the equation $D = RT$. Since the time is the unknown in this problem, it is represented by t.

Car	Rate	Time	Distance
1	55	t	$55t$
2	65	t	$65t$

Now add together the two distances from the chart and set them equal to the total distance.

$$55t + 65t = 420$$

Solve for t $120t = 420$

                      $t = 3.5$ hr

Check: $55(3.5) + 65(3.5) = 420$

             $192.5 + 227.5 = 420$

                  $420 = 420$

2.   (E)   A diagram, a chart, and the formula $D = RT$ are used to solve this problem.

Let x represent the walking rate of the second camper.

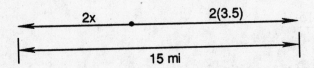

The diagram indicates that we need to add the two individual distances to equal the entire distance of 15 miles.

In the chart, we fill in the rate and the time for each camper. The formula $D = RT$ is used to find the value in the last column.

	Rate	Time	Distance
1st	3.5	2	7
2nd	x	2	$2x$

Now add the two individual distances together and set them equal to the total distance:

$$7 + 2x = 15.$$

Solve for x:

$$7 + 2x = 15$$
$$2x = 8$$
$$x = 4 \text{ mph}$$

Check: $7 + 2(4) = 15$
$$7 + 8 = 15$$
$$15 = 15$$

3.   (A)   Let r = the initial average rate and let t = the initial time. Then since $D = RT$, $75 = rt$.

If the rate is increased by 5 mph, it would be written $r + 5$. If the time is reduced by $^3/_4$, it becomes $^3/_4 t$. Using the same formula, $D = RT$,

$$75 = (r + 5)\left(\frac{3}{4}t\right).$$

Use the distributive property in the second equation.

$$75 = (r + 5)\left(\frac{3}{4}t\right)$$

$$75 = \frac{3}{4}rt + \frac{15}{4}t$$

Multiply both sides of the equation by 4.

$$300 = 3rt + 15rt$$

Since the first equation is $rt = 75$, substitute 75 for the expression rt.

$$300 = 3(75) + 15t$$

Solve for t.

$$300 = 225 + 15t$$

$$75 = 15t$$

$$5 = t$$

Since the problem asked for the rate, use t to find r.

$$rt = 75$$

$$r(5) = 75$$

$$r = 15 \text{ mph}$$

Check: $15(5) = 75$ $(15 + 5) \times {}^3/_4 (5) = 75$

$75 = 75$ $20 \times 3.75 = 75$

$75 = 75$

Drill 3 – Work

1.   **(B)** To solve this problem, decide on a convenient unit of time —
here the hour is the easiest choice. Next, write the amount of work that
each person can do in that amount of time (this is the *rate* of work).

In one hour, Marty can do $1/3$ of the job.

In one hour, Pat can do

$$\frac{1}{2\frac{1}{4}} \quad \text{or} \quad \frac{1}{\frac{9}{4}} \quad \text{or} \quad \frac{4}{9}$$

of the job.

The unknown in this problem is the amount of time it will take the two working together — call this unknown x. Then multiply each person's rate of work by the amount of time spent working together to obtain the portion of the total job each person did. Marty did $x/3$ and Pat did $4x/9$ of the work.

Then add each person's part of the work together and set it equal to 1; this represents one completed task. Now the equation looks like this:

$$\frac{x}{3} + \frac{4x}{9} = 1.$$

Find the Least Common Denominator (LCD) and multiply both sides of the equation by the LCD.

$$9\left(\frac{x}{3} + \frac{4x}{9}\right) = (1)(9)$$
$$3x + 4x = 9$$
$$7x = 9$$
$$x = \frac{9}{7} \text{ hr} \quad \text{or} \quad 1\frac{2}{7} \text{ hr}$$

2. **(D)** Let x represent the time it would take for the brother to mow the lawn alone.

Since Troy does the lawn in 3 hours, he does $1/3$ of the lawn in one hour. Since the brother takes x hours to mow the lawn, in one hour he does $1/x$ of the job. Both rates are multiplied by 2 since they complete the job in 2 hours.

	In One Hour	Time	Part of Job
Troy	$1/3$	2	$2/3$
Brother	$1/x$	2	$2/x$

Now add the part that each person does and set the sum equal to 1. The 1 represents one complete job.

$$2/3 + 2/x = 1$$

Multiply by the LCD of $3x$.

$$(^2/_3)(3x) + (^2/_x)(3x) = 1(3x)$$

$$2x + 6 = 3x$$

Solve for x.

$$6 = x$$

It would take the little brother 6 hours to mow the lawn by himself.

Check: $^2/_3 + ^2/_6 = 1$

 $^2/_3 + ^1/_3 = 1$

 $1 = 1$

3. **(D)** Let x represent the time to fill the tank.

Since it takes 15 minutes for the inlet pipe to fill the tank, in one minute it can fill $^1/_{15}$ of the tank. Since the outlet pipe drains the tank in 75 minutes, in one minute it can drain $^1/_{75}$ of the tank. The amount done in one minute is multiplied by the time to get the part of the job done in x minutes.

	In One Minute	Time	Part of Job
Inlet	$^1/_{15}$	x	$^x/_{15}$
Outlet	$^1/_{75}$	x	$^x/_{75}$

In setting up the equation, the part of the job done by the outlet pipe must be *subtracted* from that part done by the inlet pipe. The difference is set equal to one to represent one completed job.

The equation is

$$\frac{x}{15} - \frac{x}{75} = 1.$$

Multiply by the LCD, 75.

$$(75)\frac{x}{15} - (75)\frac{x}{75} = (75)1$$

$$5x - x = 75$$

$$4x = 75$$

$$x = 18\frac{3}{4} \text{ minutes}$$

Check: $\dfrac{18.75}{15} - \dfrac{18.75}{75} = 1$

$1.25 - 0.25 = 1$

$1 = 1$

Drill 4 – Mixture

1.   **(C)**   For each solution, fill in the chart with the amount of the solution, the percent of alcohol it contains, and the amount of alcohol it contains.

Solution	Amount of Solution	% of Alcohol	Amount of Alcohol
1st	x	.20	$.20x$
2nd	80	.50	$.50(80)$
mix	$(x + 80)$	.45	$.45(x + 80)$

Since we don't know how much of the first solution there is, the amount of the first solution is represented by x.

Add the first two amounts of alcohol together and set the sum equal to the amount of alcohol in the mixture. Solve the equation for x.

$$.20x + .50(80) = .45(x + 80)$$

$$.20x + 40 = .45x + 36$$

$$4 = .25x$$

$$x = 16$$

So 16 liters of the 20% alcohol solution must be added to the 50% solution.

Check: $.20(16) + .50(80) = .45(16 + 80)$

$3.2 + 40 = .45(96)$

$43.2 = 43.2$

2.   **(D)**   Fill in the chart with the amount of each solution, the percent of salt each solution is, and the amount of salt contained in each solution. Let x represent the amount of water to be evaporated.

Solution	Amount	%	Amount of Salt
Original	50	0.10	0.10(50)
Water	x	0	0
New Sol.	$(50-x)$	0.15	$0.15(50-x)$

The amount of salt in the original solution less the amount of salt in the water evaporated (which is 0) equals the amount of salt in the new solution.

$$0.10(50) - 0 = 0.15(50-x)$$

Solve for x.

$$5 - 0 = 7.5 - 0.15x$$

$$-2.5 = -0.15x$$

$$16^2/_3 = x$$

$$16.\overline{66} = x$$

Sixteen and two-thirds kilograms of water must be evaporated from the original solution.

Check: $5 = 7.5 - 0.15(16^2/_3)$

$$5 = 7.5 - \frac{15}{100} \times \frac{50}{3}$$

$$5 = 7.5 - 2.5$$

$$5 = 5$$

3.   (D)   Fill the chart in with the amount of each coffee, the price per pound of each coffee, and the total price.

Since the amount of the mixture is the unknown, call it x.

Coffee	Amount	Price/lb	Total Price
A	1.5	3.00	3(1.5)
B	2.5	4.20	2.5(4.2)
mix	(1.5 + 2.5)	x	x(1.5 + 2.5)

Add the total prices of the two coffees together and set the sum equal to the total price of the mixture. Solve for x.

$$3(1.5) + 2.5(4.2) = x(1.5 + 2.5)$$

$$4.5 + 10.50 = 4x$$

$$15 = 4x$$

$$3.75 = x$$

The cost of the mixture is $3.75 per pound.

Check: $3(1.5) + 2.5(4.2) = (2.5 + 1.5)(3.75)$

$$4.5 + 10.50 = 4(3.75)$$

$$15 = 15$$

Drill 5 – Interest

1.   (E)   Let x = the amount invested at 8%. Then, since the total amount is $3,000, the remaining part is $(3,000 - x)$.

Multiply the amount invested by the % of interest and add these two amounts together to equal the total interest.

$$0.08x + 0.07(3,000 - x) = 220$$

$$0.08x + 210 - 0.07x = 220$$

$$0.01x = 10$$

$$x = 1,000$$

$$3,000 - x = 2,000$$

The amount invested in bonds is $2,000.

Check: $0.08(1,000) + 0.07(2,000) = 220$

$$80 + 140 = 220$$

$$220 = 220$$

2.   (C)   Let x = the amount invested at 11%.

Let $4x$ = the amount invested at 7.5%.

Multiply the amount invested by the interest rate to determine the individual interest. Add these two individual interests together and set the sum equal to the total interest.

$$0.11x + 0.075(4x) = \$1,025$$
$$0.11x + 0.3x = 1,025$$
$$0.41x = 1,025$$
$$x = \$2,500$$

$2,500 was invested at 11%.

Check: $0.11(2,500) + 0.075(4 \times 2,500) = 1,025$
$$275 + 750 = 1,025$$
$$1,025 = 1,025$$

3.   **(B)**   Use the simple interest formula, $I = PRT$, to find the interest earned on each account.

Bank: $I = \$1,500 \times 0.065 \times 3 = \$292.50$

Credit Union: $I = \$1,500 \times 0.072 \times 3 = \$324$

Subtract the amounts of interest to see how much more you would earn by keeping the money in the credit union.

$$\$324 - \$292.50 = \$31.50$$

Drill 6 – Discount

1.   **(D)**   Let x be the original price of the coat.

The original price minus 20% of the original price equals $156.

Or, $x - 0.20(x) = 156.$

Or, $1.0(x) - 0.20(x) = 156.$

Or, $0.80(x) = 156$

so $x = 156/0.80 = 195.$

The coat originally cost $195.

Check: $195 - 0.20(195) = 156$
$$195 - 39 = 156$$
$$156 = 156$$

2. (E) If x = the original price of the sofa, then $0.30x$ = the amount saved, which was $225.

So, $0.30x = 225$.

Then $x = 225/0.30 = \$750$.

   The original price of the sofa was $750.

Check: $0.30(750) = 225$

                      $225 = 225$

3. (B) A good technique to use in this problem is the formula

$$\frac{\text{Percentage}}{\text{Base}} = \frac{\text{Rate}}{100}.$$

In this problem you are asked for the percent of discount which is the same as the rate — call it r.

   The percentage or discount is $9.66 and the base, or total amount, is $276.

   The equation becomes

$$\frac{9.66}{276} = \frac{r}{100}.$$

Use cross multiplication to solve.

$$9.66(100) = 276r \text{ so } r = \frac{966}{276} = 3.5.$$

The percent of discount is 3.5%.

Drill 7 – Profit

1. (B) The profit is the sale price less the initial cost. The initial cost was $50. The sale price is 15% off the advertised price.

   The advertised price is marked up 40% over the initial price — or $50 + 0.40(\$50)$. This advertised price is $70.

   Then the sale price is the advertised price less 15% of the advertised price, or $\$70 - 0.15(70)$, or $59.50.

   Finally, the profit is $\$59.50 - 50 = \$9.50$.

2. **(A)** The profit is 115% of the initial cost of the desk.

$P = 1.15(\$200) = \$230.$

3. **(B)** The profit on the stocks is the new value less the original value.

Original value = $\$27.50 \times 100 = \$2,750$

New value = $\$2,750 + 0.08(\$2,750) = \$2,970$

Profit = $\$2,970 - \$2,750 = \$220$

Drill 8 – Ratios and Proportions

1. **(A)** Let x be the number of students who take mathematics at West High. We know 4:5 take a mathematics course. Set up a ratio as follows:

$$4:5 = x:785$$

$$\frac{4}{5} = \frac{x}{785}$$

$$x = \frac{4}{5}(785)$$

$$x = 628$$

2. **(C)** Given the team won 28 games and played 32 games. Therefore, the ratio of games won to games played is

28:32.

Reduce by dividing by 4.

7:8

3. **(A)** To find the ratio of females to males, find how many females are in the class.

Total students – males = females

$24 - 16 = $ females

$8 = $ females

Set up ratio

females:males

8:16

Reduce by dividing both sides by 8.

1:2

Drill 9: Geometry

1. **(D)** Draw a sketch of the triangle and label the angles.

Two of the angles are compared to $\angle R$, so let $x =$ the measure of $\angle R$. Then

$$\angle P = 2x + 8 \text{ and } \angle Q = 3x - 2.$$

The sum of the measures of the angles of a triangle is 180°, so add the measures of all three angles and this will equal 180°.

$$x + (2x + 8) + (3x - 2) = 180°$$

$$6x + 6 = 180°$$

$$6x = 174°$$

$$x = 29°$$

The measure of $\angle R$ is 29° and the measure of $\angle Q$ is $3(29°) - 2°$ or 85°.

Check: $29° + [2(29°) + 8°] + [3(29°) - 2°] = 180°$

$$29° + 66° + 85° = 180°$$

$$180° = 180°$$

2. **(D)** Let $A =$ the measure of angle A and let $B =$ the measure of angle B. Since the two angles are supplementary, one equation is

$$A + B = 180°.$$

Since B is 5 more than four times the measure of angle A, either subtract 5 from the measure of angle B or add 5 to four times the measure of angle A. The equation becomes

$$B = 4A + 5.$$

Now substitute the value of B into the first equation to get

$$A + (4A + 5) = 180°.$$

Solve the equation for A:

$$5A + 5 = 180°$$

$$5A = 175°$$

$$A = 35°$$

Then $B = 4(35°) + 5° = 145°$.

Check: $35° + 145° = 180°$ $145° = 4(35°) + 5°$

$$180° = 180°$$ $$145° = 145°$$

3.   (C)   Draw an isosceles triangle and label each side. Let the length of the base be x. Then each leg is five times the base less 3, or $5x - 3$.

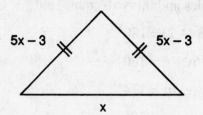

The perimeter is the sum of the sides, so the equation becomes

$$x + (5x - 3) + (5x - 3) = 60.$$

Solve for x:

$$11x - 6 = 60$$

$$11x = 66$$

$$x = 6$$

and $5(6) - 3 = 27$.

The length of each leg is 27.

Check: $6 + 27 + 27 = 60$

$$60 = 60$$

4.   **(C)**   To find the volume of a cylinder, use the formula

$$v = \pi r^2 h$$

r = radius

h = height

$$v = \pi(2)^2(6)$$

$$= 24\pi$$

The glass is $^1/_4$ full already, therefore to fill the glass you need to know what $^3/_4$ of the volume of the glass is,

$$= {}^3/_4\,(24\pi)$$

$$= 18\pi$$

Drill 10 – Averages

1.   **(D)**   To find the average height add the heights and divide by the number of boys. Average height of the boys

$$= \frac{97 + 102 + 116 + 137}{4} = \frac{452}{4} = 113 \text{ cm}.$$

2.   **(B)**   The average age is the total of the ages divided by the number of applicants. Average age of the applicants

$$= \frac{18 + 25 + 32}{3} = \frac{75}{3} = 25.$$

3.   **(D)**   To find the grade on the last test let t = the test grade.

$$\frac{85 + 90 + 94 + 82 + t}{5} = 88$$

$$\frac{351 + t}{5} = 88$$

$$351 + t = 88(5)$$

$$t = 440 - 351$$

$$t = 89$$

Drill 11 – Data Interpretation

1. **(D)** From the graph, you can see that in 1985 the amount of scholarship money is half-way between $150,000 and $200,000.

2. **(E)** To find the increase in scholarship money from 1987 to 1988, locate the amount for 1987 and 1988. In 1987 the amount of scholarship money is half-way between $50,000 and $100,000 or $75,000. In 1988 the amount of scholarship money is $150,000. The increase is $150,000 – $75,000 = $75.000.

3. **(B)** The mileage for car 2 using the old product is 32 mpg from the bar graph. Using the new product the amount increases to 38 mpg. The amount of increase is 38 mpg – 32 mpg = 6 mpg.

4. **(E)** By looking at the bar graph one can see that car 1 increases by 4 mpg, car 2 increases by 6 mpg and car 3 increases by 6 mpg. Therefore the greatest increase is for car 2 and car 3.

5. **(B)** By looking at the bar graph notice that if your car averages 25 mpg, it is like car 1. With the new product car 1 averages 29 mpg.

6. **(C)** To find the amount spent on housing locate on the pie chart the percentage allotted to housing, or 30%. 30% of $1,500 = $450.

7. **(B)** From the pie chart, the amount spent on automobile equals 15% and the amount spent on housing equals 30%. Therefore the amount spent on automobile/amount on housing equals 15%/30% or $1/2$.

8. **(D)** From the pie chart locate the amount of the budget for clothing or 8%. Eight percent of $1,240 = $99.20. The amount over the budget amount is $125 – $99.20 = $25.80.

9.   (C)   From the calorie chart dieter one who eats two ounces of French bread consumes 140 calories. From the calorie chart, dieter two who eats two ounces of bran bread eats 2 × 95 calories or 190 calories. The difference is 190 – 140 equals 50 calories.

10.   (A)   From the calorie chart locate whole wheat bread which has 115 calories per 1 oz. Oatmeal bread has 55 calories per 0.5 oz. The question was to compare 1 oz. of each type of bread. There are 2 (55 calories) = 110 in 1 oz. of oatmeal bread. There are 115 – 110 = 5 more calories in the whole wheat bread.

ELM
Entry Level Mathematics

Test 1

ELM
TEST 1

Time: 75 Minutes
   65 Questions (including 5 field test questions)

   (Answer sheets appear at the back of the book.)

> **DIRECTIONS:** Solve each problem and select the letter corresponding to the best choice to answer the question.

1. What is the area of the shaded portion of the rectangle? The heavy dot represents the center of the semicircle.

   (A) $200 - 100\pi$

   (B) $200 - 25\pi$

   (C) $30 - \dfrac{25\pi}{2}$

   (D) $\dfrac{200 - 25\pi}{2}$

   (E) $\dfrac{400 - 25\pi}{2}$

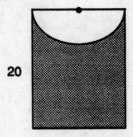

   20

   10

2. If the weight of a mass of 10 g stretches a spring 5 cm, how far will a weight of a mass 4 g stretch it?

   (A) 1 cm   (B) 2 cm

   (C) 4 cm   (D) 5 cm

   (E) 8 cm

3. $(x + 1)(3x + 4) =$

    (A) $3x^2 + 5$ (B) $3x^2 + 4$

    (C) $3x^2 - 7x - 4$ (D) $3x^2 - 7x + 5$

    (E) $3x^2 + 7x + 4$

4. The box pictured has a square base with side x and a closed top. The surface area of the box is

    (A) $4x + h.$

    (B) $4x + 4h.$

    (C) $hx^2.$

    (D) $x^2 + 4xh.$

    (E) $2x^2 + 4xh.$

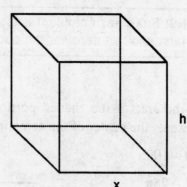

5. $\dfrac{\dfrac{1}{x} - \dfrac{1}{y}}{\dfrac{1}{x^2} - \dfrac{1}{y^2}} =$

    (A) $\dfrac{x^2 y^2}{x^2 + y^2}$ (B) $\dfrac{xy}{x + y}$

    (C) $\dfrac{xy}{(x + y)^2}$ (D) $\dfrac{xy}{y^2 - x^2}$

    (E) $\left(\dfrac{xy}{x + y}\right)^2$

6. What is t equal to if $A = P(1 + rt)$?

    (A) $A - P - Pr$ (B) $(A + P)/Pr$

    (C) $A/P - r$ (D) $(A - P)/Pr$

    (E) None of these

7. Fifteen percent of what number is 60?

    (A) 9   (B) 51

    (C) 69   (D) 200

    (E) 400

Use the following graph for Problems 8, 9, and 10.

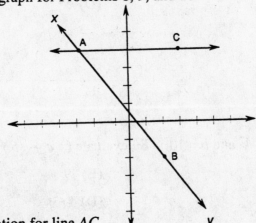

8. Find the equation for line *AC*.

    (A) $x = 4$ (B) $y = 4$

    (C) $x + y = 4$ (D) $x - y = 4$

    (E) Not enough information

9. What is the midpoint of segment *AB*?

    (A) $(-1, 2)$ (B) $(0, 0)$

    (C) $(-1/2, 1)$ (D) $(-1, 1/2)$

    (E) $(-1, -1/2)$

10. What is the slope of line *AB*?

    (A) $-2/5$ (B) $-5/2$

    (C) $5/6$ (D) $-6/5$

    (E) $-8/5$

11. Simplify $\left(\dfrac{x^2}{y}\right)^5$.

(A) $\dfrac{x^2}{y^5}$

(B) $\dfrac{x^7}{y}$

(C) $\dfrac{x^7}{y^5}$

(D) x^8

(E) $\dfrac{x^{10}}{y^5}$

12. If $a = 5^2 - 4^2$ and $b = 10^2 - 8^2$, evaluate $(\sqrt{a} - \sqrt{b})^2$.

(A) -27

(B) 9

(C) 1

(D) -3

(E) 729

13. What number must be added to 28 and 36 to get an average of 29?

(A) 23

(B) 32

(C) 21

(D) 4

(E) 5

14. If the radius of a sphere is increased by a factor of 3, then the volume of the sphere is increased by a factor of

(A) 3.

(B) 6.

(C) 9.

(D) 18.

(E) 27.

15. What is the sum of the roots in the equation $(4x - 3)^2 = 4$?

    (A) $2\frac{1}{2}$ (B) $\frac{1}{2}$

    (C) $1\frac{1}{2}$ (D) 3

    (E) $\frac{6}{5}$

16. In the figure shown (not drawn to scale) the line l and m are parallel. Then $x =$

    (A) $140°$.

    (B) $120°$.

    (C) $70°$.

    (D) $50°$.

    (E) $40°$.

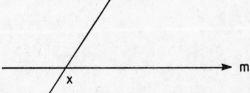

17. $\dfrac{(x^2)^{-4}(x^{-2})^3}{(x^{-3})^{-5}} =$

    (A) x^5 (B) $\dfrac{1}{x^{14}}$

    (C) $\dfrac{1}{x^{29}}$ (D) x^7

    (E) x^{29}

18. What is the product of $(\sqrt{3} + 6)$ and $(\sqrt{3} - 2)$?

    (A) $9 + 4\sqrt{3}$ (B) -9

    (C) $-9 + 4\sqrt{3}$ (D) $-9 + 2\sqrt{3}$

    (E) 9

19. If $x - (4x - 8) + 9 + (6x - 8) = 9 - x + 24$, then $x =$

    (A) 4.   (B) 2.

    (C) 8.   (D) 6.

    (E) 10.

20. Simplify $\dfrac{\frac{x-1}{x+2}}{\frac{x-x^2}{x^2+2x}}$.

    (A) -2 (B) -1

    (C) 1 (D) $\dfrac{x-1}{x+1}$

    (E) $\dfrac{x}{x+2}$

21. $\dfrac{1-\frac{1}{1-x}}{1-\frac{1}{1-\frac{1}{x}}} =$

    (A) x (B) $^1/_x$

    (C) $-^1/_x$ (D) $-x$

    (E) 1

22. Which of the following figures has exactly two lines of symmetry?

    (A) A trapezoid which is not a parallelogram

    (B) A parallelogram which is not a rectangle

    (C) A rectangle which is not a square

    (D) A square

    (E) An equilateral triangle

23. Simplify $\dfrac{5+3i}{2-i}$.

    (A) $7 + 11i$ (B) $\dfrac{7+11i}{3}$

    (C) $\dfrac{7+11i}{5}$ (D) $\dfrac{13+11i}{3}$

    (E) $\dfrac{13+11i}{5}$

24. A teacher earns \$25,000 a year and receives a 4% cost of living increase in salary, and a \$275 merit increase. His salary increased by

    (A) 4.5%.   (B) 4.9%.

    (C) 5.0%.   (D) 5.1%.

    (E) 5.2%.

25. Evaluate the expression $x^2 + 2x - y + 3$ when $x = -2$ and $y = 3$.

    (A) -5 (B) 3

    (C) 0 (D) -3

    (E) 5

26. The expression $(x + y)^2 + (x - y)^2$ is equivalent to

    (A) $2x^2$.   (B) $4x^2$.

    (C) $2(x^2 + y^2)$.   (D) $2x^2 + y^2$.

    (E) $x^2 + 2y^2$.

27. Four less than 3 times x is greater than 6. Find all values of x.

    (A) $x < {}^{10}/_3$ (B) $x > {}^{10}/_3$

    (C) $x < 5$ (D) $x > {}^2/_3$

    (E) $x > 8$

28. What is the perimeter of triangle *ABC*?

(A) 12*R*

(B) 18*R²*

(C) 12*R²*

(D) 18*R*

(E) 16*R*

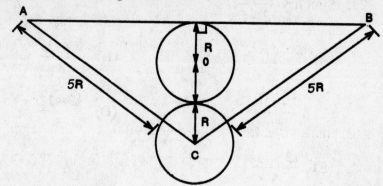

29. If $\dfrac{7a - 5b}{b} = 7$, then $\dfrac{4a + 6b}{2a} =$

(A) $^{15}/_4$.

(B) 4.

(C) $^{17}/_4$.

(D) 5.

(E) 6.

30. $^1/_4x + 3 = 15$. Find *x*.

(A) $15^1/_4$

(B) $12^1/_4$

(C) 3

(D) 12

(E) 48

31. $g(x) = x^2 + 4$, find $g(-3)$.

(A) − 3

(B) 4

(C) − 5

(D) 3

(E) 13

32. Simplify and express in factored form $6(x - 2) - 4(x + 4)$.

(A) $2(x + 1)$

(B) $2(x + 2)$

(C) $2(x + 7)$

(D) $2(x - 14)$

(E) $2(x - 8)$

33. If $x + 2y > 5$ and $x < 3$, then $y > 1$ is true
    (A) never.   (B) only if $x = 0$.
    (C) only if $x > 0$.   (D) only if $x < 0$.
    (E) always.

34. Factor $x^2 - 6x + 9$.
    (A) $x(x + 6)$ (B) $(x + 3)(x + 3)$
    (C) $(x - 3)^2$ (D) $(x + 3)^2$
    (E) $(x + 3)(x - 3)$

35. For any integer n, which of the following must be an even integer?
    I. $2n + 1$
    II. $2n + 2$
    III. $2n - 1$
    (A) I only   (B) II only
    (C) III only   (D) I and II only
    (E) II and III only

36. If $\sqrt{x - 1} = 2$, then $(x - 1)^2 =$
    (A) 4.   (B) 6.
    (C) 8.   (D) 10.
    (E) 16.

37. If $x + y = 8$ and $xy = 6$, then $\dfrac{1}{x} + \dfrac{1}{y} =$
    (A) $\frac{1}{8}$.   (B) $\frac{1}{6}$.
    (C) $\frac{1}{4}$.   (D) $\frac{4}{3}$.
    (E) 8.

38. If the hypotenuse of a right triangle is $x + 1$ and one of the legs is x, then the other leg is

   (A) $\sqrt{2x + 1}$.

   (B) $\sqrt{2x} + 1$.

   (C) $\sqrt{x^2 + (x - 1)^2}$.

   (D) 1.

   (E) $2x + 1$.

39. If a measurement of 2.25 inches on a map represents 50 miles, what distance does a measurement of 18 inches on the map represent?

   (A) 350 miles

   (B) 375 miles

   (C) 400 miles

   (D) 425 miles

   (E) 450 miles

40. The fraction $\dfrac{7x - 11}{x^2 - 2x - 15}$ was obtained by adding the two fractions $\dfrac{A}{x - 5} + \dfrac{B}{x + 3}$. The values of A and B are

   (A) $A = 7x, B = 11$.

   (B) $A = -11, B = 7x$.

   (C) $A = 3, B = 4$.

   (D) $A = 5, B = -3$.

   (E) $A = -5, B = 3$.

41. The number missing in the series 2, 6, 12, 20, x, 42, 56 is

   (A) 36.

   (B) 24.

   (C) 30.

   (D) 38.

   (E) 40.

42. If $2^x = \dfrac{16^2 \times 8^3}{2^{19}}$, then $x =$

   (A) -3.

   (B) -2.

(C) 1.

(D) 2.

(E) 3.

43. The diameter of an automobile tire is 24". How many revolutions does the tire make in traveling a mile? (1 mile = 5,280 feet.)

(A) $\dfrac{220}{\pi}$

(B) $2,640\pi$

(C) $\dfrac{2,640}{\pi}$

(D) $\dfrac{440}{\pi}$

(E) 440π

44. If $f(x) = x^2 + 3x + 2$, then $[f(x + a) - f(x)]/a =$

(A) $2x + a + 3$.

(B) $(x + a)^2 - x^2$.

(C) $a^2 + 2ax + 3a$.

(D) $2x + a$.

(E) $2x + 3$.

45. $m(\angle A) + m(\angle C) =$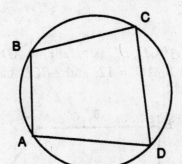

(A) $160°$

(B) $180°$

(C) $190°$

(D) $195°$

(E) $200°$

46. George is 4 years older than John, who is 4 years older than Jim, who is 4 years older than Sam, who is $^1/_2$ the age of George. How old is John?

(A) 24

(B) 8

(C) 16

(D) 20

(E) 12

47. Simplify $4x^4 \times x^6$.

   (A) $4x^{10}$

   (B) $4x^{24}$

   (C) $16x^{10}$

   (D) $24x^4$

   (E) x^{22}

48. If in $\triangle ABC$, $AB = BC$ and $\angle A = 46°$, then $\angle B =$

   (A) $46°$.

   (B) $92°$.

   (C) $88°$.

   (D) $56°$.

   (E) $23°$.

49. Laura went cruising in her motor boat. She cruised for 2 hours and 20 minutes and found she had traveled 21 nautical miles. What was her speed to the nearest knot? (One knot = one nautical mile in one hour.)

   (A) 7 knots

   (B) $2^1/_3$ knots

   (C) 21 knots

   (D) 9 knots

   (E) 49 knots

50. In quadrilateral $ABCD$, BC is parallel to AD and BA is perpendicular to AD. If $BC = 8$, $AD = 12$, and $ABCD$ has area equal to 30, then what is CD?

   (A) 3

   (B) 4

   (C) 5

   (D) 6

   (E) 25

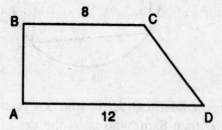

51. If $a^2 + 4 < 4a + 9$, then

   (A) $a < -1$.

   (B) $a > 5$.

(C) $a > -1$.   (D) $a < 5$.

(E) $-1 < a < 5$.

52. AB is perpendicular to BC. How many degrees are in $\angle ABD$?

(A) 90°

(B) 50°

(C) 45°

(D) 40°

(E) 100°

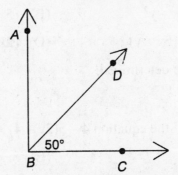

53. In the figure shown, $\triangle ABC$ is an equilateral triangle. Also, $AC = 3$ and $DB = BE = 1$. Find the perimeter of quadrilateral $ACED$.

(A) 6

(B) $6\frac{1}{2}$

(C) 7

(D) $7\frac{1}{2}$

(E) 8

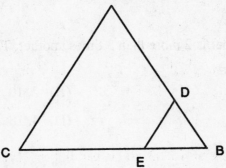

54. Joe and Jim together have 14 marbles. Jim and Tim together have 10 marbles. Joe and Tim together have 12 marbles. What is the maximum number of marbles that any one of them may have?

(A) 7   (B) 8

(C) 9   (D) 10

(E) 11

55. Reduce the following expression, where $a > b > 0$.

$$\left[\left(\sqrt{a+b} \right)^2 - \sqrt{(a-b)^2} \right]$$

(A) $2a$ (B) $2(a-b)$

(C) $2b$

(D) a

(E) b

56. Factor $10x^2 - 14xy + 5xy - 7y^2$.

(A) $10x^2 - 9xy - y^2$

(B) $(5x - 7y)(2x + y)$

(C) $(2x - 7y)(5x + y)$

(D) $(2x - 7y)(5x + 2y)$

(E) Cannot be determined

57. The solution of the equation $4 - 5(2y + 4) = 4$ is

(A) $-{}^2/_5$.

(B) 8.

(C) 4.

(D) -2.

(E) none of these.

58. One number is 2 more than 3 times another. Their sum is 22. Find the numbers.

(A) 8, 14

(B) 2, 10

(C) 5, 17

(D) 4, 18

(E) 10, 12

59. $1 + \dfrac{y}{(x - 2y)} - \dfrac{y}{(x + 2y)} =$

(A) 0

(B) 1

(C) $\dfrac{1}{(x - 2y)(x + 2y)}$

(D) $\dfrac{2x - y}{(x - 2y)(x + 2y)}$

(E) $\dfrac{x^2}{(x - 2y)(x + 2y)}$

60. What is the volume, in cubic centimeters, of this cylinder?

    (A) $2,000\pi$ cu. cm.

    (B) $8,000\pi$ cu. cm.

    (C) 400 cu. cm.

    (D) 200 cu. cm.

    (E) 200π cu. cm.

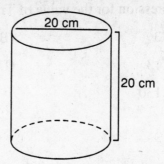

61. Multiply $(x^3yz^5)\ (x^2yz^8)$.

    (A) x^6yz^{40} (B) $x^5y^2z^{13}$

    (C) $x^6y^2z^{40}$ (D) x^5yz^{13}

    (E) $(xyz)^{40}$

62. The quotient of $(x^2 - 5x + 3)/(x + 2)$ is

    (A) $x - 7 + 17/(x + 2)$.   (B) $x - 3 + 9/(x + 2)$.

    (C) $x - 7 - 11/(x + 2)$.   (D) $x - 3 - 3/(x + 2)$.

    (E) $x + 3 - 3(x + 2)$.

63. If a and b each represent a nonzero real number and if $x = \dfrac{a}{|a|} + \dfrac{b}{|b|} + \dfrac{ab}{|ab|}$ then the set of all possible values for x is

    (A) $\{-3, -2, -1, 1, 2, 3\}$.   (B) $\{3, -1, -2\}$.

    (C) $\{3, -1, -3\}$.   (D) $\{3, -1\}$.

    (E) $\{3, 1, -1\}$.

64. Solve for all possible values of b: $b^2 - 121 > 0$.

    (A) $b = 11$ (B) $b = -11$ or $b = 11$

    (C) $b > -11$ or $b < 11$ (D) $b < -11$ or $b > 11$

    (E) $b > -11$ or $b > 11$

65. Tracey has 13 more dimes than nickels. In terms of n (for nickels), find an expression for the value of Tracey's coins.

(A) $2n + 13$

(B) $2n + 130$

(C) $15n + 13$

(D) $5n + 130$

(E) $15n + 130$

ELM
TEST 1

ANSWER KEY

1. (E)	18. (C)	35. (B)	52. (D)
2. (B)	19. (D)	36. (E)	53. (E)
3. (E)	20. (B)	37. (D)	54. (B)
4. (E)	21. (D)	38. (A)	55. (C)
5. (B)	22. (C)	39. (C)	56. (B)
6. (D)	23. (C)	40. (C)	57. (D)
7. (E)	24. (D)	41. (C)	58. (C)
8. (B)	25. (C)	42. (B)	59. (E)
9. (C)	26. (C)	43. (C)	60. (A)
10. (D)	27. (B)	44. (A)	61. (B)
11. (E)	28. (D)	45. (B)	62. (A)
12. (B)	29. (A)	46. (D)	63. (D)
13. (A)	30. (E)	47. (A)	64. (D)
14. (E)	31. (E)	48. (C)	65. (E)
15. (C)	32. (D)	49. (D)	
16. (A)	33. (E)	50. (C)	
17. (C)	34. (C)	51. (E)	

Field test questions were
4, 24, 39, 46, and 53.
Do not count them toward your final score.

DETAILED EXPLANATIONS OF ANSWERS

TEST 1

1. **(E)**

    $A = lw$

    $A = 20(10) = 200$

is the area of the rectangle. The area of the semicircle is half of πr^2 where $r = 5$ or

$$\frac{25\pi}{2}.$$

Therefore, the shaded area is

$$200 - \frac{25\pi}{2} = \frac{400 - 25\pi}{2}.$$

2. **(B)**
    The length the spring stretches is directly proportional to the weight of the mass on it.

$$\frac{L}{M} = \frac{5 \text{ cm}}{10 \text{ g}} = \frac{l}{4 \text{ g}}$$

$$l = 2 \text{ cm}$$

3. **(E)**

$$(x + 1)(3x + 4) = [x(3x) + 1(3x)] + [x(4) + 1(4)]$$
$$= [3x^2 + 3x] + [4x + 4]$$
$$= 3x^2 + 7x + 4$$

4. **(E)**

The surface area of the box equals the area of the base, plus the area of the top, plus the sum of the areas of the four faces. Hence, surface area of the box

$$= 2x^2 + 4xh.$$

5. **(B)**

$$\frac{\dfrac{1}{x} - \dfrac{1}{y}}{\dfrac{1}{x^2} - \dfrac{1}{y^2}} = \frac{\dfrac{y - x}{xy}}{\dfrac{y^2 - x^2}{x^2 y^2}}$$

$$= \frac{y - x}{xy} \times \frac{x^2 y^2}{y^2 - x^2}$$

$$= (y - x) \times \frac{xy}{(y + x)(y - x)}$$

$$= \frac{xy}{x + y}$$

6. **(D)**

$$A = P(1 + rt)$$

$$A = P + Prt$$

$$A - P = Prt$$

$$t = \frac{A - P}{Pr}$$

7. **(E)**

If x is the number, then $.15x = 60$. Therefore,

$$x = \frac{60}{.15} = 400.$$

8. **(B)**
     Identify several ordered pairs that are on line A, such as $(0, 4)$, $(1, 4)$, $(2, 4)$, and $(3, 4)$. Notice that the y-term or second term of the ordered pairs is always 4. Therefore, the equation is $y = 4$.

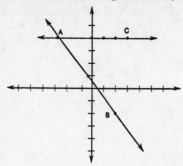

9. **(C)**
     The ordered pairs for points A and B, respectively, are $(-3, 4)$ and $(2, -2)$. The midpoint is calculated by finding the averages of the x and y coordinates. In other words, the midpoint is

$$\left(\frac{-3+2}{2}, \frac{4+(-2)}{2} \right) = \left(-\frac{1}{2}, 1 \right).$$

10. **(D)**
     The slope of a line uses the formula

$$m = \frac{y_2 - y_1}{x_2 - x_1}.$$

Assigning point $A(-3, 4)$ as (x_1, y_1) and point $B(2, -2)$ as (x_2, y_2), the formula yields

$$m = \frac{-2-4}{2-(-3)} = \frac{-6}{5} = \frac{-6}{5}.$$

11. **(E)**
     When a fraction is raised to a power, both the numerator and the denominator is raised to that power. So, x^2 taken as a factor 5 times is x^{10}, and y taken as a factor 5 times is y^5.

12. **(B)**

$$a = 25 - 16 = 9$$
$$b = 100 - 64 = 36$$
$$(\sqrt{9} - \sqrt{36})^2 = (3 - 6)^2$$
$$= (-3)^2$$
$$= 9$$

13. **(A)**

$$\frac{28 + 36 + x}{3} = 29$$
$$64 + x = 3(29)$$
$$x = 23$$

14. **(E)**
If r is the radius of the sphere, then its volume is

$$\frac{4}{3}\pi r^3.$$

If r is increased by a factor of 3, then the radius becomes $3r$ and the volume is increased to

$$\frac{4}{3}\pi(3r)^3 = \left(\frac{4}{3}\right)27\pi r^3.$$

Thus, the volume is increased by a factor of 27.

15. **(C)**
Rearrange the equation.

$$(4x - 3)^2 - 4 = 0$$
$$((4x - 3) - 2)\,((4x - 3) + 2) = 0$$

Solve each factor.

$$((4x - 3) - 2) = 0 \qquad\qquad ((4x - 3) + 2) = 0$$

$$4x - 5 = 0 \qquad\qquad 4x - 1 = 0$$
$$4x = 5 \qquad\qquad 4x = 1$$
$$x = {}^5/_4 \qquad\qquad x = {}^1/_4$$

Add the roots.

$$^5/_4 + {}^1/_4 = {}^6/_4 = 1^1/_2$$

16. **(A)**

Since lines l and m are parallel, the 40° angle and $\angle x$ are supplementary. Hence,

$$40 + x = 180$$

or $\qquad x = 140°$

17. **(C)**

$$\frac{(x^2)^{-4}(x^{-2})^3}{(x^{-3})^{-5}} = \frac{(x^{-8})(x^{-6})}{x^{15}}$$

$$= \frac{1}{x^{15}x^8x^6}$$

$$= \frac{1}{x^{29}}$$

18. **(C)**

Observe that to find the product the following multiplications should be done.

$$(\sqrt{3} + 6)(\sqrt{3} - 2) = \sqrt{3}(\sqrt{3} - 2) + 6(\sqrt{3} - 2)$$

$$= 3 - 2\sqrt{3} + 6\sqrt{3} - 12$$

$$= -9 + 4\sqrt{3}$$

19. **(D)**

The most direct way to solve this problem is to perform the indicated operations in the given equation and solve it for x. Thus,

$$x - (4x - 8) + 9 + (6x - 8) = 9 - x + 24$$
$$x - 4x + 8 + 9 + 6x - 8 = 9 - x + 24$$
$$(x + 6x - 4x) + (8 - 8 + 9) = (9 + 24) - x$$
$$(7x - 4x) + 9 = 33 - x$$
$$3x + x = 33 - 9$$
$$4x = 24$$
$$x = 6$$

20. **(B)**

$$\frac{\dfrac{x-1}{x+2}}{\dfrac{x-x^2}{x^2+2x}} = \frac{x-1}{x+2} \times \frac{x(x+2)}{x(1-x)}$$

$$= \frac{x-1}{1-x}$$

$$= \frac{-(1-x)}{1-x}$$

$$= -1$$

21. **(D)**

$$\frac{1 - \frac{1}{1-x}}{1 - \frac{1}{1-\frac{1}{x}}} = \frac{1 - \frac{1}{1-x}}{1 - \frac{x}{x-1}}$$

$$= \frac{(1-x)\left(1 - \frac{1}{1-x}\right)}{(1-x)\left(1 - \frac{x}{x-1}\right)}$$

$$= \frac{1 - x - 1}{1 - x + x}$$

$$= -x$$

22. **(C)**

Trapezoids and parallelograms have zero lines of symmetry, squares have four lines of symmetry, equilateral triangles have three lines of symmetry, and rectangles which are not squares have two lines of symmetry.

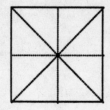 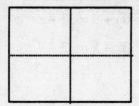 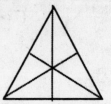

23. **(C)**

$$\frac{5+3i}{2-i} = \frac{5+3i}{2-i} \times \frac{2+i}{2+i}$$

Multiply by complex conjugate.

$$\frac{5(2+i)+3i(2+i)}{4-i^2} = \frac{10+5i+6i+3i^2}{4-i^2}$$

$$= \frac{10+11i+3i^2}{4-i^2}$$

$$= \frac{10+11i-3}{4+1} = \frac{7+11i}{5}$$

Remember $i^2 = -1$.

24. **(D)**

Cost of living increase on $25,000

$$= 25,000\,(.04) = 1,000.$$

Hence, total increase in salary

$$= 1,000 + 275 = 1,275$$

and the percent increase

$$= (1,275/25,000)/100 = 5.1.$$

25. **(C)**

To evaluate an expression, simply replace the x and y with the equivalent numbers,

$$(-2)^2 + 2(-2) - 3 + 3 = 4 - 4 - 3 + 3 = 0.$$

26. **(C)**

$$(x + y)^2 + (x - y)^2 = [x^2 + 2xy + y^2] + [x^2 - 2xy + y^2]$$
$$= 2x^2 + 2y^2$$
$$= 2(x^2 + y^2)$$

27. **(B)**

Set up the inequality in mathematical symbols and solve.

$$3x - 4 > 6$$
$$3x > 6 + 4$$
$$3x > 10$$
$$x > {}^{10}/_3$$

28. **(D)**

Redraw the figure. Given

$$AC = BC = 5R.$$

Let $x = BD$, then $AB = 2x$. Using the Pythagorean Theorem in triangle BCD

$$(3R)^2 + x^2 = (5R)^2$$
$$9R^2 + x^2 = 25R^2$$
$$x^2 = 16R^2$$
$$x = 4R$$

and the perimeter of triangle ABC will be

$$5R + 5R + 2(4R) = 18R.$$

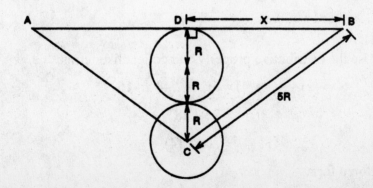

29. **(A)**

$$\frac{7a - 5b}{b} = 7$$

$$\frac{7a}{b} - \frac{5b}{b} = 7$$

$$7 \times \frac{a}{b} - 5 = 7$$

$$7\frac{a}{b} = 12$$

$$\frac{a}{b} = \frac{12}{7}$$

$$\frac{b}{a} = \frac{7}{12}$$

$$\frac{4a + 6b}{2a} = \frac{4a}{2a} + \frac{6b}{2a}$$

$$= 2 + 3 \times \frac{b}{a}$$

$$= 2 + 3 \times \frac{7}{12}$$

$$= \frac{15}{4}$$

30. **(E)**

$$\frac{1}{4}x + 3 = 15$$

$$\frac{1}{4}x = 15 - 3$$

$$x = 4(12)$$

$$= 48$$

31. **(E)**

$$g(x) = x^2 + 4$$

$$g(-3) = (-3)^2 + 4$$

$$= 9 + 4$$

$$= 13$$

32. **(D)**

Use the distributive property and collect like terms:

$$6(x - 2) - 4(x + 4) = 6x - 12 - 4x - 16$$

$$= 2x - 28$$

$$= 2(x - 14)$$

in factored form.

33. **(E)**

If $x + 2y > 5$ and $x < 3$,

then $5 < x + 2y < 3 + 2y$.

Thus, $5 - 3 < 2y$, or $y > 1$.

34. **(C)**

This expression is of the form

$$A^2 - 2AB + B^2,$$

which is the square of a binomial $(A - B)^2$. So the answer is $(x - 3)^2$.

35. **(B)**

For any integer n, $2n + 1$ as well as $2n - 1$ must always be odd integers and

$$2n + 2 = 2(n + 1)$$

must be an even integer.

36. **(E)**

Since

$$\sqrt{x-1} = (x-1)^{1/2}$$

and since

$$\left[(x-1)^{1/2}\right]^4 = (x-1)^2$$

$$(\sqrt{x-1})^4 = 2^4$$

or $(x-1)^2 = 16$

37. **(D)**

$$\frac{1}{x} + \frac{1}{y} = \frac{x+y}{xy}$$

$$= \frac{8}{6}$$

$$= \frac{4}{3}$$

38. **(A)**

By the Pythagorean Theorem the square of the length of the hypotenuse is equal to the sum of the squares of the lengths of the legs. Therefore, if y is the length of the other leg then

$$(x + 1)^2 = x^2 + y^2$$

or

$$y^2 = (x + 1)^2 - x^2$$

$$= 2x + 1$$

Hence

$$y = \sqrt{2x + 1}.$$

39. **(C)**

Since 2.25 inches on the map represent 50 miles, each one inch on the map represents 50/2.25 miles. Therefore, 18 inches represent

$$\frac{18 \times 50}{2.25} = 400 \text{ miles.}$$

40. **(C)**

$$\frac{A}{x - 5} + \frac{B}{x + 3} = \frac{7x - 11}{(x - 5)(x + 3)}$$

On the left side of the equation, add fractions using the LCD in the usual manner, obtaining

$$\frac{Ax + 3A + Bx - 5B}{(x - 5)(x + 3)},$$

$$Ax + 3A + Bx - 5B = 7x - 11;$$

equating coefficients of like terms gives the system

$$A + B = 7$$

$$3A - 5B = -11.$$

Solving simultaneously gives $A = 3$ and $B = 4$. Check:

$$\frac{3}{x - 5} + \frac{4}{x + 3} = \frac{3x + 9 + 4x - 20}{(x - 5)(x + 3)}$$

$$= \frac{7x - 11}{(x - 5)(x + 3)}.$$

41. **(C)**

   The difference between the first two numbers is 4(6 − 2); the difference between the second and third numbers is 6(12 − 6) which is two more than the first difference; the difference between the third and fourth numbers is 8(20 − 12) which is two more than the second difference; the difference between the fourth and fifth numbers is 10(x − 20). Thus, the value of x is given by

$$x - 20 = 10$$

$$x = 30$$

42. **(B)**

$$\frac{16^2 \times 8^3}{2^{19}} = \frac{(2^4)^2 \times (2^3)^3}{2^{19}}$$

$$= \frac{2^8 \times 2^9}{2^{19}}$$

$$= \frac{2^{17}}{2^{19}}$$

$$= 2^{-2}.$$

43. **(C)**

   One mile = 5,280 ft × 12 in/ft = 63,360 inches.

The circumference of the tire is found by the formula

$$c = \pi d = 2\pi \text{ feet.}$$

Therefore, the number of revolutions is

$$\frac{63,360}{24\pi} = \frac{5,280}{2\pi} = \frac{2,640}{\pi}.$$

44. **(A)**

$$\frac{[f(x+a) - f(x)]}{a} = \frac{[((x+a)^2 + 3(x+a) + 2) - (x^2 + 3x + 2)]}{a}$$

$$= \frac{[(x^2 \pm 2xa + a^2 + 3x + 3a + 2) - x^2 - 3x - 2]}{a}$$

$$= \frac{[2xa + a^2 + 3a]}{a}$$

$$= \frac{a(2x + a + 3)}{a}$$

$$= 2x + a + 3$$

45. (B)

Since $\angle A$ and $\angle C$ are inscribed angles, the measure of each of these angles is half the measure of the intercepted arc. Since the two arcs comprise the entire circle, the sum of the measures of these angles is $\frac{1}{2} \times 360° = 180°$.

46. (D)

The ages of each man may be represented as follows:

$$x = \text{George}$$

$$\tfrac{1}{2}x = \text{Sam}$$

$$\tfrac{1}{2}x + 4 = \text{Jim}$$

$$\tfrac{1}{2}x + 4 + 4 = \text{John or John} = \tfrac{1}{2}x + 8$$

George is 4 years older than John:

$$x = \tfrac{1}{2}x + 8 + 4$$

$$x = \tfrac{1}{2}x + 12$$

Multiplying each term by 2 gives

$$2x = x + 24$$

$$x = 24$$

Therefore, George is 24, John is 20, Jim is 16, and Sam is 12.

47. (A)

The form

$$a^m a^n = a^{m + n}.$$

This is the same form as

$$4(x^4 \times x^6),$$

which equals $4x^{10}$.

48. **(C)**
Since $AB = BC$, $\angle C = 46°$. However, the sum of the measures of the angles of a triangle is 180° and

$$180 - (46 + 46) = 88$$

so the measure of $\angle B$ is 88°.

49. **(D)**
The formula

$$D = rt$$

is the one to use for this problem.

$$21 = r \times 2^{1}/_{3} \text{ and } r = 9 \text{ knots/hour.}$$

50. **(C)**
Since BC is parallel to AD, the quadrilateral $ABCD$ is a trapezoid with

Area = (average of the length of the bases) × height.

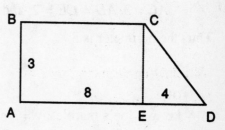

Hence,

$$30 = (^{1}/_{2}) (8 + 12) \times \text{(height)},$$

giving

$$AB = \text{height} = 3.$$

If CE is the perpendicular from C to AD, then

$$AE = BC = 8, \text{ and } ED = 12 - 8 = 4.$$

By Pythagorean Theorem

$$(CD)^2 = (3)^2 + (4)^2 = 25.$$

Therefore, $CD = 5$.

51. **(E)**

If
$$a^2 + 4 < 4a + 9,$$

then
$$a^2 - 4a + 4 < 9,$$

or
$$(a - 2)^2 < 3^2.$$

It follows that
$$|a - 2| < 3,$$

and hence
$$-3 < a - 2 < 3, \text{ or } -1 < a < 5.$$

52. **(D)**

Since the two segments are perpendicular, they form a right angle. A right angle measures $90°$, so the two marked angles must add up to $90°$.

$$50 + \angle ABD = 90,$$

therefore $\angle ABD = 40°$.

53. **(E)**

In this case

$$AC = 3, AD = CE = 2, \text{ and } DE = 1.$$

Thus the perimeter is 8.

54. **(B)**

Let x = Joe's marbles, y = Jim's marbles, and z = Tim's marbles. It is given that

$$x + y = 14 \tag{1}$$
$$y + z = 10 \tag{2}$$
$$x + z = 12 \tag{3}$$

Solve equation (2) for y and equation (3) for x. Then substitute their values in equation (1) and solve for z.

$$y + z = 10$$
$$y = 10 - z$$

and $x + z = 12$

$$x = 12 - z$$

Thus,

$$x + y = 14 \Rightarrow (12 - z) + (10 - z) = 14$$
$$-2z + 22 = 14$$
$$-2z + 22 + (-22) = 14 + (-22)$$
$$-2z = -8$$
$$z = 4 \text{ (Tim's marbles)}$$

Now substitute the value of z in equations (2) and (3), respectively, and solve. The results are

$$y = 10 - z$$
$$= 10 - 4$$
$$y = 6 \text{ (Jim's marbles)}$$

and

$$x = 12 - z$$
$$= 12 - 4$$
$$x = 8 \text{ (Joe's marbles)}$$

Joe's marbles, 8, is the maximum number of marbles anyone can have.

55. **(C)**

$$(\sqrt{a + b})^2 = a + b, \sqrt{(a - b)^2} = a - b$$

since $a > b$. So,

$$\left[\left(\sqrt{a + b} \right)^2 - \sqrt{(a - b)^2} \right] = [(a + b) - (a - b)]$$
$$= [a + b - a + b]$$
$$= 2b$$

56. **(B)**
Group pairs of terms that have a common variable.

$$(10x^2 - 14xy) + (5xy - 7y^2)$$

Factoring both of these terms,

$$2x(5x - 7y) + y(5x - 7y).$$

Since there is a common term, it can be rewritten,

$$(5x - 7y)(2x + y).$$

57. **(D)**

$$4 - 5(2y + 4) = 4$$

$$4 - 10y - 20 = 4$$

$$-10y = 4 + 16$$

$$-10y = 20$$

$$y = -2$$

58. **(C)**

Let x and y = two numbers

$$3x + 2 = y$$

$$x + y = 22$$

$$x + (3x + 2) = 22$$

$$4x = 20$$

$$x = 5$$

$$3(5) + 2 = y$$

$$17 = y$$

59. **(E)**

$$1 + \frac{y}{(x - 2y)} - \frac{y}{x + 2y}$$

$$= \frac{(x - 2y)(x + 2y)}{(x - 2y)(x + 2y)} + \frac{y(x + 2y)}{(x - 2y)(x + 2y)} - \frac{y(x - 2y)}{(x - 2y)(x + 2y)}$$

$$= \frac{x^2 - 4y^2 + xy + 2y^2 - xy + 2y^2}{(x - 2y)(x + 2y)}$$

$$= \frac{x^2}{(x - 2y)(x + 2y)}$$

60. (A)

The volume of any solid is the area of the base multiplied by the height. The base of a cylinder is a circle. The formula for the area of a circle is

$$A = \pi r^2.$$

The diameter is marked 20 cm on the figure, so the radius is 10 cm.

$$10 \times 10 = 100 \text{ and } 100 \times \pi = 100\pi.$$

This is the area of the base. Now multiply by the height, 20, and the answer is $2,000\pi$ cubic cm.

61. (B)

$$(x^3 y z^5)(x^2 y z^8) = (x^3)(x^2)(y)(y)(z^5)(z^8)$$
$$= (x^{3+2})(y^{1+1})(z^{5+8})$$
$$= x^5 y^2 z^{13}$$

62. (A)

$$\frac{(x^2 - 5x + 3)}{(x + 2)}$$

$$
\begin{array}{r}
x - 7 \\
x + 2 \overline{\smash{\big)}\, x^2 - 5x + 3} \\
\underline{x^2 + 2x} \\
-7x + 3 \\
\underline{-7x - 14} \\
17
\end{array}
$$

$$x - 7 + \frac{17}{(x + 2)}$$

63. **(D)**

If a is positive and b is positive then

$$x = \frac{a}{|a|} + \frac{b}{|b|} + \frac{ab}{|ab|}$$

$$= 1 + 1 + 1$$

$$= 3$$

If a is positive and b is negative then

$$x = \frac{a}{|a|} + \frac{b}{|b|} + \frac{ab}{|ab|}$$

$$= 1 + (-1) + (-1)$$

$$= -1$$

If a is negative and b is positive then

$$x = \frac{a}{|a|} + \frac{b}{|b|} + \frac{ab}{|ab|}$$

$$= 1 + 1 + (-1)$$

$$= -1$$

If a is negative and b is negative then

$$x = \frac{a}{|a|} + \frac{b}{|b|} + \frac{ab}{|ab|}$$

$$= -1 + (-1) + 1$$

$$= -1$$

64. **(D)**

The interpretation of the sign "> 0" means that all the answers derived from the inequality $b^2 - 121 > 0$ must be of positive value. Therefore, the values of b when it is squared must be greater than 121 in order for the difference to be positive. Because the product of two negative numbers is positive, negative values less than -11 must be considered, as well as all the positive values greater than $+11$.

65. **(E)**

Let n equal the number of nickels and $n + 13$ equal the number of dimes. Then let $5n$ equal the value of the n nickels and $10(n + 13)$ equal the value of the dimes. The total value of Tracey's coins may now be represented by the expression:

$$5n + 10(n + 13) = 5n + 10n + 130$$

$$= 15n + 130$$

ELM

Entry Level Mathematics

Test 2

ELM
TEST 2

Time: 75 Minutes
  65 Questions (including 5 field test questions)

  (Answer sheets appear at the back of the book.)

DIRECTIONS: Solve each problem and select the letter corresponding to the best choice to answer the question.

---

1. Evaluate $\left(2^{1-\sqrt{3}}\right)^{1+\sqrt{3}}$.

    (A) 4   (B) -4

    (C) 16   (D) $\frac{1}{2}$

    (E) $\frac{1}{4}$

2. A first square has a side of length x while the length of a side of a second square is two units greater than the length of a side of the first square. What is an expression for the sum of the areas of the two squares?

    (A) $2x^2 + 4x + 4$ (B) $x^2 + 2$

    (C) $x^2 + 4$ (D) $2x^2 + 2x + 2$

    (E) $2x^2 + 3x + 4$

3. $\dfrac{3y}{y+1} + \dfrac{2y}{y-1} =$

    (A) $\dfrac{5y}{y^2-1}$ (B) $\dfrac{5y}{y+1}$

(C) $\dfrac{5y^2 - y}{y^2 - 1}$ (D) $\dfrac{5y^2}{y + 1}$

(E) $\dfrac{5y}{y^2 + 2y + 1}$

Question 4 refers to the graph below.

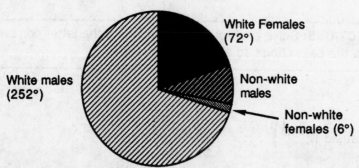

White Females (72°)

White males (252°)

Non-white males

Non-white females (6°)

4. What percent of the Ph.D. degrees were awarded in 1986 to males who are non-white?

    (A) 30   (B) $8^{1}/_{3}$

    (C) $4^{1}/_{6}$ (D) 20

    (E) None of these

5. Simplify $15 - 4(x + 2) + (6x + 2)$.

    (A) $2x + 7$ (B) $2x + 9$

    (C) $10x + 25$ (D) $10x + 9$

    (E) $2x + 25$

6. What is the solution of x for the following system?

    $x - 3y = 9$
    $3x + y = 7$

    (A) -3 (B) 3

    (C) -2 (D) No solutions

    (E) Infinite number of solutions

7. Find the length of the body-diagonal of the rectangular solid shown in the following figure.

    (A) 7

    (B) $2\sqrt{10}$

    (C) $3\sqrt{5}$

    (D) 11

    (E) None of these

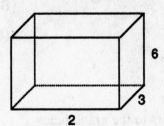

8. One endpoint of a line segment is $(5, -3)$. The midpoint is $(-1, 6)$. What is the other endpoint?

    (A) $(7, 3)$ (B) $(2, 1.5)$

    (C) $(-7, 15)$ (D) $(-2, 1.5)$

    (E) $(-7, 12)$

9. To make lemonade 5 scoops of crystals are needed to make 4 liters. How many scoops are needed to make 10 liters of lemonade?

    (A) $2^1/_2$ (B) 4

    (C) 8   (D) 10

    (E) $12^1/_2$

10. The statement that $.3$ is between $^3/_n$ and $^6/_n$ is equivalent to

    (A) $.1 < n < .2.$ (B) $.3 < n < .6.$

    (C) $1 < n < 2.$ (D) $10 < n < 20.$

    (E) $n > 10.$

11. One solution of the equation $2x^2 - 3x - 2 = 0$ is

    (A) $-^3/_2.$ (B) $-2.$

    (C) $^1/_2.$ (D) $2.$

    (E) no solution.

12. A cube has 96 square feet of surface area. What is the volume of the cube in cubic feet?

(A) 16   (B) 36

(C) 64   (D) 96

(E) 216

Question 13 refers to the graph below.

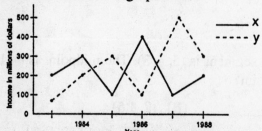

13. By how much was the largest difference between the income earnings of the companies in a given year?

(A) 100   (B) 200

(C) 300   (D) 400

(E) 500

14. $(x^2 - x - 2) \times \left(\dfrac{x^2 + 3x + 2}{x^2 - 4} \right) =$

(A) $(x - 2)^2$ (B) $(x + 1)(x + 2)$

(C) $(x + 2)^2$ (D) $(x + 1)^2$

(E) $\dfrac{(x + 1)^2}{x - 2}$

15. If $f(x) = 3x - 2$ and $g(x) = x^2 + x$, what is $(f \circ g)(4)$?

(A) 10   (B) 30

(C) 58   (D) 110

(E) 200

16. I filled $^2/_3$ of my swimming pool with 1,800 ft^3 of water. What is the total capacity of my swimming pool?

(A) 2,400 ft^3 (B) 2,700 ft^3

(C) 3,000 ft^3 (D) 3,600 ft^3

(E) 3,200 ft^3

17. Solve for the value of x: $4x + 7 = 27$.

(A) $^{27}/_4$ (B) $^{17}/_2$

(C) 4   (D) 5

(E) -5

18. A line segment is drawn from the point $(3, 5)$ to the point $(9, 13)$. What are the coordinates of the midpoint of the line segment?

(A) $(9, 6)$ (B) $(12, 18)$

(C) $(6, 9)$ (D) $(6, 8)$

(E) $(3, 4)$

19. The length of a rectangle is twice its height. What is the perimeter of the rectangle in terms of the height, h?

(A) $8h$ (B) $6h$

(C) $3h$ (D) $9h^2$

(E) $2h^2$

20. $\left[\left(\dfrac{x}{y}\right)^{-1} - \left(\dfrac{y}{x}\right)^{-1}\right]^{-1} =$

(A) xy (B) $\dfrac{1}{xy}$

(C) $x^2 - y^2$ (D) $y^2 - x^2$

(E) $\dfrac{xy}{(y^2 - x^2)}$

21. Laura spent $3.89 for milk, $1.29 for bread, and $4.99 for lunch meat. Lana spent $3.45 for milk, $1.39 for bread, and $5.50 for lunch meat. Who spent more and how much more?

(A) Laura spent 27¢ more.

(B) Lana spent 27¢ more.

(C) Laura spent 17¢ more.

(D) Lana spent 17¢ more.

(E) They spent the same amount.

22. $(2 + 3i)(4 + 5i) =$

(A) $22 - 7i$ (B) $8 - 15i$

(C) $-7 - 22i$ (D) $23 + 22i$

(E) $-7 + 22i$

23. Find the area of the shaded portion in the figure shown.

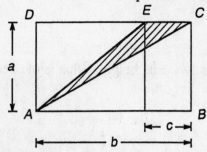

(A) $\dfrac{ac}{2}$ (B) $\dfrac{ab}{2}$

(C) $\dfrac{bc}{2}$ (D) ac

(E) Cannot be determined

24. Simplify $\dfrac{x^{11}}{x^4}$.

(A) x^{44} (B) x^7

(C) x^6

(D) $\dfrac{1}{x^4}$

(E) $\dfrac{1}{x^7}$

25. $\dfrac{2x^2 - x - 3}{x^2 - 1} \times \dfrac{x^2 + x - 2}{2x^2 + x - 6} =$

(A) $(x + 1)^2$

(B) 1

(C) $\dfrac{3x^2 - 5}{3x^2 + x - 7}$

(D) $\dfrac{1}{x - 2}$

(E) $\dfrac{(2x - 3)^2}{(x - 1)^2}$

26. $\dfrac{x + 2}{x + 5} - \dfrac{x - 3}{x + 7} =$

(A) $\dfrac{5}{(x + 5)(x + 7)}$

(B) $\dfrac{7x + 29}{(x + 5)(x + 7)}$

(C) $\dfrac{2x - 1}{(x + 5)(x + 7)}$

(D) $x^2 - x - 6$

(E) -2

27. An airplane made a 6-hour trip with the wind which blew in the same direction as the airplane. The return flight against the wind took 8 hours. The wind speed was 60 km per hour. What was the speed of the airplane in still air?

(A) 420 km per hr.

(B) 480 km per hr.

(C) 360 km per hr.

(D) 400 km per hr.

(E) 500 km per hr.

28. Find the area of a circle with a diameter 10 inches.

(A) 5π sq. in.

(B) 10π sq. in.

(C) 15π sq. in.

(D) 25π sq. in.

(E) 28π sq. in.

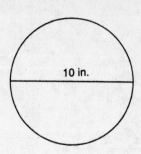

29. $5 + 10 + 15 + 20 + \dots + 100 =$

(A) 2,100

(B) 1,050

(C) 5,050

(D) 25,250

(E) 210

30. Simplify $\dfrac{\frac{1}{3}}{1+\frac{2}{4+5}}$.

(A) $^7/_{24}$

(B) $^3/_{11}$

(C) $^8/_{21}$

(D) 1

(E) $^1/_3$

31. $(a + 3)^3 =$

(A) $3a^3 + 9$

(B) $a^3 + 27$

(C) $a^3 + 9a^2 + 27a + 27$

(D) $a^3 + 9a^2 + 9a + 9$

(E) $a^3 + 27a + 27$

32. If $x = -3$, then $x^x =$

(A) $-^1/_{27}$.

(B) $^1/_{27}$.

(C) 27.

(D) -27.

(E) 9.

33. What is the length of side *BC*?

    (A) 3

    (B) 5

    (C) $\sqrt{34}$

    (D) 7

    (E) None of these

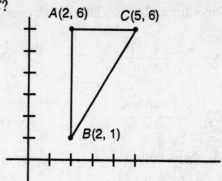

34. Multiply $(x + 1)(4x + 3)$.

    (A) $4x^2 + 4$ (B) $4x^2 + 3$

    (C) $4x^2 + 4x + 3$ (D) $4x^2 + 7x + 3$

    (E) $4x^2 - 7x - 4$

35. Factor completely $x^4 - 81$.

    (A) $(x^2 + 9)(x^2 + 9)$ (B) $(x^2 + 3)(x^2 - 3)$

    (C) $(x^2 + 9)(x - 3)(x - 3)$ (D) $(x^2 + 9)(x + 3)(x - 3)$

    (E) $(x^2 - 9)(x^2 - 9)$

36. Two cars 660 miles apart start traveling toward each other, agreeing to meet midway. One car averages 40 mph, the other 55 mph. How long will the faster car have to wait in order to meet the slower car at the halfway point?

    (A) 2 hours (B) $2^1/_4$ hours

    (C) 4 hours (D) 6 hours

    (E) $8^1/_4$ hours

37. $(-a^2 + 2b + 3) - (4a^2 - 2b - 1) =$

    (A) $5a^2b$ (B) $3a^2b$

    (C) $4a^2 + 4b - 3$ (D) $-5a^2 + 4b + 4$

    (E) $3a^2 + 2$

38. Solve for x: $2x^2 + \sqrt{3}x - 4 = 0$.

(A) $\dfrac{-\sqrt{3} \pm \sqrt{35}}{4}$

(B) $\dfrac{\sqrt{3} \pm \sqrt{35}}{2}$

(C) $\dfrac{-\sqrt{3} \pm \sqrt{35}}{2}$

(D) $\dfrac{\sqrt{3} \pm \sqrt{35}}{4}$

(E) No solution

39. In the figure shown, line r is parallel to line l. Find the measure of angle RBC.

(A) 30°

(B) 80°

(C) 90°

(D) 100°

(E) 110°

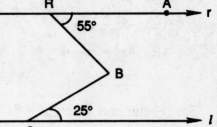

40. What is the distance between $A(3, 4)$ and $B(-1, 1)$?

(A) $\sqrt{7}$

(B) 5

(C) $\sqrt{29}$

(D) $\sqrt{41}$

(E) 6

41. $\dfrac{x+1-\frac{6}{x}}{\frac{1}{x}} =$

(A) $\dfrac{x^2 + x - 6}{x}$

(B) $\dfrac{x-5}{x^2}$

(C) $\dfrac{x-5}{x}$

(D) $x^2 + x - 6$

(E) $x - 5$

42. What is the equation that passes through (6, 4) and has a slope of $^1/_2$?

    (A) $y = 4 + ^1/_2x$ (B) $6y + ^1/_2 = 4x$

    (C) $4y + 6x = ^1/_2$ (D) $^1/_2y = 1 + x$

    (E) $y = 1 + ^1/_2x$

43. Mary wants to cover a small chest with contact paper. The chest is 24" × 12" × 10". How much contact paper is needed?

    (A) 5 sq. ft.

    (B) 4 sq. ft.

    (C) 9 sq. ft.

    (D) $1^2/_3$ sq. ft.

    (E) 720 sq. ft.

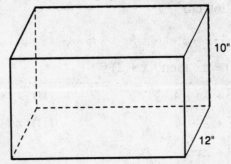

44. Harry bought a sofa priced at $995 and a chair priced at $149. The sales tax is 8%. How much must he pay for the sofa and chair and tax?

    (A) $1,144   (B) $91.52

    (C) $1,134   (D) $1,224.72

    (E) $1,235.52

45. $15 > 2x - 7 > 9$ is equivalent to

    (A) $7.5 > x > 11.5$.   (B) $4 > x > 1$.

    (C) $8 > x > 2$.   (D) $22 > x > 16$.

    (E) $11 > x > 8$.

46. Robert's fish tank is 48 centimeters long, 35 centimeters wide, and 52 centimeters high. What is the volume of the water in the tank if he leaves 2 centimeters at the top without water?

(A) 1,680 cm³

(B) 87,360 cm³

(C) 83,720 cm³

(D) 84,000 cm³

(E) 3,360 cm³

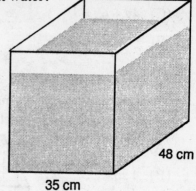

52 cm

48 cm

35 cm

47. Let $f(x) = x^2$, then $f(x + 2) =$

(A) $x^2 + 4x + 4$.   (B) $x^2 + 2x + 4$.

(C) $x^2 + 2$.   (D) $x^2 + 4$.

(E) $x^3 + 2x^2$.

48. Triangles ABC and $A'B'C'$ are similar right triangles. Find the length of side AC.

(A) 10

(B) 12

(C) 13

(D) 16

(E) 26

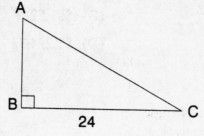
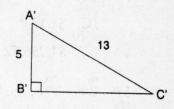

49. $\dfrac{x^2 - y^2}{x^2 + 3y + 2y^2} \times \dfrac{2x + 4y}{x^2 - xy} =$

(A) $\dfrac{2x^3 - 4y^3}{x}$ (B) $\dfrac{2}{x}$

(C) 2   (D) $\dfrac{x + y}{x^3 + y^2}$

(E) $\dfrac{2(x + 2y)}{x}$

50. Ira has enough seed to plant a garden 220 square feet. He has a place 20 feet long to put the garden. How wide must it be to have exactly 220 square feet?

    (A) 20 ft.

    (B) 10 ft.

    (C) 12 ft.

    (D) 11 ft.

    (E) 9.5 ft.

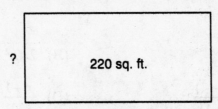

? 220 sq. ft.

20 feet

51. One of the solutions to the equation $(3s + 1)(s - 2) = 0$ is

    (A) -2. (B) $-1/3$.

    (C) 0. (D) $1/3$.

    (E) 6.

52. Solve for x: $2x - 7 = 3x + 2$.

    (A) -14 (B) -9

    (C) 1 (D) $9/5$

    (E) $14/5$

53. What is the measure of angle A?

    (A) $43°$

    (B) $47°$

    (C) $90°$

    (D) $137°$

    (E) $57°$

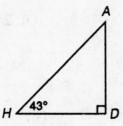

54. $\dfrac{\dfrac{x^2 - xy}{3x - 3}}{\dfrac{xy - y^2}{6x + 6}} =$

(A) xy

(B) $2x(x^2 - 1)$

(C) $\dfrac{2x(x + 1)}{y(x - 1)}$

(D) $\dfrac{x + 1}{x - 1}$

(E) $\dfrac{2x}{y}$

55. Find the area of the isosceles trapezoid.

(A) n^2

(B) $2n^2$

(C) $4n^2$

(D) $4n$

(E) $4n + 2n\sqrt{2}$

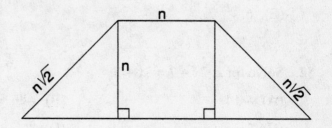

56. If $\dfrac{x}{y} = 5$, then $\dfrac{x^2 - y^2}{y^2} =$

(A) -25.

(B) -24.

(C) 25.

(D) 24.

(E) 26.

57. If $\log_x 27 = 3$, then

(A) $x = 9$.

(B) $x = 27$.

(C) $x^3 = 27$.

(D) $x = 2$.

(E) $x = 81$.

58. $(3x)^2 - \dfrac{x^2}{9} =$

   (A) $\dfrac{8x^2}{9}$ (B) $2x^2$

   (C) $\dfrac{26x^2}{9}$ (D) $\dfrac{80x^2}{9}$

   (E) $9x^2$

59. Which of the following is equivalent to $x^2 - 2x - 3 < 0$?
   (A) $x < -3$ or $x > 1$ (B) $x = 3$
   (C) $x = -1$ (D) $-1 > x$ or $x > 3$
   (E) $-1 < x < 3$

60. Let $a \times b = a^2 + 2b$. Find $3 \times \frac{1}{2}$.
   (A) -8 (B) -5
   (C) 7 (D) 8
   (E) 10

61. What is the least common multiple of $18x$ and $24xy$?
   (A) 2 (B) $2xy$
   (C) $6x$ (D) 48
   (E) $72xy$

62. The angles of a triangle are in a ratio of 3:5:10. How many degrees is the largest angle?
   (A) $10°$ (B) $18°$
   (C) $100°$ (D) $150°$
   (E) $180°$

63. Find the product of the roots of $3x^2 + 3x - 6 = 0$.

    (A) -18 (B) -6

    (C) -3 (D) -2

    (E) 6

64. $x^{1/4} \div x^{1/2} =$

    (A) $x^{3/4}$ (B) $x^{1/2}$

    (C) $x^{1/4}$ (D) $\dfrac{1}{x^{1/4}}$

    (E) $\dfrac{1}{x^{1/2}}$

65. If

$$a + b = 15$$
$$a + c = 16$$
$$b + c = 11$$

    then $a =$

    (A) 10.   (B) 5.

    (C) 6.   (D) 15.

    (E) 11.

ELM
TEST 2

ANSWER KEY

1. (E)	18. (C)	35. (D)	52. (B)
2. (A)	19. (B)	36. (B)	53. (B)
3. (C)	20. (E)	37. (D)	54. (C)
4. (B)	21. (D)	38. (A)	55. (B)
5. (B)	22. (E)	39. (B)	56. (D)
6. (B)	23. (A)	40. (B)	57. (C)
7. (A)	24. (B)	41. (D)	58. (D)
8. (C)	25. (B)	42. (E)	59. (E)
9. (E)	26. (B)	43. (C)	60. (E)
10. (D)	27. (A)	44. (E)	61. (E)
11. (D)	28. (D)	45. (E)	62. (C)
12. (C)	29. (B)	46. (D)	63. (D)
13. (D)	30. (B)	47. (A)	64. (D)
14. (D)	31. (C)	48. (E)	65. (A)
15. (C)	32. (A)	49. (B)	
16. (B)	33. (C)	50. (D)	
17. (D)	34. (D)	51. (B)	

Field test questions were
9, 23, 36, 46, and 50.
Do not count them toward your final score.

DETAILED EXPLANATIONS
OF ANSWERS

TEST 2

1. **(E)**

$$(1 - \sqrt{3})(1 + \sqrt{3}) = 1 - 3 = -2.$$

And

$$2^{-2} = \frac{1}{2^2} = \frac{1}{4}.$$

2. **(A)**

The area of the first square is x^2 and the area of the second square is $(x + 2)^2$. Thus, the sum of the areas is

$$x^2 + (x + 2)^2 = x^2 + (x^2 + 4x + 4)$$

$$= 2x^2 + 4x + 4$$

3. **(C)**

$$\frac{3y}{y+1} + \frac{2y}{y-1} = \frac{(y-1)3y + (y+1)(2y)}{(y+1)(y-1)}$$

$$= \frac{3y^2 - 3y + 2y^2 + 2y}{y^2 - 1}$$

$$= \frac{5y^2 - y}{y^2 - 1}$$

4. **(B)**

Since the non-white males category is the only portion (in degrees) not shown in the graph, simply add the given degrees in the circle and subtract the sum from 360° to obtain 30°. Then form the ratio of 30 to 360 and find the percent which is simply $8^1/_3\%$.

5. **(B)**

To simplify, remove the parentheses and collect like terms.

$$15 - 4x - 8 + 6x + 2 = 2x + 9.$$

The most common error is failure to distribute the minus sign with the 4.

6. **(B)**

The correct solution may be obtained by solving the system by the substitution or addition methods. To use the substitution method, solve the second equation for y by transposing the $(3x)$ to the right side of the equation, thus

$$y = 7 - 3x.$$

Substitute this expression in the first equation, which gives

$$x - 3(7 - 3x) = 7$$

and solve for x. Use of the addition method employs the addition property of equality, which says that if equals are added to equals, then the results are equal. First multiply the second equation by 3. This gives

$$9x + 3y = 21.$$

If this new equation is added to the first equation, the result is

$$10x = 30.$$

The terms containing the y variable disappeared. Now if both sides are divided by 10, $x = 3$.

7. **(A)**

$$\text{Diagonal} = \sqrt{4 + 9 + 36} = \sqrt{49} = 7.$$

8. **(C)**

$$\text{midpoint} = \left(\frac{x_1 + x_2}{2}, \frac{y_1 + y_2}{2}\right)$$

$$x_2 \qquad -1 = \frac{5 + x_2}{2}$$

$$-2 = 5 + x_2$$

$$x_2 = -7$$

$$y_2 \qquad 6 = \frac{-3 + y_2}{2}$$

$$12 = -3 + y_2$$

$$y_2 = 15$$

9. **(E)**

Let x = the number of scoops needed to make 10 liters. Set up the proportion.

$$\frac{\text{\# scoops}}{\text{\# liters}} = \frac{5}{4} = \frac{x}{10}$$

Solve for x.

$$4x = 50$$

$$x = 12\tfrac{1}{2}$$

10. **(D)**

$$\tfrac{3}{n} < .3 < \tfrac{6}{n}$$

is equivalent to

$$3 < (.3)n < 6.$$

Multiplying the inequality by 10 we get

$$30 < 3n < 60, \text{ or } 10 < n < 20.$$

11. **(D)**

$$2x^2 - 3x - 2 = 0$$

Use the quadratic formula to solve.

$$x = \frac{-b \pm \sqrt{b^2 - 4ac}}{2a}$$

$$= \frac{-(-3) \pm \sqrt{(-3)^2 - 4(2)(-2)}}{2(2)}$$

$$= \frac{3 \pm \sqrt{9 + 16}}{4}$$

$$= \frac{3 \pm \sqrt{25}}{4}$$

$$= \frac{3 \pm 5}{4}$$

$$= 2 \text{ or } -\frac{1}{2}$$

12. (C)

One needs to first recall that a cube has 6 equal sized faces. Thus, the area of each face is found by dividing 6 into 96 to obtain 16 square feet. Since each face contains 16 square feet, then one can conclude that each edge of a face is 4 feet long. So, the volume of the cube, given by the formula,

$V = $ (length of edge)^3 is found to be

$V = (4 \text{ ft})^3 = 64$ cu. ft.

13. (D)

By observation one needs only to find the largest spread between corresponding plotted points on the two lines representing the companies. Thus, the largest difference occurred in 1987 where the difference was 400 million (500 – 100).

14. (D)

$$(x^2 - x - 2) \times \frac{x^2 + 3x + 2}{x^2 - 4} =$$

Multiply the fractions.

$$= \frac{(x^2 - x - 2)(x^2 + 3x + 2)}{x^2 - 4}$$

Factor each polynomial.

$$= \frac{(x-2)(x+1)(x+1)(x+2)}{(x-2)(x+2)}$$

Divide the common factors and simplify.

$$= (x+1)^2$$

15. **(C)**

$$(f \circ g)(4) = f(g(4))$$

$$g(x) = x^2 + x$$

Substitute the value of x.

$$g(4) = 4^2 + 4$$

$$= 16 + 4$$

$$= 20$$

$$f(x) = 3x - 2$$

Substitute the value of $g(4)$ in $f(x)$.

$$f(20) = 3(20) - 2$$

$$= 60 - 2$$

$$= 58$$

16. **(B)**

Let x be the total capacity of the swimming pool, then

$$\frac{2}{3}x = 1,800$$

$$x = \frac{1,800 \times 3}{2} = 2,700 \text{ ft}^3$$

17. **(D)**

$$4x + 7 = 27$$

$$4x = 27 - 7$$

$$4x = 20$$

$$x = {}^{20}/_4$$

$$x = 5$$

18. (C)

In order to find the midpoint of the line segment between two points one must know the formula. It is given by an ordered pair (x, y) where x is formed by the average of the x-coordinates and y is formed by the average of the y-coordinates of the two points. Thus, the midpoint is

$$x = \frac{3+9}{2} = \frac{12}{2} = 6$$

and

$$y = \frac{5+13}{2} = \frac{18}{2} = 9$$

or the ordered pair $(6, 9)$.

19. (B)

$$h = \text{height}$$

$$2h = \text{length}$$

$$\text{The perimeter} = 2h + 2(2h)$$

$$= 2h + 4h$$

$$= 6h$$

20. (E)

$$\left[\left(\frac{x}{y} \right)^{-1} - \left(\frac{y}{x} \right)^{-1} \right]^{-1} = \left[\left(\frac{y}{x} \right)^{1} - \left(\frac{x}{y} \right)^{1} \right]^{-1}$$

$$= \left[\frac{y}{x} - \frac{x}{y} \right]^{-1}$$

$$= \left[\frac{y^2 - x^2}{xy} \right]^{-1} = \frac{xy}{y^2 - x^2}$$

21. **(D)**

   Laura spent \$10.17 and Lana spent \$10.34, so Lana spent \$.17 more than Laura.

22. **(E)**

$$(2 + 3i)(4 + 5i) = 8 + 12i + 10i + 15i^2$$
$$= 8 + 22i + 15(-1)$$
$$= 8 + 22i - 15$$
$$= -7 + 22i$$

23. **(A)**

   The shaded portion is a triangle AEC, so

$$\text{shaded portion} = \frac{\text{height} \times \text{base}}{2} = \frac{ac}{2}$$

24. **(B)**

$$\frac{x^{11}}{x^4} = x^{11-4}$$
$$= x^7$$

25. **(B)**

$$\frac{2x^2 - x - 3}{x^2 - 1} \times \frac{x^2 + x - 2}{2x^2 + x - 6} =$$

Multiply the fractions.

$$= \frac{(2x^2 - x - 3)(x^2 + x - 2)}{(x^2 - 1)(2x^2 + x - 6)}$$

Factor each polynomial.

$$= \frac{(2x - 3)(x + 1)(x + 2)(x - 1)}{(x + 1)(x - 1)(2x - 3)(x + 2)}$$
$$= 1$$

26. **(B)**

$$\frac{x+2}{x+5} - \frac{x-3}{x+7} =$$

Find a common denominator.

$$= \frac{(x+2)(x+7) - (x-3)(x+5)}{(x+5)(x+7)}$$

$$= \frac{x^2 + 9x + 14 - (x^2 + 2x - 15)}{(x+5)(x+7)}$$

$$= \frac{x^2 + 9x + 14 - x^2 - 2x + 15}{(x+5)(x+7)}$$

$$= \frac{7x + 29}{(x+5)(x+7)}$$

27. **(A)**

The easiest way to solve this is with a chart. The chart below represents the trip going and the trip returning. The distance is the same for both trips. The trip going has the speed of the airplane plus the tail wind. The trip returning has the speed of the airplane minus the tail wind. The times are as stated.

	D =	r	t
going ⟹	D	r + 60	6
returning ⟸	D	r − 60	8

Since the distance equals the rate times the time and the distances are equal, set up an equation of representations of the equal distances and solve:

$$6(r + 60) = 8(r - 60)$$

$$6r + 360 = 8r - 480$$

Then $r = 420$.

28. **(D)**

    The formula for the area of a circle is

    $A = \pi r^2.$

Since the diameter is 10, the radius is 5. Completing the formula:

    $A = \pi \times 25 = 25\pi$ sq. in.

29. **(B)**

    $5 + 10 + 15 + 20 + \ldots + 100 =$

    $5(1 + 2 + 3 + 4 + \ldots + 20)$

Sum of all of the integers from 1 to n equals

$$\frac{n}{2}(n+1) = 5\left[\frac{20}{2}(20+1)\right]$$

$$= 5(10(21))$$

$$= 1{,}050$$

30. **(B)**

$$\frac{\frac{1}{3}}{1+\frac{2}{4+5}} = \frac{\frac{1}{3}}{1+\frac{2}{9}}$$

$$= \frac{\frac{1}{3}}{\frac{11}{9}}$$

$$= \left(\frac{1}{3}\right)\left(\frac{9}{11}\right)$$

$$= \frac{3}{11}$$

31. **(C)**

    Using the binomial formula

$$(a+b)^n = \binom{n}{0}a^n + \binom{n}{1}a^{n-1}b + \binom{n}{2}a^{n-2}b^2 + \ldots + \binom{n}{n-1}ab^{n-1} + \binom{n}{n}b^n$$

$$= a^n + na^{-1}b + \binom{n}{2}a^{n-2}b^2 + \ldots + nab^{n-1} + b^n$$

$$(a + 3)^3 = a^3 + 3a^2(3) + \binom{3}{2}a(3)^2 + 3^3$$

$$= a^3 + 9a^2 + \frac{3(2)}{2(1)}(a\,9) + 27$$

$$= a^3 + 9a^2 + 27a + 27$$

32. **(A)**

$$-3^{-3} = \frac{1}{(-3)^3}$$

$$= -\frac{1}{27}$$

33. **(C)**

Notice that triangle ABC is a right triangle and that distance $AC = 5 - 2 = 3$ and distance $AB = 6 - 1 = 5$. Use the Pythagorean Theorem to find the length of side BC as follows:

$$(BC)^2 = (AC)^2 + (AB)^2$$

$$(BC)^2 = 3^2 + 5^2$$

$$(BC)^2 = 9 + 25$$

$$BC = \sqrt{34}$$

34. **(D)**

$$(x + 1)(4x + 3) = [(x)(4x) + (1)(4x)] + [(x)(3) + (1)(3)]$$

$$= (4x^2 + 4x) + (3x + 3)$$

$$= 4x^2 + 7x + 3$$

35. **(D)**

We want to find what binomials multiplied together would give

$(x^4 - 81)$. $(x^2 + 9)$ and $(x^2 - 9)$ would give the results, but $(x^2 - 9)$ can also be factored into $(x + 3)$ and $(x - 3)$, so $(x^2 + 9)(x + 3)(x - 3)$ are the prime factors.

36. **(B)**

The car traveling 55 mph can get to the halfway point 330 miles away in

$$\frac{330}{55} = 6 \text{ hours.}$$

The 40 mph car covers the same distance in

$$\frac{330}{40} = 8\frac{1}{4} \text{ hours.}$$

The faster car will have to wait

$$8\frac{1}{4} - 6 = 2\frac{1}{4} \text{ hours.}$$

37. **(D)**

$$(-a^2 + 2b + 3) - (4a^2 - 2b - 1)$$
$$= -a^2 + 2b + 3 - 4a^2 + 2b + 1$$
$$= -5a^2 + 4b + 4$$

38. **(A)**

$$2x^2 + \sqrt{3}x - 4$$

Use the quadratic formula to solve.

$$x = \frac{-b \pm \sqrt{b^2 - 4ac}}{2a}$$

$$a = 2, b = \sqrt{3}, c = -4$$

$$x = \frac{-\sqrt{3} \pm \sqrt{3 - 4(2)(-4)}}{2(2)}$$

$$= \frac{-\sqrt{3} \pm \sqrt{3 + 32}}{4}$$

$$= \frac{-\sqrt{3} \pm \sqrt{35}}{4}$$

39. **(B)**

Extend *RB* to meet line *l* at point *E*, then angle *ARB* and angle *CER* are alternate interior angles. Since *r* is parallel to *l*, it follows that the measure of angle *ARB* is equal to the measure of angle *CER*. Thus, the measure of angle *CER* = 55°.

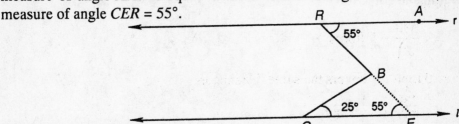

Since angle *RBC* is an exterior angle of triangle *BEC*, and the measure of an exterior angle of a triangle is equal to the sum of the measures of the two non-adjacent interior angles of the triangles, it follows that the measure of angle *RBC* is equal to the sum of the measures of angle *BEC* and angle *BCE*. Thus,

$$\text{measure of angle } RBC = 55° + 25°$$

$$= 80°$$

40. **(B)**

The distance between *A*(3, 4) and *B*(−1, 1) is found by using the following formula where the subscript 1 refers to coordinates in point *A* and the subscript 2 refers to coordinates in point *B*.

$$\sqrt{(x_2 - x_1)^2 + (y_2 - y_1)^2} = \sqrt{(-1-3)^2 + (1-4)^2}$$

$$= \sqrt{16 + 9}$$

$$= \sqrt{25}$$

$$= 5$$

41. **(D)**

$$\frac{x + 1 - \frac{6}{x}}{\frac{1}{x}} = \frac{\frac{x^2 + x - 6}{x}}{\frac{1}{x}}$$

$$= \frac{x^2 + x - 6}{x} \times \frac{x}{1}$$

$$= x^2 + x - 6$$

42. (E)

To solve, use the formula to find the slope of the line and put the point in and solve for y.

$$m = \frac{y_2 - y_1}{x_2 - x_1}$$

$$\frac{1}{2} = \frac{4 - y}{6 - x}$$

$$\frac{1}{2}(6 - x) = 4 - y$$

$$y = 1 + \frac{1}{2}x$$

43. (C)

The problem is to find the surface area of the rectangular solid. This is done by finding the sum of the areas of every side, including the top and bottom. This problem is complicated by the fact that the measurements in the problem are given in inches, and the answers are given in square feet. We must convert to the same unit of measure. If we convert the inches to feet, the dimensions of the chest are $1 \times 2 \times \frac{5}{6}$. A formula to find the lateral area (area of all the sides, but not the top and bottom) is

$$L = ph,$$

where p = perimeter of the base and h = the height. The perimeter of the base is

$$1 + 2 + 1 + 2 \text{ or } 6.$$

Then

$$6 \times \frac{5}{6} = 5 \text{ sq. ft.}$$

for the sides. Now find the area of the top and bottom and add it to the sides. The bottom is a rectangle and the

$$\text{Area} = lw,$$

where l = length and w = width. So the area is

    2 × 1 or 2 sq. ft.

This is the bottom, but the top is the same. Finally, add the area of the sides and the top and the bottom:

    5 + 2 + 2 = 9 sq. ft.

44. **(E)**

    995 + 149 = 1,144

and

    1,144 × .08 = 91.52 tax

    $1,144 + $91.52 = $1,235.52

45. **(E)**

    $15 > 2x - 7 > 9$

    $22 > 2x > 16$ Add 7 to all three sides.

    $11 > x > 8$ Divide all three sides by 2.

46. **(D)**

    The tank is a rectangular solid with length = 48 cm, width = 35 cm, and height = 52 cm. 2 cm at the top will be without water, so the actual height of the water will be only 50 cm. The formula for the volume of a solid is

    V = Length × Width × Height.

    $V = 48 × 35 × 50$

    $= 84,000 \text{ cm}^3$

47. **(A)**

    $f(x) = x^2$

    $f(x + 2) = (x + 2)^2$

    $= x^2 + 4x + 4$

48. **(E)**

The sides of similar triangles are in proportion. Using the Pythagorean Theorem the length of $B'C'$ is:

$$5^2 + (B'C')^2 = 13^2$$

$$25 + (B'C')^2 = 169$$

$$(B'C')^2 = 144$$

$$B'C' = 12$$

BC and $B'C'$ are corresponding sides of similar triangles in a ratio of 24:12 or 2:1. Similarly, side AC and $A'C'$ have the same ratio; AC must be twice as long as $A'C'$. In other words, $AC = 2(13) = 26$.

49. **(B)**

$$\frac{x^2 - y^2}{x^2 + 3y + 2y^2} \times \frac{2x + 4y}{x^2 - xy}$$

$$= \frac{(x+y)(x-y)}{(x+y)(x+2y)} \times \frac{2(x+2y)}{x(x-y)}$$

$$= \frac{2}{x}$$

50. **(D)**

The problem is asking, "20 times what equals 220." You must know that the length times the width of a rectangle is the area, and then use algebra to solve for the unknown.

$$20x = 220$$

Divide both sides by 20 to find $x = 11$. Also, for a problem like this, you may try each answer to find the one which gives 220.

51. **(B)**

$$(3s + 1)(s - 2) = 0$$

To find the solutions, set each factor equal to 0.

$$3s + 1 = 0 \quad \text{and} \quad s - 2 = 0$$
$$s = -\tfrac{1}{3} \qquad\qquad s = 2$$

52. **(B)**
   To solve any equation, use some simple rules of algebra. First, get the like terms on one side of the equation, then simplify to solve for the variable.

$$2x - 7 = 3x + 2$$
$$2x - 3x = 2 + 7$$
$$-x = 9$$

or
$$x = -9$$

53. **(B)**
   The sum of the measures of the angles of a triangle is 180°. Angle D is marked as a right angle, which is 90°. This leaves the other two angles to make up the other 90°. So the correct answer is obtained by subtracting 43° from 90°. Also, you could add 90° and 43° to get 133° and subtract 133° from 180°. The answer is the same.

54. **(C)**

$$\frac{\dfrac{x^2 - xy}{3x - 3}}{\dfrac{xy - y^2}{6x + 6}} = \frac{x(x - y)}{3(x - 1)} \times \frac{6(x + 1)}{y(x - y)}$$

$$= \frac{2x(x + 1)}{y(x - 1)}$$

55. **(B)**

The formula for the area of the trapezoid is

$$A = (^1/_2) \, (\text{height}) \, (\text{first base} + \text{second base}).$$

To find the length of the second base, use the Pythagorean Theorem to find the bases of the two congruent triangles on either side of the square.

$$(\text{base})^2 + n^2 = (n\sqrt{2})^2$$

$$(\text{base})^2 + n^2 = 2n^2$$

$$\text{base}^2 = n^2$$

$$\text{base} = n$$

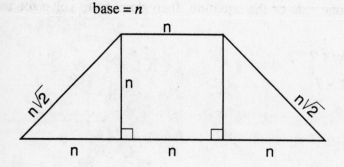

The base of the trapezoid is $3n$. Using the area formula:

$$A = (^1/_2) \, (n) \, (n + 3n)$$

$$A = (^1/_2) \, (n) \, (4n)$$

$$A = 2n^2$$

56. **(D)**

If $^x/_y = 5$, then $x = 5y$. Substitute in

$$\frac{x^2 - y^2}{y^2} = \frac{(5y)^2 - y^2}{y^2}$$

$$= \frac{25y^2 - y^2}{y^2}$$

$$= \frac{24y^2}{y^2}$$

$$= 24$$

57. **(C)**

$$\log_x 27 = 3$$

$$x^3 = 27$$

58. **(D)**

$$(3x)^2 - \frac{x^2}{9} = 9x^2 - \frac{x^2}{9}$$

$$= \frac{81x^2 - x^2}{9}$$

$$= \frac{80x^2}{9}$$

59. **(E)**

$$x^2 - 2x - 3 < 0$$

$$(x - 3)(x + 1) < 0$$

$$x = 3, -1$$

makes the equation equal 0. Since the product must be less than zero, one of the equations must be positive and the other negative. So

$$-1 < x < 3.$$

60. **(E)**
What is needed here is some substitution: $a = 3$ and $b = \frac{1}{2}$. Now simplify:

$$a \times b = a^2 + 2b$$

$$3 \times \frac{1}{2} = 3^2 + 2(\frac{1}{2})$$

$$= 9 + 1 = 10$$

61. **(E)**
The least common multiple or LCM of $18x$ and $24xy$ is the smallest number the both of these numbers can divide into evenly without a re-

mainder. To find the LCM, prime factorize $18x$ and $24xy$ into:

$$18x = (2)\,(3)\,(3)\,(x)$$

$$24xy = (2)\,(2)\,(2)\,(3)\,(x)\,(y)$$

Now, take the largest group of each number and variable represented. Of the 2's, the larger group is the (2) (2) (2) from the $24xy$. Of the 3's, the larger group is the (3) (3) from the $18x$. There is also one x and one y to be represented. Therefore, the LCM of $18x$ and $24xy$ is

$$(2)\,(2)\,(2)\,(3)\,(3)\,(xy) = 72xy.$$

62. **(C)**
    The ratio 3:5:10 indicates that the 180° of the triangle must be divided into

$$3 + 5 + 10 = 18$$

equal parts or 10° for each part. The largest angle is made up of ten 10° parts or 100°.

63. **(D)**
    Find the roots for

$$3x^2 + 3x - 6 = 0$$

$$(3x + 6)\,(x - 1) = 0$$

$$3x + 6 = 0 \qquad x - 1 = 0$$

$$x = -2 \qquad x = 1$$

The roots are -2 and 1. Therefore, the product of the roots equals

$$(-2)\,(1) = -2$$

64. **(D)**

$$\frac{x^{1/4}}{x^{1/2}} = x^{1/4 - 1/2}$$

$$= x^{-1/4}$$

$$= \frac{1}{x^{1/4}}$$

65. **(A)**

Solve for a.

$$a + b = 15$$

$$a + c = 16$$

$$b + c = 11$$

$$c = 16 - a$$

$$b = 15 - a$$

Therefore, $b + c = 11$

$$(15 - a) + (16 - a) = 11$$

$$31 - 2a = 11$$

$$20 = 2a$$

$$10 = a$$

ELM

Entry Level Mathematics

Test 3

ELM
TEST 3

Time: 75 Minutes
65 Questions (including 5 field test questions)

(Answer sheets appear at the back of the book.)

DIRECTIONS: Solve each problem and select the letter corresponding to the best choice to answer the question.

1. Simplify $(m^6n^5q^3)^2$.

    (A) $2m^6n^5q^3$ (B) m^4n^3q

    (C) $m^8n^7q^5$ (D) $m^{12}n^{10}q^6$

    (E) $2m^{12}n^{10}q^6$

2. Jay and his brother Ray own a janitorial service. Jay can do a cleaning job alone in 5 hours and Ray can do the same job in 4 hours. How long will it take them to do the cleaning job together?

    (A) 5 hours   (B) 1 hour

    (C) 4 hours   (D) $2^2/_9$ hours

    (E) $4^1/_2$ hours

3. Find the area of $\triangle xyz$.

    (A) 20 cm²

    (B) 50 cm²

    (C) $50\sqrt{2}$ cm²

    (D) 100 cm²

    (E) 200 cm²

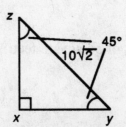

4. $\dfrac{15,561}{25} + \dfrac{9,439}{25} =$

(A) 997　　　　　　　　　　　(B) 1,000

(C) 1,002　　　　　　　　　　(D) 1,005

(E) 1,005.08

5. $\dfrac{1}{1 \times 2} + \dfrac{1}{2 \times 3} + \dfrac{1}{3 \times 4} + \ldots + \dfrac{1}{99 \times 100} =$

(A) $\dfrac{49}{50}$　　　　　　　　　　(B) $\dfrac{74}{75}$

(C) $\dfrac{98}{99}$　　　　　　　　　　(D) $\dfrac{99}{100}$

(E) $\dfrac{101}{100}$

6. If $i = \sqrt{-1}$ and $f(x) = x^2 + 3x + 5$, find $f(2 + i)$.

(A) $6 + 5i$　　　　　　　　　(B) $14 + 7i$

(C) $10 + 8i$　　　　　　　　(D) $3 + 9i$

(E) $11 + 10i$

7. If $z > 0$ and $z^2 + z - 2 = 0$, then z is

(A) -2.　　　　　　　　　　(B) -1.

(C) 0.　　　　　　　　　　　(D) 1.

(E) 2.

8. A cube consists of 54 square feet. What is the volume of the cube in cubic feet?

(A) 9　　　　　　　　　　　(B) 18

(C) 27　　　　　　　　　　　(D) 54

(E) 216

9. Mary lives 6 miles east of Dave and 8 miles south of Joan. If you could fly from Joan's house to Dave's house how far would you have to fly?

(A) 4   (B) 5

(C) 7   (D) 10

(E) 12

10. The simplest expression for

$$\frac{a^2 - 3ab + 2b^2}{2b^2 + ab - a^2} \text{ is}$$

(A) 1.   (B) $a + b$.

(C) $\dfrac{2a + b}{b - a}$.   (D) $a - b$.

(E) $\dfrac{b - a}{b + a}$.

11. The figure shown below is a sketch of $y = f(x)$. What is $f(f(6))$?

(A) -2

(B) 1

(C) 2

(D) 3

(E) 0

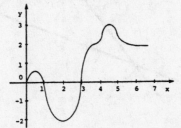

12. Find the area of parallelogram *MNOP*.

(A) 19

(B) 32

(C) $32\sqrt{3}$

(D) 44

(E) $44\sqrt{3}$

13. Simplify $\dfrac{x^{10}y^8}{x^7y^3}$.

(A) x^2y^5 (B) x^3y^4

(C) x^3y^5 (D) x^2y^4

(E) x^5y^3

14. In which equation does P vary directly with the square of x, and inversely with the cube of s?

(A) $P = \dfrac{2s^3}{x^2}$ (B) $P = \dfrac{2x^2}{s^3}$

(C) $P = 2x^2s^3$ (D) $P = 2x^3s^2$

(E) $P = \dfrac{2x^3}{s^2}$

15. What is the measurement of $\angle x$?

(A) 30°

(B) 60°

(C) 90°

(D) 120°

(E) 150°

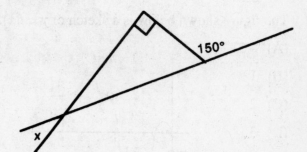

16. Which of the following equations correspond to the graph below?

(A) $y = x^2$

(B) $y = 2x^2$

(C) $y = 2x^2 + 1$

(D) $y = 2(x^2 + 1)$

(E) $y = 2(x^2 - 1)$

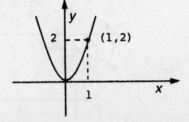

17. If $\log_2(x-1) + \log_2(x+1) = 3$, then $x =$

    (A) -1.   (B) 1.

    (C) 2.   (D) 3.

    (E) 4.

18. At a factory, three out of every 1,000 parts produced are defective. In a day, the factory can produce 25,000 parts. How many of these parts would be defective?

    (A) 7   (B) 75

    (C) 750   (D) 7,500

    (E) 75,000

19. $4x + 3y - z - 10y + x =$

    (A) $5x + 3y - 11z$ (B) $-6x + 2y$

    (C) $5x - 7y - z$ (D) $-3xyz$

    (E) $5x - 7y$

20. If one root of $x^2 - ax + 12 = 0$ is 6, then the other root is

    (A) 2.   (B) -4.

    (C) -6.   (D) 8.

    (E) 12.

21. If $f(x) = 3x^2 - x + 5$, then $f(3) =$

    (A) 15.   (B) 17.

    (C) 23.   (D) 27.

    (E) 29.

22. If $x^2 - 3x - 4 < 0$, then the solution set is

    (A) $-4 < x < 1$.   (B) $-4 < x < -3$.

    (C) $-3 < x < 0$.   (D) $-1 < x < 0$.

    (E) $-1 < x < 4$.

23. The fraction

    $$\frac{\frac{2}{a^2 b^2}}{\frac{1}{b^2 - 2b}}$$

    may be expressed more compactly as

    (A) $\dfrac{2a}{b}$.   (B) $\dfrac{b-4}{b}$.

    (C) $\dfrac{ab}{b^2 - a}$.   (D) $\dfrac{b-a}{a}$.

    (E) $\dfrac{2b-4}{a^2 b}$.

24. Which of the following alternatives is correct?

    (A) $\alpha + \beta + \gamma = 180°$

    (B) $\gamma - \alpha + 180° = \beta$

    (C) $\alpha = \beta + \gamma$

    (D) $\gamma = \alpha + \beta$

    (E) $\alpha = 180° - \beta - \alpha$

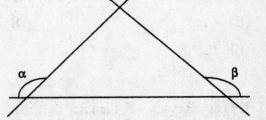

25. Find a solution to $|2x - 18| = -6$.

    (A) -6 (B) -3

    (C) 6 (D) 12

    (E) No solution

26. Evaluate $10 - 5[2^3 + 27/3 - 2(8 - 10)]$.

   (A) -95 (B) 105

   (C) 65   (D) -55

   (E) -85

27. In the figure, if $BD \parallel AE$, then the following must be true:

   (A) $\angle CBD = \angle CDB$.

   (B) $\angle CAE = \angle CEA$.

   (C) $\dfrac{CB}{CA} = \dfrac{CD}{AE}$.

   (D) $\dfrac{CD}{CE} = \dfrac{BD}{AE}$.

   (E) $\dfrac{CB}{BD} = \dfrac{CD}{CA}$.

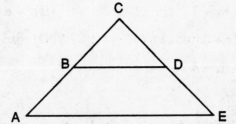

28. If $f(x) = x + 1$, $g(x) = 2x - 3$, and an operation $*$ is defined for all real numbers a and b by the equation $a * b = 2a + b - ab$, then $f(3) * g(4) =$

   (A) -9.   (B) -7.

   (C) -1.   (D) 0.

   (E) 5.

29. In the following figure, 0 is the center of the circle. If arc ABC has length 2π, what is the area of the circle?

   (A) 3π

   (B) 6π

   (C) 9π

   (D) 12π

   (E) 15π

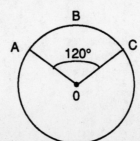

30. What is the sixth number in the series:

   3, 7, 11, ... ?

   (A) 20   (B) 22

   (C) 23   (D) 24

   (E) 26

31. If $f(x) = -2x + 5$ and $g(x) = 4x - 1$. What is $(g \circ f)(x)$?

   (A) $-8x + 7$ (B) $-8x + 19$

   (C) $2x + 4$ (D) $8x^2 - 5$

   (E) $-6x + 4$

32. If a triangle of base 6 units has the same area as a circle of radius 6 units, what is the altitude of the triangle?

   (A) π (B) 3π

   (C) 6π (D) 12π

   (E) 36π

33. Given the expression

   $$\frac{3}{x + 4} + \frac{5}{x - 4} = \frac{8}{x^2 - 16},$$

   solve for x.

   (A) 4   (B) 5

   (C) 0   (D) 1

   (E) 2

34. What is the distance between the points (3, 4) and (− 2, 1)?

    (A) $\sqrt{34}$ (B) 7

    (C) $\frac{1}{3}$ (D) 17

    (E) $\sqrt{43}$

35. What is the value of x?

    (A) 20°

    (B) 40°

    (C) 60°

    (D) 90°

    (E) 30°

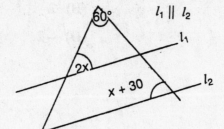

36. The roots of $x^2 + 2x + 5 = 0$ are

    (A) 3, 4.   (B) $-1 \pm 2i$.

    (C) $3 \pm 4i$.   (D) 6, 3.

    (E) $2 \pm 3i$.

Use the following table for question 37.

ANNUAL INCOME BY SEX OF HEAD OF THE HOUSEHOLD

Sex	Number of heads of households with income			
	Less than $15,000	$15,000– $35,000	$35,000– $50,000	$50,000 and above
Male	12	25	35	8
Female	22	10	6	2

37. What percent of the males earn less than $35,000?

    (A) 31%   (B) $46\frac{1}{4}$%

    (C) $57\frac{1}{2}$%   (D) 60%

    (E) 90%

38. If $6x^2 - 5x < -1$, then

(A) $x > {}^1/_2$.   (B) $x < 3$.

(C) $x > 2$.   (D) $2 < x < 3$.

(E) ${}^1/_3 < x < {}^1/_2$.

39. What is the sum of the roots of $x^2 - 2x - 8$?

(A) 8   (B) 2

(C) 0   (D) -2

(E) -6

40. $$\frac{m^2 - n^2}{2x^2 + 3x - 2} \div \frac{n^2 - m^2}{2x^2 + 5x - 3} =$$

(A) $-\dfrac{x+3}{x+2}$ (B) $-\dfrac{x+2}{x+3}$

(C) $\dfrac{x+3}{x+2}$ (D) $\dfrac{x+2}{x+3}$

(E) $-\dfrac{1}{2x+1}$

41. Find the value of y if

$$0 = x - 3y$$

$$y + 3x = 20$$

(A) -6 (B) -2

(C) 0   (D) 2

(E) 6

42. If $3^x > 1$ then $x =$

(A) $0 < x < 1$.   (B) $x \geq 0$.

(C) $x \geq 1$.　　　　　　　(D) $x > 0$.

(E) $x > 1$.

43. Planes P and Q leave an airport at the same time and travel in opposite directions. Plane P travels 50 miles per hour faster than plane Q. How fast is plane Q traveling if they are 1,600 miles apart after 2 hours?

(A) 350　　　　　　　　(B) 375

(C) 425　　　　　　　　(D) 475

(E) 500

44. If $abc \neq 0$, then $\dfrac{3a^2bc^3 + 9a^3b^2c}{27ab^2c + 15a^2b^2c^3} =$

(A) $\dfrac{ab(c^2 + 3)}{c(9 + 5a)}$.　　　　　(B) $\dfrac{a(c^2 + 3ab)}{b(9 + 5ac^2)}$.

(C) $\dfrac{a(c^2 + 3ab)}{c(9 + ac^2)}$.　　　　　(D) $\dfrac{c^2 + 3ab}{9 + 5ac^2}$.

(E) $\dfrac{a}{b(9 + 5ac^2)}$.

45. Find the $f^{-1}(x)$ for $4x - 5y^2 = 20$.

(A) $20 - 4x$　　　　　　(B) $4 + y^2$

(C) $\sqrt{4y - 4}$　　　　　　(D) $5 + {}^5/_4x^2$

(E) $4 + \dfrac{y^2}{5}$

407

46. Given $\angle CBA = 75°$, what is $\angle CAB$ equal to?

(A) 15°

(B) 25°

(C) 30°

(D) 35°

(E) 45°

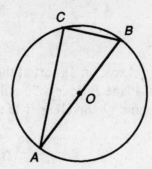

47. What percent of 260 is 13?

(A) .05% (B) 5%

(C) 50% (D) .5%

(E) 20%

48. What is the range of values for which $|6x - 5| \leq 8$ is satisfied?

(A) $-\dfrac{1}{2} \leq x \leq \dfrac{1}{2}$

(B) $0 \leq x \leq \dfrac{5}{6}$

(C) $-1 \leq x \leq \dfrac{1}{2}$

(D) $-\dfrac{1}{2} \leq x \leq \dfrac{13}{6}$

(E) $-\dfrac{1}{2} \leq x \leq \dfrac{1}{3}$

49. If $2^{(6x - 8)} = 16$, then $x =$

(A) 2. (B) 4.

(C) 10. (D) 1.

(E) 6.

50. What is the sum of the roots of $y^2 + 12y + 27 = 0$?

(A) − 12 (B) − 6

(C) 6 (D) 12

(E) No unique solution

51. The value of *B* in the equation $a = (h/2)(B + b)$ is

    (A) $(2a - b)/h$.

    (B) $2h/a - b$.

    (C) $2a - b$.

    (D) $2a/h - b$.

    (E) none of these.

52. The length of a rectangle is twice the width. If the perimeter is 72 centimeters, what is the area of the rectangle in square centimeters?

    (A) 72

    (B) 216

    (C) 288

    (D) 324

    (E) 1,152

53. When a number is multiplied by 6 and that product is subtracted from 70 the difference is 4. What is the number?

    (A) -11

    (B) 10

    (C) 11

    (D) $12^1/_3$

    (E) 14

54. Solve $|3x - 5| \leq 2$.

    (A) $-2 \leq x \leq 2$

    (B) $3 \leq x \leq 7$

    (C) $x \leq 1$

    (D) $1 \leq x \leq {}^7/_3$

    (E) ${}^7/_3 \leq x$

55. Peter has five rulers of 30 cm each and three of 20 cm each. What is the average height of Peter's rulers?

    (A) 25

    (B) 27

    (C) 23

    (D) 26.25

    (E) 27.25

56. Simplify $\dfrac{\frac{1}{x-1}+\frac{1}{x+1}}{\frac{2}{x}}$.

(A) 1

(B) $\dfrac{x}{x^2-1}$

(C) $\dfrac{x^2}{x^2-1}$

(D) $\dfrac{x}{2(x^2-1)}$

(E) $\dfrac{4}{x^2-1}$

57. The quotient of
$$\dfrac{(x^2-5x+3)}{(x+2)} \text{ is}$$

(A) $x-7+\dfrac{17}{x+2}$.

(B) $x-3+\dfrac{9}{x+2}$.

(C) $x-7-\dfrac{11}{x+2}$.

(D) $x-3-\dfrac{3}{x+2}$.

(E) $x+3-\dfrac{3}{x+2}$.

58. $\dfrac{x-4}{x-3}+\dfrac{6}{x^2-9}=$

(A) $\dfrac{x+2}{x^2+x-12}$

(B) $\dfrac{x+2}{x^2-9}$

(C) $\dfrac{x-3}{x+3}$

(D) $\dfrac{x}{x+3}$

(E) $\dfrac{x+2}{x+3}$

59. If point P has coordinates $(3, -6)$ and point Q has coordinates $(15, 5)$, the coordinates of the midpoint of the line segment between the two points is

    (A) $(9, -1/2)$.   (B) $(18, 1/2)$.

    (C) $(15, 3)$.   (D) $(-1/2, 1)$.

    (E) $(15, -1/2)$.

60. If the measure of an angle exceeds its complement by $40°$, then its measure is

    (A) $65°$.   (B) $50°$.

    (C) $45°$.   (D) $40°$.

    (E) $30°$.

61. Which of the following statements are true, if

    $$x + y + z = 10$$

    $$y \geq 5$$

    $$4 \geq z \geq 3$$

    I. $x < z$

    II. $x > y$

    III. $x + z \leq y$

    (A) I only   (B) II only

    (C) III only   (D) I and III only

    (E) I, II, and III

62. Write the formula in terms of y. y varies inversely as the square root of x, and $y = 2$ when $x = 9$.

(A) $y = 6x^2$

(B) $y = \dfrac{9}{\sqrt{x}}$

(C) $y = 2x^2$

(D) $y = \dfrac{6}{\sqrt{x}}$

(E) $y = \dfrac{2}{\sqrt{x}}$

63. The length of a rectangle is $6L$ and the width is $4W$. What is the perimeter?

(A) $12L + 8W$

(B) $12L^2 + 8W^2$

(C) $6L + 4W$

(D) $20LW$

(E) $24LW$

64. $(2x - 8)/(x + 1)$ divided by $(3x^2 - 12x)/(x^2 - 1)$ equals

(A) $\dfrac{2}{x^2}$.

(B) $\dfrac{3x^2}{2}$.

(C) $\dfrac{2}{3}(16 - x)$.

(D) $\dfrac{2(x - 1)}{3x}$.

(E) $\dfrac{x - 5}{6x}$.

65. Which of the following represents the graph of the equation $y = |x - 2|$?

(A)

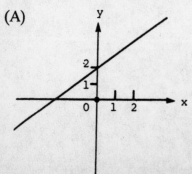

(B)

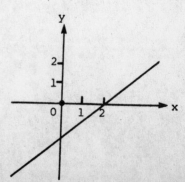

(C)

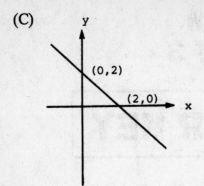

(D)

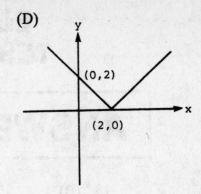

(E)

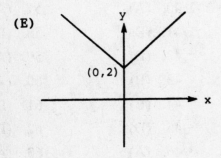

ELM
TEST 3

ANSWER KEY

1. (D)	18. (B)	35. (E)	52. (C)
2. (D)	19. (C)	36. (B)	53. (C)
3. (B)	20. (A)	37. (B)	54. (D)
4. (B)	21. (E)	38. (E)	55. (D)
5. (D)	22. (E)	39. (B)	56. (C)
6. (B)	23. (E)	40. (A)	57. (A)
7. (D)	24. (B)	41. (D)	58. (E)
8. (C)	25. (E)	42. (D)	59. (A)
9. (D)	26. (A)	43. (B)	60. (A)
10. (E)	27. (D)	44. (B)	61. (D)
11. (A)	28. (B)	45. (D)	62. (D)
12. (E)	29. (C)	46. (A)	63. (A)
13. (C)	30. (C)	47. (B)	64. (D)
14. (B)	31. (B)	48. (D)	65. (D)
15. (B)	32. (D)	49. (A)	
16. (B)	33. (C)	50. (A)	
17. (D)	34. (A)	51. (D)	

Field test questions were
9, 21, 30, 43, and 52.
Do not count them toward your final score.

DETAILED EXPLANATIONS OF ANSWERS

TEST 3

1. **(D)**

$$(m^6 n^5 q^3)^2 = m^{(6)(2)} n^{(5)(2)} q^{(3)(2)}$$
$$= m^{12} n^{10} q^6$$

2. **(D)**

The traditional way to solve this problem is to set up and solve an equation. Consider what part of the job could be done in 1 hour by each person. Thus, Jay could do $^1/_5$ of the job in 1 hour and Ray could do $^1/_4$ of the job in the same amount of time. What is unknown is the part of the job they could do together in 1 hour, which can be represented by $^1/_x$. The x represents the amount of time the brothers can do the job together.

The sum of the amount of the job each brother can do in 1 hour equals the amount of the job they can do together in 1 hour. Hence, the equation is given by:

$$\frac{1}{5} + \frac{1}{4} = \frac{1}{x}$$

Solving for x you calculate as follows:

$$\frac{1}{5} \times \frac{4}{4} + \frac{1}{4} \times \frac{5}{5} = \frac{1}{x}$$

$$\frac{4}{20} + \frac{5}{20} = \frac{1}{x}$$

$$\frac{9}{20} = \frac{1}{x}$$

$$9x = 20$$

$$\frac{9x}{9} = \frac{20}{9}$$

$$x = \frac{20}{9} \text{ or } 2\frac{2}{9} \text{ hours}$$

3. **(B)**

Use the Pythagorean Theorem to find the base and the height of the right triangle.

$$b = h$$

since it is a 45°–45°–90° triangle.

$$b^2 + b^2 = (10\sqrt{2})^2$$
$$2b^2 = (100)(2)$$
$$b = 10$$
$$A = \tfrac{1}{2}bh$$
$$= (\tfrac{1}{2})(10)(10)$$
$$= 50 \text{ cm}^2$$

4. **(B)**

When $c \neq 0$

$$\frac{a}{c} + \frac{b}{c} = \frac{a+b}{c}$$

Thus,

$$\frac{15,561}{25} + \frac{9,439}{25} = \frac{(15,561 + 9,439)}{25}$$
$$= \frac{25,000}{25}$$
$$= 1,000$$

5. **(D)**

$$\frac{1}{1 \times 2} + \frac{1}{2 \times 3} = \frac{1}{2} + \frac{1}{6}$$
$$= \frac{2}{3}$$

$$\frac{1}{1 \times 2} + \frac{1}{2 \times 3} + \frac{1}{3 \times 4} = \frac{1}{2} + \frac{1}{6} + \frac{1}{12}$$
$$= \frac{3}{4}$$

$$\frac{1}{1 \times 2} + \frac{1}{2 \times 3} + \frac{1}{3 \times 4} + \frac{1}{4 \times 5} = \frac{1}{2} + \frac{1}{6} + \frac{1}{12} + \frac{1}{20}$$

$$= \frac{4}{5}$$

and

$$\frac{1}{1 \times 2} + \frac{1}{2 \times 3} + \frac{1}{3 \times 4} + \dots + \frac{1}{99 \times 100} = \frac{99}{100}$$

6. **(B)**

$$f(x) = x^2 + 3x + 5$$

$f(2 + i)$ is obtained by substituting $(2 + i)$ for x:

$$f(2 + i) = (2 + i)^2 + 3(2 + i) + 5$$

Multiplying out:

$$f(2 + i) = 4 + 4i - 1 + 6 + 3i + 5$$

$$f(2 + i) = 14 + 7i$$

7. **(D)**
    Solve the quadratic equation by factoring.

$$z^2 + z - 2 = 0$$

$$(z + 2)(z - 1) = 0$$

Set each factor equal to 0 to find the solution to the equation.

$$z + 2 = 0 \qquad z - 1 = 0$$

$$z = -2 \qquad z = 1$$

$z = -2$ and 1 but the first equation states z must be greater than 0. Therefore the answer is 1.

8. **(C)**
    One needs to first recall that a cube has 6 equal-sized faces. Thus, the area of each face is found by dividing 6 into 54 to obtain 9 square feet. Since each face contains 9 square feet, then one can conclude that each

edge of a face is 3 feet long. So, the volume of the cube, given by the formula,

$$V = (\text{length of edge})^3$$

is found to be

$$V = (3 \text{ feet})^3 = 27 \text{ cubic feet.}$$

9.   **(D)**
   Make a diagram from the given information to see that the distance from Joan's house to Dave's house is the hypotenuse of a right triangle.
   Let d = the distance from Joan's house to Dave's house.

$$6^2 + 8^2 = d^2$$

$$36 + 64 = d^2$$

$$100 = d^2$$

$$10 = d$$

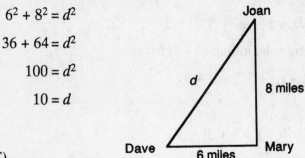

10.   **(E)**

$$\frac{a^2 - 3ab + 2b^2}{2b^2 + ab - a^2}$$

Factoring the numerator:

$$a^2 - 3ab + 2b^2 = (a - 2b)(a - b).$$

Factoring the denominator:

$$2b^2 + ab - a^2 = (2b - a)(b + a).$$

Rewriting the expression:

$$\frac{(a - 2b)(a - b)}{(2b - a)(b + a)} = \frac{a - 2b}{2b - a} \times \frac{a - b}{b + a}.$$

We note that $a - 2b = -1(2b - a)$. Therefore,

$$\frac{a - 2b}{2b - a} = -1.$$

The expression reduces to

$$-1\left(\frac{a - b}{b + a}\right) = \frac{b - a}{b + a}.$$

11. **(A)**

This is an example of a composite function. First we must evaluate $f(6)$. From the figure, we see that

$$f(6) = 2.$$

Thus,

$$f(f(6)) = f(2).$$

From the figure $f(2) = -2$, so that

$$f(f(6)) = -2.$$

12. **(E)**

To find the height use the Pythagorean Theorem,

$$a^2 + b^2 = c^2.$$

$$4^2 + b^2 = 8^2$$

$$16 + b^2 = 64$$

$$b^2 = 64 - 16$$

$$b^2 = 48$$

Height $\quad b = 4\sqrt{3}$

$$A = bh$$

$$= (11)(4\sqrt{3})$$

$$= 44\sqrt{3}$$

13. **(C)**

$$\frac{x^{10}y^8}{x^7y^3} = x^{(10-7)}y^{(8-3)}$$

$$= x^3 y^5$$

14. **(B)**

When translating words into equations remember: x varies directly with y means

$$x = ky$$

where k equals some constant. x varies inversely with y means

$$x = \frac{k}{y}$$

where k equals some constant. The square of x equals x^2 and the cube of x equals x^3. Therefore, the equation is

$$P = \frac{2x^2}{s^3}.$$

15. **(B)**
    From the properties of a straight line

$$y + 150° = 180°$$

$$y = 30°$$

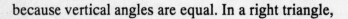

Also

$$\angle x = \angle z$$

because vertical angles are equal. In a right triangle,

$$\angle z + \angle y = 90°$$

or $\quad \angle x + \angle y = 90°$

$$\angle x + 30° = 90°$$

$$\angle x = 60°$$

16. **(B)**
    The general equation of a parabola with vertex at the origin and symmetrical about the y-axis is

$$y = ax^2.$$

Use the point $(1, 2)$ to find a:

$$2 = a(1)^2$$

$$a = 2$$

Therefore, the equation should be $y = 2x^2$.

17. **(D)**

$$\log_2(x - 1) + \log_2(x + 1) = 3$$
$$\log_2(x - 1)(x + 1) = 3$$
$$(x - 1)(x + 1) = 2^3$$
$$x^2 - 1 = 8$$
$$x^2 = 9$$
$$x = 3$$

18. **(B)**
3:1,000 is the ratio of defective parts to parts produced.
Let x = defective parts

$$3/1{,}000 = x/25{,}000$$
$$1{,}000x = 3(25{,}000)$$
$$x = 75{,}000/1{,}000$$
$$x = 75$$

19. **(C)**

$$4x + 3y - z - 10y + x = (4x + x) + (3y - 10y) - z$$
$$= 5x - 7y - z$$

20. **(A)**
To find the other root of the quadratic equation, we must first solve for the coefficient a.
Substituting 6 for x we obtain:

$$x^2 - ax + 12 = 0$$
$$6^2 - a(6) + 12 = 0$$
$$36 + 12 = 6a$$
$$48 = 6a$$
$$8 = a$$

The quadratic equation that we obtain is:

$$x^2 - 8x + 12 = 0.$$

Factoring:

$$(x - 6)(x - 2) = 0,$$

therefore, the roots are 6 and 2.

21. **(E)**

$$f(3) = 3(3)^2 - (3) + 5$$
$$= 27 - 3 + 5$$
$$= 29$$

22. **(E)**

$$x^2 - 3x - 4 < 0$$
$$(x + 1)(x - 4) < 0$$
$$-1 < x < 4$$

23. **(E)**

The fraction is a complex fraction. To simplify, we must multiply both the numerator and the denominator by $b^2 - 2b$:

$$\frac{\frac{2}{a^2b^2}}{\frac{1}{b^2-2b}} \times \frac{b^2 - 2b}{b^2 - 2b} = \frac{2(b^2 - 2b)}{a^2b^2}.$$

Multiplying through in the numerator:

$$\frac{2b^2 - 4b}{a^2b^2}.$$

The numerator is factored and like terms are canceled:

$$\frac{b(2b - 4)}{a^2b^2} = \frac{2b - 4}{a^2b}.$$

24. **(B)**

Redraw the figure and put the interior angles in the triangle. The sum of the interior angles is 180°.

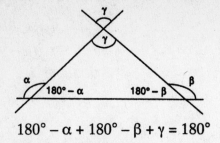

$$180° - \alpha + 180° - \beta + \gamma = 180°$$

Rearranging and simplifying:

$$180° - \alpha + \gamma = \beta, \text{ or } \gamma - \alpha + 180° = \beta.$$

25. **(E)**

$$|2x - 18| = -6$$

There is no solution, since an absolute number cannot equal a negative number.

26. **(A)**

Remember the order of operation rules are PEMDAS, meaning parentheses, exponents, multiplication, division, addition, and subtraction. The correct solution is

$$10 - 5[8 + 9 - 2(-2)] = 10 - 5(21)$$

$$10 - 105 = -95.$$

27. **(D)**

We are told that segments *BD* and *AE* are parallel. This implies that $\angle CBD = \angle CAE$ and $\angle CAE$ and $\angle CDB = \angle CEA$ (corresponding angles formed by parallel lines cut by a transversal are congruent).

$$\angle ACE = \angle BCD \text{ (same angle)}$$

Thus $\triangle BCD$ and $\triangle ACE$ are equiangular and similar. From a theorem, we know that the sides of similar triangles that correspond to each other are proportional. Sides *CD* and *CE* and *BD* and *AE* are corresponding sides and are thus proportional:

$$\frac{CD}{CE} = \frac{BD}{AE}.$$

28. **(B)**

$$f(3) = 3 + 1$$

$$= 4$$

$$g(4) = 2(4) - 3$$

$$= 5$$

$$f(3) * g(4) = 4 * 5$$

$$= 2(4) + 5 - (4)\,(5)$$

$$= -7$$

29. **(C)**

$$\frac{2\pi}{120°} = \frac{2\pi r}{360°}$$

$$r = 3$$

$$\text{Area} = \pi r^2 = 9\pi.$$

30. **(C)**

To find the sixth term in an arithmetic progression, find a, the first term, and d, the common difference. The difference between the first two numbers is $7 - 3 = 4$ and $a = 3$.

The nth term of an arithmetic progression equals

$$a + (n - 1)d.$$

Therefore the 6th term

$$= 3 + (6 - 1)4$$

$$= 3 + 5(4)$$

$$= 23$$

31. **(B)**

$$g(x) = 4x - 1 \qquad f(x) = -2x + 5$$

$$(g \circ f)\,(x) = g(f(x))$$

$$= 4(-2x + 5) - 1$$
$$= -8x + 20 - 1$$
$$= -8x + 19$$

32. **(D)**

To find the altitude of the triangle one must recall that the area of a triangle is given by

$$A = (1/2)bh,$$

where b denotes the base and h denotes the altitude. Also, one must recall that the area of a circle is given by

$$A = \pi r^2,$$

where r denotes the radius of the circle.

Since $b = 6$ units then

$$(1/2)(6)h = 3h = A,$$

the area of the triangle. In addition, since $r = 6$ units, then

$$A = \pi r^2 = \pi(6) = 36\pi,$$

the area of the circle. But the area is the same for both figures. Thus,

$$3h = 36\pi$$
$$h = 12\pi$$

is the altitude of the triangle.

33. **(C)**

Given the expression:

$$\frac{3}{x + 4} + \frac{5}{x - 4} = \frac{8}{x^2 - 16}$$

factor the denominator of the right side:

$$\frac{3}{x + 4} + \frac{5}{x - 4} = \frac{8}{(x + 4)(x - 4)}$$

Multiply both sides by $(x + 4)(x - 4)$:

$$3(x - 4) + 5(x + 4) = 8$$

Simplifying:

$$3x - 12 + 5x + 20 = 8$$
$$8x + 8 = 8$$
$$8x = 0$$
$$x = 0$$

34. (A)

$$\text{Distance} = \sqrt{(x_1 - x_2)^2 + (y_1 - y_2)^2}$$
$$= \sqrt{(3-2)^2 + (4-1)^2}$$
$$= \sqrt{25 + 9}$$
$$= \sqrt{34}$$

35. (E)
   Redraw the figure as below since $l_1 \parallel l_2$.

$$2x + x + 30° + 60° = 180°$$
$$3x + 90° = 180°$$
$$3x = 90°$$
$$x = 30°$$

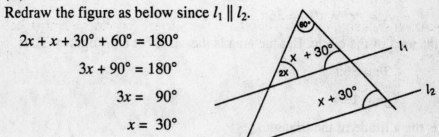

36. (B)
   The polynomial is not factorable, so we must use the quadratic formula:

$$x = \frac{-b \pm \sqrt{b^2 - 4ac}}{2a}$$

In the polynomial $a = 1$, $b = 2$, and $c = 5$. Substituting, we get:

$$x = \frac{-2 \pm \sqrt{2^2 - 4(1)(5)}}{2(1)}.$$

Simplifying:

$$x = \frac{-2 \pm \sqrt{-16}}{2}$$

$$= \frac{-2 \pm 4\sqrt{-1}}{2}$$

$$= -1 \pm 2\sqrt{-1}$$

We know $\sqrt{-1} = i$, so:

$$x = -1 \pm 2i.$$

37. **(B)**

The number of males

$$= 12 + 25 + 35 + 8 = 80.$$

Of these

$$12 + 25 = 37$$

earn less than \$35,000. Therefore, the percent of males earning less than \$35,000 is

$$\left(\frac{37}{80}\right) 100 = 46\frac{1}{4}.$$

38. **(E)**

$$6x^2 - 5x < -1$$

Put inequality in a form with 0 on one side.

$$6x^2 - 5x + 1 < 0$$

Factor the non-zero side.

$$(2x - 1)(3x - 1) < 0$$

$$x = {}^1\!/_2, \text{ and } x = {}^1\!/_3$$

are critical points. Check the intervals

$$(-\infty, {}^1\!/_3); \; ({}^1\!/_3, {}^1\!/_2); \text{ and } ({}^1\!/_2, \infty)$$

to see if the interval is in the solution set.

$$\frac{1}{3} < x < \frac{1}{2}$$

39. **(B)**

First factor.

$$x^2 - 2x - 8 = 0$$

$$(x - 4)(x + 2) = 0$$

Find the roots.

$$x - 4 = 0 \qquad\qquad x + 2 = 0$$

$$x = 4 \qquad\qquad x = -2$$

The sum of the roots $= 4 - 2 = 2$.

40. **(A)**

$$\frac{m^2 - n^2}{2x^2 + 3x - 2} \div \frac{n^2 - m^2}{2x^2 + 5x - 3}$$

Invert divisor and multiply.

$$= \frac{m^2 - n^2}{2x^2 + 3x - 2} \times \frac{2x^2 + 5x - 3}{n^2 - m^2}$$

Factor the polynomials.

$$= \frac{(m - n)(m + n)}{(2x - 1)(x + 2)} \times \frac{(2x - 1)(x + 3)}{(n - m)(n + m)} = \frac{(m - n)}{x + 2} \times \frac{(x + 3)}{-1(m - n)}$$

$$= -\frac{x + 3}{x + 2}$$

41. **(D)**

$$0 = x - 3y \qquad\qquad\qquad (1)$$

$$y + 3x = 20 \qquad\qquad\qquad (2)$$

Change

$$0 = x - 3y$$

$$3y = x$$

Substitute into equation (2) and solve for y.

$$y + 3(3y) = 20$$
$$y + 9y = 20$$
$$10y = 20$$
$$y = 2$$

42. **(D)**

We need to find the value of x, where $3^x > 1$.

If $x = 0$, then $3^0 = 1$.

If $x = 1$, then $3^1 = 3$.

Given that 3^x must be bigger than 1, $x > 0$.

43. **(B)**

If plane P travels x miles per hour (mph), then Q travels at $(x + 50)$ mph. In two hours P travels $2x$ and Q travels $(2x + 50)$ and since they travel in opposite directions the distance between P and Q is

$$2x + 2(x + 50) = 1,600.$$

Therefore,
$$4x + 100 = 1,600, \text{ or } x = 1,500/4 = 375.$$

44. **(B)**

$$\frac{3a^2bc^3 + 9a^3b^2c}{27ab^2c + 15a^2b^2c^3} = \frac{3a^2bc(c^2 + 3ab)}{3ab^2c(9 + 5ac^2)}$$
$$= \frac{a(c^2 + 3ab)}{b(9 + 5ac^2)}$$

45. **(D)**

$$4x - 5y^2 = 20$$

To find the $f^{-1}(x)$ interchange variables x and y to obtain

$$4y - 5x^2 = 20.$$

Solve for y.

$$4y = 20 + 5x^2$$

$$y = 5 + {}^5/_4 x^2$$

46. (A)

Since $\angle ACB$ is an inscribed angle intercepting a semicircle, it is 90°. Know that

$$\angle CAB + \angle ACB + \angle CBA = 180°$$

since the angles of a triangle equal 180°.

$$\angle CAB + 75° + 90° = 180°$$

$$\angle CAB = 180° - 165°$$

$$\angle CAB = 15°$$

47. (B)

In order to find what percent of 260 is 13 one needs only to form the following equation:

$$x\%(260) = 13$$

$$\frac{x(260)}{100} = 13$$

$$260x = 13(100)$$

$$x = \frac{1,300}{260}$$

$$= 5\%$$

48. (D)

When given an inequality with an absolute value, recall the definition of absolute value:

$$|x| \equiv \begin{cases} x \text{ if } x \geq 0 \\ -x \text{ if } x < 0 \end{cases}$$

$$6x - 5 \leq 8 \text{ if } 6x - 5 \geq 0$$

$$-6x + 5 \leq 8 \text{ if } 6x - 5 < 0$$

$$-6x + 5 \leq 8 \text{ can be written as } 6x - 5 \geq -8.$$

We can set up both of these equations as follows:

$$-8 \leq 6x - 5 \leq 8$$

adding 5:

$$-3 \leq 6x \leq 13$$

dividing by 6:

$$-\tfrac{1}{2} \leq x \leq \tfrac{13}{6}$$

49. **(A)**

$$2^{(6x - 8)} = 16,$$

2 raised to the 4th power equals 16. Thus

$$6x - 8 = 4.$$

Add 8 to both sides.

$$6x = 12$$

Divide both sides by 6.

$$x = 2$$

50. **(A)**

First factor the left-hand side of the equation as follows:

$$y^2 + 12y + 27 = (y + 9)(y + 3) = 0$$

$$y + 9 = 0 \qquad y + 3 = 0$$

$$y = -9 \qquad y = -3$$

The sum of the roots

$$= -9 + (-3)$$

$$= -12$$

51. **(D)**

Simplify the equation by first expanding by 2 on both sides and expand the right-hand side as follows:

$$a = (h/2) (B + b) \text{ or } 2a = 2(h/2) (B + b)$$

$$2a = h(B + b)$$

$$2a = hB + hb$$

Then, solve for B as follows:

$$hB + hb = 2a$$

$$hB = 2a - hb$$

$$B = 2a/h - hb/h$$

$$B = 2a/h - b$$

52. **(C)**

$$\text{Let width} = w$$

$$\text{length} = 2w$$

$$2w + 4w = \text{perimeter} = 72$$

$$6w = 72$$

$$w = 12$$

$$\text{length} = 24$$

$$\text{Area} = wl$$

$$= (12)(24)$$

$$= 288$$

53. **(C)**

Let x = the number

$$70 - 6x = 4$$

$$70 - 4 = 6x$$

$$66 = 6x$$

$$11 = x$$

54. **(D)**

$$|3x - 5| \leq 2$$

Replace the absolute value.

$$-2 \leq 3x - 5 \leq 2$$

Add 5.

$$3 \leq 3x \leq 7$$

Divide by 3.

$$1 \leq x \leq {}^7/_3$$

55. **(D)**

$$\text{Average} = \frac{5 \times 30 + 3 \times 20}{8}$$

$$= \frac{150 + 60}{8}$$

$$= \frac{210}{8} = 26.25$$

56. **(C)**

$$\frac{\frac{1}{x-1} + \frac{1}{x+1}}{\frac{2}{x}} = \frac{\frac{(x+1)+(x-1)}{(x-1)(x+1)}}{\frac{2}{x}}$$

$$= \frac{x+1+x-1}{x^2-1} \times \frac{x}{2}$$

$$= \frac{2x}{x^2-1} \times \frac{x}{2}$$

$$= \frac{x^2}{x^2-1}$$

57. **(A)**

Use long division to find the quotient and the remainder.

$$\begin{array}{r} x-7 \\ x+2\overline{)x^2-5x+3} \\ \underline{x^2+2x} \\ -7x+3 \\ \underline{-7x-14} \\ 17 \end{array}$$

$$x-7+\dfrac{17}{(x+2)}$$

58. **(E)**

$$\dfrac{x-4}{x-3}+\dfrac{6}{x^2-9}=\dfrac{x-4}{x-3}+\dfrac{6}{(x-3)(x+3)}$$

Factor to find a common denominator.

$$=\dfrac{(x-4)(x+3)+6}{(x-3)(x+3)}$$

$$=\dfrac{x^2-x-12+6}{(x-3)(x+3)}$$

$$=\dfrac{x^2-x-6}{(x-3)(x+3)}$$

$$=\dfrac{(x-3)(x+2)}{(x-3)(x+3)}$$

$$=\dfrac{x+2}{x+3}$$

59. **(A)**

$$P(x_1, y_1), Q(x_2, y_2)$$

From the equation for midpoint,

$$x_m = {}^1\!/_2(x_1+x_2) = {}^1\!/_2(3+15) = 9$$

$$y_m = {}^1\!/_2(-6+5) = -{}^1\!/_2$$

Thus the midpoint is:

$$P_{\text{mid}} = (9, -\tfrac{1}{2}).$$

60. (A)

Two angles that are complementary must have measures that add up to 90°. Let the angle $= x$, its complement $= x - 40$.

These angles must add up to 90°. Therefore,

$$x + x - 40° = 90°$$
$$2x = 130°$$
$$x = 65°$$

Therefore, the angle is 65°.

61. (D)

Rearrange the first equation.

$$x = 10 - y - z$$

If we use the smallest values for y and z, we obtain the biggest one for x, that is

$$x = 10 - 5 - 3$$
$$x = 2$$

Therefore, $x < z$ and also $x < y$.

Now rearrange the expression to analyze proposition III.

$$x + z = 10 - y$$

If $\quad y = 5$ (the smallest one), $x + z = 5$

but if $\quad y > 5$

then $\quad x + z < 5$

Therefore, $\quad x + z \leq y$.

62. (D)

$$y \propto \frac{a}{\sqrt{x}}$$

Let k = constant

$$y = \frac{k}{\sqrt{x}}$$

Given $y = 2$ when $x = 9$

$$2 = \frac{k}{\sqrt{9}}$$

$$2 = \frac{k}{3}$$

$$k = 6$$

Therefore,

$$y = \frac{6}{\sqrt{x}}.$$

63. **(A)**

In order to find the perimeter of the rectangle it is important first to understand the definition, that is, perimeter equals the sum of the dimensions of the rectangle. Hence, for the given rectangle,

$$\text{Perimeter} = 6L + 4W + 6L + 4W$$

Add like terms

$$= 12L + 8W$$

64. **(D)**

$$(2x - 8)/(x + 1) + (3x^2 - 12x)/(x^2 - 1)$$

Convert to a complex fraction:

$$\frac{\frac{2x-8}{x+1}}{\frac{3x^2-12x}{x^2-1}}$$

Invert the denominator and multiply by the numerator:

$$\left[\frac{2x-8}{x+1}\right]\left[\frac{(x+1)(x-1)}{3x^2-12x}\right]$$

$$= [2(x-4)]\left[\frac{(x-1)}{3x(x-4)}\right] = \frac{2(x-1)}{3x}$$

65. **(D)**

$$y = |x - 2|$$

Points were obtained by putting different values of x into the equation. Notice there are no negative values of y since the equation has absolute value symbols around it.

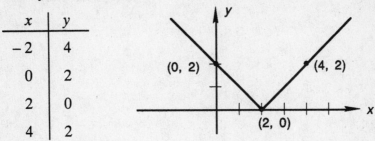

x	y
-2	4
0	2
2	0
4	2

ELM

Entry Level Mathematics

Answer Sheets

ELM – Test 1
ANSWER SHEET

1. Ⓐ Ⓑ Ⓒ Ⓓ Ⓔ
2. Ⓐ Ⓑ Ⓒ Ⓓ Ⓔ
3. Ⓐ Ⓑ Ⓒ Ⓓ Ⓔ
4. Ⓐ Ⓑ Ⓒ Ⓓ Ⓔ
5. Ⓐ Ⓑ Ⓒ Ⓓ Ⓔ
6. Ⓐ Ⓑ Ⓒ Ⓓ Ⓔ
7. Ⓐ Ⓑ Ⓒ Ⓓ Ⓔ
8. Ⓐ Ⓑ Ⓒ Ⓓ Ⓔ
9. Ⓐ Ⓑ Ⓒ Ⓓ Ⓔ
10. Ⓐ Ⓑ Ⓒ Ⓓ Ⓔ
11. Ⓐ Ⓑ Ⓒ Ⓓ Ⓔ
12. Ⓐ Ⓑ Ⓒ Ⓓ Ⓔ
13. Ⓐ Ⓑ Ⓒ Ⓓ Ⓔ
14. Ⓐ Ⓑ Ⓒ Ⓓ Ⓔ
15. Ⓐ Ⓑ Ⓒ Ⓓ Ⓔ
16. Ⓐ Ⓑ Ⓒ Ⓓ Ⓔ
17. Ⓐ Ⓑ Ⓒ Ⓓ Ⓔ
18. Ⓐ Ⓑ Ⓒ Ⓓ Ⓔ
19. Ⓐ Ⓑ Ⓒ Ⓓ Ⓔ
20. Ⓐ Ⓑ Ⓒ Ⓓ Ⓔ
21. Ⓐ Ⓑ Ⓒ Ⓓ Ⓔ
22. Ⓐ Ⓑ Ⓒ Ⓓ Ⓔ

23. Ⓐ Ⓑ Ⓒ Ⓓ Ⓔ
24. Ⓐ Ⓑ Ⓒ Ⓓ Ⓔ
25. Ⓐ Ⓑ Ⓒ Ⓓ Ⓔ
26. Ⓐ Ⓑ Ⓒ Ⓓ Ⓔ
27. Ⓐ Ⓑ Ⓒ Ⓓ Ⓔ
28. Ⓐ Ⓑ Ⓒ Ⓓ Ⓔ
29. Ⓐ Ⓑ Ⓒ Ⓓ Ⓔ
30. Ⓐ Ⓑ Ⓒ Ⓓ Ⓔ
31. Ⓐ Ⓑ Ⓒ Ⓓ Ⓔ
32. Ⓐ Ⓑ Ⓒ Ⓓ Ⓔ
33. Ⓐ Ⓑ Ⓒ Ⓓ Ⓔ
34. Ⓐ Ⓑ Ⓒ Ⓓ Ⓔ
35. Ⓐ Ⓑ Ⓒ Ⓓ Ⓔ
36. Ⓐ Ⓑ Ⓒ Ⓓ Ⓔ
37. Ⓐ Ⓑ Ⓒ Ⓓ Ⓔ
38. Ⓐ Ⓑ Ⓒ Ⓓ Ⓔ
39. Ⓐ Ⓑ Ⓒ Ⓓ Ⓔ
40. Ⓐ Ⓑ Ⓒ Ⓓ Ⓔ
41. Ⓐ Ⓑ Ⓒ Ⓓ Ⓔ
42. Ⓐ Ⓑ Ⓒ Ⓓ Ⓔ
43. Ⓐ Ⓑ Ⓒ Ⓓ Ⓔ

44. Ⓐ Ⓑ Ⓒ Ⓓ Ⓔ
45. Ⓐ Ⓑ Ⓒ Ⓓ Ⓔ
46. Ⓐ Ⓑ Ⓒ Ⓓ Ⓔ
47. Ⓐ Ⓑ Ⓒ Ⓓ Ⓔ
48. Ⓐ Ⓑ Ⓒ Ⓓ Ⓔ
49. Ⓐ Ⓑ Ⓒ Ⓓ Ⓔ
50. Ⓐ Ⓑ Ⓒ Ⓓ Ⓔ
51. Ⓐ Ⓑ Ⓒ Ⓓ Ⓔ
52. Ⓐ Ⓑ Ⓒ Ⓓ Ⓔ
53. Ⓐ Ⓑ Ⓒ Ⓓ Ⓔ
54. Ⓐ Ⓑ Ⓒ Ⓓ Ⓔ
55. Ⓐ Ⓑ Ⓒ Ⓓ Ⓔ
56. Ⓐ Ⓑ Ⓒ Ⓓ Ⓔ
57. Ⓐ Ⓑ Ⓒ Ⓓ Ⓔ
58. Ⓐ Ⓑ Ⓒ Ⓓ Ⓔ
59. Ⓐ Ⓑ Ⓒ Ⓓ Ⓔ
60. Ⓐ Ⓑ Ⓒ Ⓓ Ⓔ
61. Ⓐ Ⓑ Ⓒ Ⓓ Ⓔ
62. Ⓐ Ⓑ Ⓒ Ⓓ Ⓔ
63. Ⓐ Ⓑ Ⓒ Ⓓ Ⓔ
64. Ⓐ Ⓑ Ⓒ Ⓓ Ⓔ
65. Ⓐ Ⓑ Ⓒ Ⓓ Ⓔ

ELM – Test 2
ANSWER SHEET

1. Ⓐ Ⓑ Ⓒ Ⓓ Ⓔ	23. Ⓐ Ⓑ Ⓒ Ⓓ Ⓔ	44. Ⓐ Ⓑ Ⓒ Ⓓ Ⓔ
2. Ⓐ Ⓑ Ⓒ Ⓓ Ⓔ	24. Ⓐ Ⓑ Ⓒ Ⓓ Ⓔ	45. Ⓐ Ⓑ Ⓒ Ⓓ Ⓔ
3. Ⓐ Ⓑ Ⓒ Ⓓ Ⓔ	25. Ⓐ Ⓑ Ⓒ Ⓓ Ⓔ	46. Ⓐ Ⓑ Ⓒ Ⓓ Ⓔ
4. Ⓐ Ⓑ Ⓒ Ⓓ Ⓔ	26. Ⓐ Ⓑ Ⓒ Ⓓ Ⓔ	47. Ⓐ Ⓑ Ⓒ Ⓓ Ⓔ
5. Ⓐ Ⓑ Ⓒ Ⓓ Ⓔ	27. Ⓐ Ⓑ Ⓒ Ⓓ Ⓔ	48. Ⓐ Ⓑ Ⓒ Ⓓ Ⓔ
6. Ⓐ Ⓑ Ⓒ Ⓓ Ⓔ	28. Ⓐ Ⓑ Ⓒ Ⓓ Ⓔ	49. Ⓐ Ⓑ Ⓒ Ⓓ Ⓔ
7. Ⓐ Ⓑ Ⓒ Ⓓ Ⓔ	29. Ⓐ Ⓑ Ⓒ Ⓓ Ⓔ	50. Ⓐ Ⓑ Ⓒ Ⓓ Ⓔ
8. Ⓐ Ⓑ Ⓒ Ⓓ Ⓔ	30. Ⓐ Ⓑ Ⓒ Ⓓ Ⓔ	51. Ⓐ Ⓑ Ⓒ Ⓓ Ⓔ
9. Ⓐ Ⓑ Ⓒ Ⓓ Ⓔ	31. Ⓐ Ⓑ Ⓒ Ⓓ Ⓔ	52. Ⓐ Ⓑ Ⓒ Ⓓ Ⓔ
10. Ⓐ Ⓑ Ⓒ Ⓓ Ⓔ	32. Ⓐ Ⓑ Ⓒ Ⓓ Ⓔ	53. Ⓐ Ⓑ Ⓒ Ⓓ Ⓔ
11. Ⓐ Ⓑ Ⓒ Ⓓ Ⓔ	33. Ⓐ Ⓑ Ⓒ Ⓓ Ⓔ	54. Ⓐ Ⓑ Ⓒ Ⓓ Ⓔ
12. Ⓐ Ⓑ Ⓒ Ⓓ Ⓔ	34. Ⓐ Ⓑ Ⓒ Ⓓ Ⓔ	55. Ⓐ Ⓑ Ⓒ Ⓓ Ⓔ
13. Ⓐ Ⓑ Ⓒ Ⓓ Ⓔ	35. Ⓐ Ⓑ Ⓒ Ⓓ Ⓔ	56. Ⓐ Ⓑ Ⓒ Ⓓ Ⓔ
14. Ⓐ Ⓑ Ⓒ Ⓓ Ⓔ	36. Ⓐ Ⓑ Ⓒ Ⓓ Ⓔ	57. Ⓐ Ⓑ Ⓒ Ⓓ Ⓔ
15. Ⓐ Ⓑ Ⓒ Ⓓ Ⓔ	37. Ⓐ Ⓑ Ⓒ Ⓓ Ⓔ	58. Ⓐ Ⓑ Ⓒ Ⓓ Ⓔ
16. Ⓐ Ⓑ Ⓒ Ⓓ Ⓔ	38. Ⓐ Ⓑ Ⓒ Ⓓ Ⓔ	59. Ⓐ Ⓑ Ⓒ Ⓓ Ⓔ
17. Ⓐ Ⓑ Ⓒ Ⓓ Ⓔ	39. Ⓐ Ⓑ Ⓒ Ⓓ Ⓔ	60. Ⓐ Ⓑ Ⓒ Ⓓ Ⓔ
18. Ⓐ Ⓑ Ⓒ Ⓓ Ⓔ	40. Ⓐ Ⓑ Ⓒ Ⓓ Ⓔ	61. Ⓐ Ⓑ Ⓒ Ⓓ Ⓔ
19. Ⓐ Ⓑ Ⓒ Ⓓ Ⓔ	41. Ⓐ Ⓑ Ⓒ Ⓓ Ⓔ	62. Ⓐ Ⓑ Ⓒ Ⓓ Ⓔ
20. Ⓐ Ⓑ Ⓒ Ⓓ Ⓔ	42. Ⓐ Ⓑ Ⓒ Ⓓ Ⓔ	63. Ⓐ Ⓑ Ⓒ Ⓓ Ⓔ
21. Ⓐ Ⓑ Ⓒ Ⓓ Ⓔ	43. Ⓐ Ⓑ Ⓒ Ⓓ Ⓔ	64. Ⓐ Ⓑ Ⓒ Ⓓ Ⓔ
22. Ⓐ Ⓑ Ⓒ Ⓓ Ⓔ		65. Ⓐ Ⓑ Ⓒ Ⓓ Ⓔ

ELM – Test 3
ANSWER SHEET

1. Ⓐ Ⓑ Ⓒ Ⓓ Ⓔ
2. Ⓐ Ⓑ Ⓒ Ⓓ Ⓔ
3. Ⓐ Ⓑ Ⓒ Ⓓ Ⓔ
4. Ⓐ Ⓑ Ⓒ Ⓓ Ⓔ
5. Ⓐ Ⓑ Ⓒ Ⓓ Ⓔ
6. Ⓐ Ⓑ Ⓒ Ⓓ Ⓔ
7. Ⓐ Ⓑ Ⓒ Ⓓ Ⓔ
8. Ⓐ Ⓑ Ⓒ Ⓓ Ⓔ
9. Ⓐ Ⓑ Ⓒ Ⓓ Ⓔ
10. Ⓐ Ⓑ Ⓒ Ⓓ Ⓔ
11. Ⓐ Ⓑ Ⓒ Ⓓ Ⓔ
12. Ⓐ Ⓑ Ⓒ Ⓓ Ⓔ
13. Ⓐ Ⓑ Ⓒ Ⓓ Ⓔ
14. Ⓐ Ⓑ Ⓒ Ⓓ Ⓔ
15. Ⓐ Ⓑ Ⓒ Ⓓ Ⓔ
16. Ⓐ Ⓑ Ⓒ Ⓓ Ⓔ
17. Ⓐ Ⓑ Ⓒ Ⓓ Ⓔ
18. Ⓐ Ⓑ Ⓒ Ⓓ Ⓔ
19. Ⓐ Ⓑ Ⓒ Ⓓ Ⓔ
20. Ⓐ Ⓑ Ⓒ Ⓓ Ⓔ
21. Ⓐ Ⓑ Ⓒ Ⓓ Ⓔ
22. Ⓐ Ⓑ Ⓒ Ⓓ Ⓔ

23. Ⓐ Ⓑ Ⓒ Ⓓ Ⓔ
24. Ⓐ Ⓑ Ⓒ Ⓓ Ⓔ
25. Ⓐ Ⓑ Ⓒ Ⓓ Ⓔ
26. Ⓐ Ⓑ Ⓒ Ⓓ Ⓔ
27. Ⓐ Ⓑ Ⓒ Ⓓ Ⓔ
28. Ⓐ Ⓑ Ⓒ Ⓓ Ⓔ
29. Ⓐ Ⓑ Ⓒ Ⓓ Ⓔ
30. Ⓐ Ⓑ Ⓒ Ⓓ Ⓔ
31. Ⓐ Ⓑ Ⓒ Ⓓ Ⓔ
32. Ⓐ Ⓑ Ⓒ Ⓓ Ⓔ
33. Ⓐ Ⓑ Ⓒ Ⓓ Ⓔ
34. Ⓐ Ⓑ Ⓒ Ⓓ Ⓔ
35. Ⓐ Ⓑ Ⓒ Ⓓ Ⓔ
36. Ⓐ Ⓑ Ⓒ Ⓓ Ⓔ
37. Ⓐ Ⓑ Ⓒ Ⓓ Ⓔ
38. Ⓐ Ⓑ Ⓒ Ⓓ Ⓔ
39. Ⓐ Ⓑ Ⓒ Ⓓ Ⓔ
40. Ⓐ Ⓑ Ⓒ Ⓓ Ⓔ
41. Ⓐ Ⓑ Ⓒ Ⓓ Ⓔ
42. Ⓐ Ⓑ Ⓒ Ⓓ Ⓔ
43. Ⓐ Ⓑ Ⓒ Ⓓ Ⓔ

44. Ⓐ Ⓑ Ⓒ Ⓓ Ⓔ
45. Ⓐ Ⓑ Ⓒ Ⓓ Ⓔ
46. Ⓐ Ⓑ Ⓒ Ⓓ Ⓔ
47. Ⓐ Ⓑ Ⓒ Ⓓ Ⓔ
48. Ⓐ Ⓑ Ⓒ Ⓓ Ⓔ
49. Ⓐ Ⓑ Ⓒ Ⓓ Ⓔ
50. Ⓐ Ⓑ Ⓒ Ⓓ Ⓔ
51. Ⓐ Ⓑ Ⓒ Ⓓ Ⓔ
52. Ⓐ Ⓑ Ⓒ Ⓓ Ⓔ
53. Ⓐ Ⓑ Ⓒ Ⓓ Ⓔ
54. Ⓐ Ⓑ Ⓒ Ⓓ Ⓔ
55. Ⓐ Ⓑ Ⓒ Ⓓ Ⓔ
56. Ⓐ Ⓑ Ⓒ Ⓓ Ⓔ
57. Ⓐ Ⓑ Ⓒ Ⓓ Ⓔ
58. Ⓐ Ⓑ Ⓒ Ⓓ Ⓔ
59. Ⓐ Ⓑ Ⓒ Ⓓ Ⓔ
60. Ⓐ Ⓑ Ⓒ Ⓓ Ⓔ
61. Ⓐ Ⓑ Ⓒ Ⓓ Ⓔ
62. Ⓐ Ⓑ Ⓒ Ⓓ Ⓔ
63. Ⓐ Ⓑ Ⓒ Ⓓ Ⓔ
64. Ⓐ Ⓑ Ⓒ Ⓓ Ⓔ
65. Ⓐ Ⓑ Ⓒ Ⓓ Ⓔ

ELM – Test ____
Additional Answer Sheet

1. Ⓐ Ⓑ Ⓒ Ⓓ Ⓔ
2. Ⓐ Ⓑ Ⓒ Ⓓ Ⓔ
3. Ⓐ Ⓑ Ⓒ Ⓓ Ⓔ
4. Ⓐ Ⓑ Ⓒ Ⓓ Ⓔ
5. Ⓐ Ⓑ Ⓒ Ⓓ Ⓔ
6. Ⓐ Ⓑ Ⓒ Ⓓ Ⓔ
7. Ⓐ Ⓑ Ⓒ Ⓓ Ⓔ
8. Ⓐ Ⓑ Ⓒ Ⓓ Ⓔ
9. Ⓐ Ⓑ Ⓒ Ⓓ Ⓔ
10. Ⓐ Ⓑ Ⓒ Ⓓ Ⓔ
11. Ⓐ Ⓑ Ⓒ Ⓓ Ⓔ
12. Ⓐ Ⓑ Ⓒ Ⓓ Ⓔ
13. Ⓐ Ⓑ Ⓒ Ⓓ Ⓔ
14. Ⓐ Ⓑ Ⓒ Ⓓ Ⓔ
15. Ⓐ Ⓑ Ⓒ Ⓓ Ⓔ
16. Ⓐ Ⓑ Ⓒ Ⓓ Ⓔ
17. Ⓐ Ⓑ Ⓒ Ⓓ Ⓔ
18. Ⓐ Ⓑ Ⓒ Ⓓ Ⓔ
19. Ⓐ Ⓑ Ⓒ Ⓓ Ⓔ
20. Ⓐ Ⓑ Ⓒ Ⓓ Ⓔ
21. Ⓐ Ⓑ Ⓒ Ⓓ Ⓔ
22. Ⓐ Ⓑ Ⓒ Ⓓ Ⓔ

23. Ⓐ Ⓑ Ⓒ Ⓓ Ⓔ
24. Ⓐ Ⓑ Ⓒ Ⓓ Ⓔ
25. Ⓐ Ⓑ Ⓒ Ⓓ Ⓔ
26. Ⓐ Ⓑ Ⓒ Ⓓ Ⓔ
27. Ⓐ Ⓑ Ⓒ Ⓓ Ⓔ
28. Ⓐ Ⓑ Ⓒ Ⓓ Ⓔ
29. Ⓐ Ⓑ Ⓒ Ⓓ Ⓔ
30. Ⓐ Ⓑ Ⓒ Ⓓ Ⓔ
31. Ⓐ Ⓑ Ⓒ Ⓓ Ⓔ
32. Ⓐ Ⓑ Ⓒ Ⓓ Ⓔ
33. Ⓐ Ⓑ Ⓒ Ⓓ Ⓔ
34. Ⓐ Ⓑ Ⓒ Ⓓ Ⓔ
35. Ⓐ Ⓑ Ⓒ Ⓓ Ⓔ
36. Ⓐ Ⓑ Ⓒ Ⓓ Ⓔ
37. Ⓐ Ⓑ Ⓒ Ⓓ Ⓔ
38. Ⓐ Ⓑ Ⓒ Ⓓ Ⓔ
39. Ⓐ Ⓑ Ⓒ Ⓓ Ⓔ
40. Ⓐ Ⓑ Ⓒ Ⓓ Ⓔ
41. Ⓐ Ⓑ Ⓒ Ⓓ Ⓔ
42. Ⓐ Ⓑ Ⓒ Ⓓ Ⓔ
43. Ⓐ Ⓑ Ⓒ Ⓓ Ⓔ

44. Ⓐ Ⓑ Ⓒ Ⓓ Ⓔ
45. Ⓐ Ⓑ Ⓒ Ⓓ Ⓔ
46. Ⓐ Ⓑ Ⓒ Ⓓ Ⓔ
47. Ⓐ Ⓑ Ⓒ Ⓓ Ⓔ
48. Ⓐ Ⓑ Ⓒ Ⓓ Ⓔ
49. Ⓐ Ⓑ Ⓒ Ⓓ Ⓔ
50. Ⓐ Ⓑ Ⓒ Ⓓ Ⓔ
51. Ⓐ Ⓑ Ⓒ Ⓓ Ⓔ
52. Ⓐ Ⓑ Ⓒ Ⓓ Ⓔ
53. Ⓐ Ⓑ Ⓒ Ⓓ Ⓔ
54. Ⓐ Ⓑ Ⓒ Ⓓ Ⓔ
55. Ⓐ Ⓑ Ⓒ Ⓓ Ⓔ
56. Ⓐ Ⓑ Ⓒ Ⓓ Ⓔ
57. Ⓐ Ⓑ Ⓒ Ⓓ Ⓔ
58. Ⓐ Ⓑ Ⓒ Ⓓ Ⓔ
59. Ⓐ Ⓑ Ⓒ Ⓓ Ⓔ
60. Ⓐ Ⓑ Ⓒ Ⓓ Ⓔ
61. Ⓐ Ⓑ Ⓒ Ⓓ Ⓔ
62. Ⓐ Ⓑ Ⓒ Ⓓ Ⓔ
63. Ⓐ Ⓑ Ⓒ Ⓓ Ⓔ
64. Ⓐ Ⓑ Ⓒ Ⓓ Ⓔ
65. Ⓐ Ⓑ Ⓒ Ⓓ Ⓔ

ELM – Test ___
Additional Answer Sheet

1. Ⓐ Ⓑ Ⓒ Ⓓ Ⓔ	23. Ⓐ Ⓑ Ⓒ Ⓓ Ⓔ	44. Ⓐ Ⓑ Ⓒ Ⓓ Ⓔ
2. Ⓐ Ⓑ Ⓒ Ⓓ Ⓔ	24. Ⓐ Ⓑ Ⓒ Ⓓ Ⓔ	45. Ⓐ Ⓑ Ⓒ Ⓓ Ⓔ
3. Ⓐ Ⓑ Ⓒ Ⓓ Ⓔ	25. Ⓐ Ⓑ Ⓒ Ⓓ Ⓔ	46. Ⓐ Ⓑ Ⓒ Ⓓ Ⓔ
4. Ⓐ Ⓑ Ⓒ Ⓓ Ⓔ	26. Ⓐ Ⓑ Ⓒ Ⓓ Ⓔ	47. Ⓐ Ⓑ Ⓒ Ⓓ Ⓔ
5. Ⓐ Ⓑ Ⓒ Ⓓ Ⓔ	27. Ⓐ Ⓑ Ⓒ Ⓓ Ⓔ	48. Ⓐ Ⓑ Ⓒ Ⓓ Ⓔ
6. Ⓐ Ⓑ Ⓒ Ⓓ Ⓔ	28. Ⓐ Ⓑ Ⓒ Ⓓ Ⓔ	49. Ⓐ Ⓑ Ⓒ Ⓓ Ⓔ
7. Ⓐ Ⓑ Ⓒ Ⓓ Ⓔ	29. Ⓐ Ⓑ Ⓒ Ⓓ Ⓔ	50. Ⓐ Ⓑ Ⓒ Ⓓ Ⓔ
8. Ⓐ Ⓑ Ⓒ Ⓓ Ⓔ	30. Ⓐ Ⓑ Ⓒ Ⓓ Ⓔ	51. Ⓐ Ⓑ Ⓒ Ⓓ Ⓔ
9. Ⓐ Ⓑ Ⓒ Ⓓ Ⓔ	31. Ⓐ Ⓑ Ⓒ Ⓓ Ⓔ	52. Ⓐ Ⓑ Ⓒ Ⓓ Ⓔ
10. Ⓐ Ⓑ Ⓒ Ⓓ Ⓔ	32. Ⓐ Ⓑ Ⓒ Ⓓ Ⓔ	53. Ⓐ Ⓑ Ⓒ Ⓓ Ⓔ
11. Ⓐ Ⓑ Ⓒ Ⓓ Ⓔ	33. Ⓐ Ⓑ Ⓒ Ⓓ Ⓔ	54. Ⓐ Ⓑ Ⓒ Ⓓ Ⓔ
12. Ⓐ Ⓑ Ⓒ Ⓓ Ⓔ	34. Ⓐ Ⓑ Ⓒ Ⓓ Ⓔ	55. Ⓐ Ⓑ Ⓒ Ⓓ Ⓔ
13. Ⓐ Ⓑ Ⓒ Ⓓ Ⓔ	35. Ⓐ Ⓑ Ⓒ Ⓓ Ⓔ	56. Ⓐ Ⓑ Ⓒ Ⓓ Ⓔ
14. Ⓐ Ⓑ Ⓒ Ⓓ Ⓔ	36. Ⓐ Ⓑ Ⓒ Ⓓ Ⓔ	57. Ⓐ Ⓑ Ⓒ Ⓓ Ⓔ
15. Ⓐ Ⓑ Ⓒ Ⓓ Ⓔ	37. Ⓐ Ⓑ Ⓒ Ⓓ Ⓔ	58. Ⓐ Ⓑ Ⓒ Ⓓ Ⓔ
16. Ⓐ Ⓑ Ⓒ Ⓓ Ⓔ	38. Ⓐ Ⓑ Ⓒ Ⓓ Ⓔ	59. Ⓐ Ⓑ Ⓒ Ⓓ Ⓔ
17. Ⓐ Ⓑ Ⓒ Ⓓ Ⓔ	39. Ⓐ Ⓑ Ⓒ Ⓓ Ⓔ	60. Ⓐ Ⓑ Ⓒ Ⓓ Ⓔ
18. Ⓐ Ⓑ Ⓒ Ⓓ Ⓔ	40. Ⓐ Ⓑ Ⓒ Ⓓ Ⓔ	61. Ⓐ Ⓑ Ⓒ Ⓓ Ⓔ
19. Ⓐ Ⓑ Ⓒ Ⓓ Ⓔ	41. Ⓐ Ⓑ Ⓒ Ⓓ Ⓔ	62. Ⓐ Ⓑ Ⓒ Ⓓ Ⓔ
20. Ⓐ Ⓑ Ⓒ Ⓓ Ⓔ	42. Ⓐ Ⓑ Ⓒ Ⓓ Ⓔ	63. Ⓐ Ⓑ Ⓒ Ⓓ Ⓔ
21. Ⓐ Ⓑ Ⓒ Ⓓ Ⓔ	43. Ⓐ Ⓑ Ⓒ Ⓓ Ⓔ	64. Ⓐ Ⓑ Ⓒ Ⓓ Ⓔ
22. Ⓐ Ⓑ Ⓒ Ⓓ Ⓔ		65. Ⓐ Ⓑ Ⓒ Ⓓ Ⓔ

ELM – Test ___
Additional Answer Sheet

1. Ⓐ Ⓑ Ⓒ Ⓓ Ⓔ	23. Ⓐ Ⓑ Ⓒ Ⓓ Ⓔ	44. Ⓐ Ⓑ Ⓒ Ⓓ Ⓔ
2. Ⓐ Ⓑ Ⓒ Ⓓ Ⓔ	24. Ⓐ Ⓑ Ⓒ Ⓓ Ⓔ	45. Ⓐ Ⓑ Ⓒ Ⓓ Ⓔ
3. Ⓐ Ⓑ Ⓒ Ⓓ Ⓔ	25. Ⓐ Ⓑ Ⓒ Ⓓ Ⓔ	46. Ⓐ Ⓑ Ⓒ Ⓓ Ⓔ
4. Ⓐ Ⓑ Ⓒ Ⓓ Ⓔ	26. Ⓐ Ⓑ Ⓒ Ⓓ Ⓔ	47. Ⓐ Ⓑ Ⓒ Ⓓ Ⓔ
5. Ⓐ Ⓑ Ⓒ Ⓓ Ⓔ	27. Ⓐ Ⓑ Ⓒ Ⓓ Ⓔ	48. Ⓐ Ⓑ Ⓒ Ⓓ Ⓔ
6. Ⓐ Ⓑ Ⓒ Ⓓ Ⓔ	28. Ⓐ Ⓑ Ⓒ Ⓓ Ⓔ	49. Ⓐ Ⓑ Ⓒ Ⓓ Ⓔ
7. Ⓐ Ⓑ Ⓒ Ⓓ Ⓔ	29. Ⓐ Ⓑ Ⓒ Ⓓ Ⓔ	50. Ⓐ Ⓑ Ⓒ Ⓓ Ⓔ
8. Ⓐ Ⓑ Ⓒ Ⓓ Ⓔ	30. Ⓐ Ⓑ Ⓒ Ⓓ Ⓔ	51. Ⓐ Ⓑ Ⓒ Ⓓ Ⓔ
9. Ⓐ Ⓑ Ⓒ Ⓓ Ⓔ	31. Ⓐ Ⓑ Ⓒ Ⓓ Ⓔ	52. Ⓐ Ⓑ Ⓒ Ⓓ Ⓔ
10. Ⓐ Ⓑ Ⓒ Ⓓ Ⓔ	32. Ⓐ Ⓑ Ⓒ Ⓓ Ⓔ	53. Ⓐ Ⓑ Ⓒ Ⓓ Ⓔ
11. Ⓐ Ⓑ Ⓒ Ⓓ Ⓔ	33. Ⓐ Ⓑ Ⓒ Ⓓ Ⓔ	54. Ⓐ Ⓑ Ⓒ Ⓓ Ⓔ
12. Ⓐ Ⓑ Ⓒ Ⓓ Ⓔ	34. Ⓐ Ⓑ Ⓒ Ⓓ Ⓔ	55. Ⓐ Ⓑ Ⓒ Ⓓ Ⓔ
13. Ⓐ Ⓑ Ⓒ Ⓓ Ⓔ	35. Ⓐ Ⓑ Ⓒ Ⓓ Ⓔ	56. Ⓐ Ⓑ Ⓒ Ⓓ Ⓔ
14. Ⓐ Ⓑ Ⓒ Ⓓ Ⓔ	36. Ⓐ Ⓑ Ⓒ Ⓓ Ⓔ	57. Ⓐ Ⓑ Ⓒ Ⓓ Ⓔ
15. Ⓐ Ⓑ Ⓒ Ⓓ Ⓔ	37. Ⓐ Ⓑ Ⓒ Ⓓ Ⓔ	58. Ⓐ Ⓑ Ⓒ Ⓓ Ⓔ
16. Ⓐ Ⓑ Ⓒ Ⓓ Ⓔ	38. Ⓐ Ⓑ Ⓒ Ⓓ Ⓔ	59. Ⓐ Ⓑ Ⓒ Ⓓ Ⓔ
17. Ⓐ Ⓑ Ⓒ Ⓓ Ⓔ	39. Ⓐ Ⓑ Ⓒ Ⓓ Ⓔ	60. Ⓐ Ⓑ Ⓒ Ⓓ Ⓔ
18. Ⓐ Ⓑ Ⓒ Ⓓ Ⓔ	40. Ⓐ Ⓑ Ⓒ Ⓓ Ⓔ	61. Ⓐ Ⓑ Ⓒ Ⓓ Ⓔ
19. Ⓐ Ⓑ Ⓒ Ⓓ Ⓔ	41. Ⓐ Ⓑ Ⓒ Ⓓ Ⓔ	62. Ⓐ Ⓑ Ⓒ Ⓓ Ⓔ
20. Ⓐ Ⓑ Ⓒ Ⓓ Ⓔ	42. Ⓐ Ⓑ Ⓒ Ⓓ Ⓔ	63. Ⓐ Ⓑ Ⓒ Ⓓ Ⓔ
21. Ⓐ Ⓑ Ⓒ Ⓓ Ⓔ	43. Ⓐ Ⓑ Ⓒ Ⓓ Ⓔ	64. Ⓐ Ⓑ Ⓒ Ⓓ Ⓔ
22. Ⓐ Ⓑ Ⓒ Ⓓ Ⓔ		65. Ⓐ Ⓑ Ⓒ Ⓓ Ⓔ